Innovative
MACHINE
QUILTING

HETTIE RISINGER

Sterling Publishing Co., Inc.   New York
Oak Tree Press Co., Ltd.   London & Sydney

OTHER BOOKS OF INTEREST

Appliqué & Reverse Appliqué
Classic American Patchwork Quilt Patterns
One-Stitch Stitchery
Pictures in Patchwork

Dedication

To my husband,

William Oliver Risinger

Photographs on pages 94, 96, 100, 101, 102, 103, 111, 149, and color pages C (lower right photo) and D (lower right photo) by Mike Doran. All other photographs by Leroy Hayes.

Fourth Printing, 1980

Copyright © 1980 by Sterling Publishing Co., Inc.
Two Park Avenue, New York, N.Y. 10016
Distributed in Australia by Oak Tree Press Co., Ltd.
P.O. Box J34, Brickfield Hill, Sydney 2000, N.S.W.
Distributed in the United Kingdom by Ward Lock Ltd.
116 Baker Street, London W.1
Manufactured in the United States of America
All rights reserved
Library of Congress Catalog Card No.: 79-91393
Sterling ISBN 0-8069-5398-5 Trade   Oak Tree 7061-2688-2
0-8069-5399-3 Library

ACKNOWLEDGMENTS

Many thanks! One of the nicest things about writing a book is that it gives one the opportunity of working with such wonderful people. Everyone I have called upon has been more than willing to help. Many have even been eager to be a part of this exciting project. They have given very generously of both time and energy. Appreciation for such friendship can only be expressed with a responding friendship of the same sincerity. This it is my joy to do. In addition, I am happy to take this opportunity to express my gratitude to those who have been most actively involved.

The one person who has contributed most to this book has done so indirectly. He has made every effort to free my time for this activity, often at the expense of his own. He has supported my aims very generously in other ways as well and has shared the pleasure of my successes along the way. Without this, they would not have glowed half so brightly for me. Many thanks to my husband.

Betty Hartman has graciously done all the typing involved in the project. She has willingly adapted her schedule to my needs and met deadlines without hesitation.

Glenda Sims, an instructor in extemporaneous writing, has proofread the manuscript. Her encouragement and comments have been most helpful.

Phyllis Adelman, owner of The Walrus Quilt Shop in Rockford, Illinois, gave me my professional start as a teacher of machine quilting. From the first, she has offered all possible help in making my work on the book easier and has encouraged me in every way.

Charlot Rainey, formerly of The Walrus Quilt Shop, was the first to see some of the early designs planned for the book. I value her encouragement as a professional and as an instructor of hand quilting.

Gracie Hendricks was very helpful in some special ways which I appreciate very much.

LeRoy Hayes, assisted by his wife, Grace, took many of the photographs used in the book. They gave most generously of their time and talents on several occasions.

My thanks to Leo Doran and to his son Mike, for their cooperation in taking many of the photographs for the book.

My appreciation to Dorothy Bross, machine embroidery instructor, who graciously loaned several pieces of embroidery and quilting for photographing.

My thanks to Zaltan of Zaltan's Sewing Center and Minta Minor, of Picatoruca, Illinois, who increased my knowledge in the use and mechanics of the sewing machine.

Dean Trafton, of Rockford College, deserves my special thanks for his advice and counsel.

Many others have been helpful and encouraging and have added to my pleasure in the work by their enthusiasm for it. All these people have not only eased my way in completing the book, but have enriched my life with their friendship. Many thanks to each one of them.

Contents

Color pages A-D follow page 32
Color pages E-L follow page 96

Metric Conversion Chart

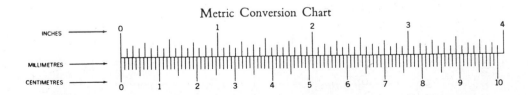

FOREWORD

Quilting pursued me through the years until I finally "caught" it. Like many things we do for the joy of doing, quilting can become an all-absorbing pastime. Some of us are even fortunate enough to be attracted to more than one of these activities. Whether there are one or more, however, we are happier people because of them. We know how to work out our frustrations, to calm our jangled nerves, to face up to empty hours, to release our creativity. We have found a help in times of sorrow. We have found a means of sharing and giving of ourselves. Even strangers are drawn together through a common interest in quilting, tapestry, knitting—or perhaps painting, cooking or any other activity which permits us to lose ourselves in a happy venture of self-involvement, self-expression and creativity.

My mother, bless her, introduced me to sewing at an early age. The summer that I turned five, she began an embroidered bedspread. It was in a beautiful wisteria pattern with lots of lovely colors and fascinating stitches. Each time she began to work on it, I lost interest in playing and was right by her side, watching the colored threads become blossoms and leaves and tendrils—and asking for something of my own to embroider. Perhaps it was in self defense that she drew a squirrel on a circle of linen and taught me to outline stitch. I still have that little fellow tucked away among my keepsakes. Not too bad for five!

My sixth summer I was introduced to the sewing machine, contributing a set of batiste underwear to my new school wardrobe. So it went from year to year. My mother, a wise teacher, always encouraged my interests, sometimes suggesting new possibilities to expand my horizons. She was good at finding a new pattern that was just enough of a challenge but not too difficult—yet she never pushed me in these things.

It was many years, however, before quilting caught up with me. I had been interested in quilts, admiring the many beautiful ones in Grandma's quilt box and appreciating the colorful "Sunbonnet Sue" quilt that Aunt Ida made for my hope chest. But I was so caught up in the many demands of my new married life that I seldom found time to work on the lovely appliqué quilt kit she gave me soon after my wedding. It still isn't finished to this day!

My specialty became the sewing machine, and it has served my family and me well, giving me many hours of pleasure at the same time. When the children were grown, I accepted a job instructing women in the use of their new sewing machines and teaching sewing classes. Later, I found that my earlier years of education and training, together with all those years of experience in sewing, qualified me to teach advanced sewing and tailoring classes for Rock Valley College Adult Continuing Education.

Seemingly unrelated things sometimes work together to open doors we never dreamed of passing through. My daughter, Susie, was piecing an original quilt design which caught my interest. I began buying and borrowing books on the subject. I dug out my old appliqué quilt, which lay about making me feel frustrated because the work progressed so slowly.

While I enjoyed my clothing classes, I still had stirrings of something unsatisfied, something unexpressed. There was a feeling of too much time and energy devoted to outside demands and not enough to all the things I had wanted to do over the years yet couldn't find the time for.

Then one cold January day I had a phone call from Phyllis Adelman, a former student of mine. "I don't know whether or not you know that I now own The Walrus Quilt Shop," she said. I didn't. "I remember how much I enjoyed your class and how well you handled your sewing machine. When I decided to add machine quilting to the classes I offer at the shop, I knew you were just the one I wanted to teach them for me. Would you be interested?"

Suddenly that dreary, humdrum day began to glow with opportunity and possibility. "Yes," I said. "I am interested." Plans for my "Quickie Quilt Class" were underway.

The days and weeks flew by as I prepared for my classes. It was no great problem that I could find practically nothing written to help me. I had spent many years figuring out solutions to sewing problems. I just developed my own methods and enjoyed trying them out to be sure they were right. The classes went like a dream! I was thrilled and the students were excited about being able to make a whole quilt in two weeks.

At first I taught simple patterns and quilting methods for beginners. Later I began branching out, trying all the types of patterns on my machine. I found that I could do virtually all the things on my machine that others told me could only be done by hand: 1" (25 mm) hexagons for "Grandmother's Flower Garden"; curved seams for "Drunkard's Path"; set-in corners for "Rolling Star"; easy ways with diamonds and triangles and apartment quilts —yes, and even easily pieced circles and rings. I also found that very beautiful and effective quilting can be done by machine.

In some ways, I feel it has been an advantage to have been a machine sewer first, for when a problem in method or construction has come up, I have approached it from the point of view of a machine sewer, not that of a quilter. I was not bound by what had been done in the past or what could not be done according to hand-quilting procedures. Sometimes I did not learn until after I had solved a problem that the method I had developed for the machine would not work for hand quilting. If I had been a quilter first, these methods would likely not have occurred to me.

Quilting has now become the art I enjoy most. In fabric shops I now find I am more interested in cotton prints than in knits, woolens and silks. I am delighted to happen upon a quilt show in a shopping mall. I "doodle" quilt designs while I travel or watch T.V., and I am never without a small pad of graph paper in my handbag to use in such emergencies as a sudden idea for a new design or for "doodling" while waiting. Time on my hands is never a bore anymore! Quilting, in short, brings me so much pleasure and satisfaction that it is a further joy to have this opportunity to share it with you. I hope it is very contagious and that you find it as fulfilling as I do.

HETTIE RISINGER

INTRODUCTION

BACKGROUND OF QUILTING

Quilting has developed over a period of many centuries, first as a craft, out of necessity for warmth and protection, and finally as an art form as well. A great deal has been written in much detail and from various points of view about all that has happened to quilting and about its progress. Truly, it has blossomed forth from its earliest seedling-beginnings into a many-branched and many-flowered form. Quilting has been aided and nudged and influenced by many other developments: the opening up of a new source of materials, the use of more permanent dyes, the colonization of a New World, the development of faster and better weaving machines, better communication and transportation, growing trade, the easing of hard times, the migration across our continent. These are only a few of the many contributions to quilting and other needlework, as well as to life itself, as it is known today.

The great movements in the field of the fine arts have also had their influence upon quilting. The period, for instance, of oil-painted miniatures and small, exquisite pieces of sculpture is the same period out of which came size 000 knitting needles and petit point, tiny quilt pieces the size of a fingernail and trapunto cording every 1/8" (3 mm) on the fabric. More recently, just the opposite trend developed, so that we have jumbo knitting yarn and needles an inch (25 mm) in diameter, quick point, and sculpture on so gigantic a scale that it is dug into the earth or cut into the side of a mountain. One is not necessarily better than the other, only a different concept. Each is the outgrowth of the times in which it developed.

New ways and ideas are always met with cries of fearful protest and discredit by those who still value the old ways or who are reluctant to see the advent of change. It is true that new ways are not always good, nor are they always a threat to the old, which often overlap the new and are sometimes "rediscovered" at a later time and applied in a new context.

One important "new" thing in quilting has been creeping up on us, as change usually does, for some years—the sewing machine. Women have not been able to resist experimenting with this new tool since it was first introduced into their homes. Their skills in its use have developed along with the improvement of the machine itself until this method of sewing has finally come into its own. Now, with the renewed interest in quilting, talented and busy people naturally turn to their machines in making fine quilts. This does not endanger the old ways, nor should it. Rather, it complements and supplements them. It is a new area to be explored and developed side by side with the continuing advancement of other fine handwork of all types. These are still rightly being promoted and encouraged by those who appreciate beautiful things produced one at a time with loving care. This is the true attitude of the artisan. It is also the feeling of many who make quilts with the use of the sewing machine.

The use of the sewing machine does not necessarily mean poor workmanship or mass production, any more than the use of the many tools and pieces of equipment used by the makers of fine furniture or paintings or objects of crystal or silver or any other art indicates that these artists and craftsmen have fallen from their inner commitment to create objects of worth and beauty to the best of their skill and ability to conceive. For a sewing machine is a tool—nothing more and nothing less. It is the hands and the mind and the spirit of the one who uses the tool that determine the quality of the results. It has the same relationship to quilting that the electric oven has to the baking of bread or that the typewriter has to the writing of a book.

This book is written to help those who are interested in developing their skills and conserving their efforts in making quilts by machine. With its use you can progress to whatever level is your personal aim. You will not be pushed to become a fine artisan if you only want to make a quick everyday floor quilt for the children. On the other hand, this book will instruct you in the basic skills needed to produce quilts of great beauty and fine workmanship—yes, even of true artistic achievement. If that is your desire, something from within yourself must build upon these skills for its fulfillment.

This view is in complete accord with the attitudes of quilters in the past. Not all quilts were planned for presentation to some honored person or for use only when company came. Most were planned for, and completely worn out in, everyday use. The time and care in workmanship used for making quilts was adapted to their intended use, and the quilter made no pretenses about it.

It seems to me that quilting has something to offer people with all types of interest: the casual interest in working with color and fabric and pattern; the interest in producing a quilt of exceptionally fine and lasting quality; and also to the many whose interest lies somewhere between. Each of these needs is real and the satisfaction of achievement for each one is fulfilling. Happiness results from working toward, and sometimes achieving, your own goals without being limited by those of some or pressured beyond your aims by others. If you will apply this attitude to quilting, you will have a wonderful time.

A Word about Original Design and Giving Credit Where Credit Is Due

Scarcely had I begun to take an active interest in quilting than I started getting ideas for designs of my own. Since then I have made them by the score and more. No sooner do I pick up a pencil and a pad of graph paper and begin to make a few lines than the patterns begin to flow. Sometimes ideas come faster than I can get them down. One design often leads to one or more variations which develop from the first idea (see Illus. 1). It is not too surprising that, as I enjoy the many books and magazines on quilting which are increasingly available, I sometimes come across one of "my" designs proclaimed as an old and cherished pattern of generations gone by. This does not mean that I did not "create" it as a part of my developing ability. It simply means that I did not create it first. This is not an uncommon thing. It happens to all creative thinkers every now and then. I understand, for instance, that the invention of television occurred in two parts of the world at the same time.

This does not mean that there is no such thing as an original idea or design or that the one who is creative enough to come up with one should have no credit. Nor does it mean that none of my designs are original. I believe that many of them are original, which pleases me, but I am equally pleased to give the credit to someone else if it is due. It is certainly not my intention or desire to claim credit for the original creation of any design which is not truly mine. There are uncounted numbers of patterns in existence, however, and I have not seen them all—nor do I know of any way to check my collection against all those patterns which have been done by others over the centuries.

There also seems to be some difference of opinion as to just what qualifies as an original design. Some recognize only designs which have never been published or used before by anyone. Some concede that variations of an old design may be claimed as original or at least as an original variation. Another school of thought accepts any design that has been given a new appearance—that has been made to look different by a new way of combining colors or values—as being a new design, and perhaps they should be. Only slight variation seems to be needed in the realm of fashion for a designer to claim a design as his or her "own." It seems equally reasonable to apply this same qualification to quilt design.

The pros and cons of this issue will not likely affect many quilters in a very earth-shaking way. I offer these variations in thinking on the subject merely as an insight into the dilemma I have encountered in offering the many designs in this book which I have not seen anywhere before, so far as I know, and which I feel to be original. I feel that the important thing is for quilt patterns to be shared, as quilters have shared them from the beginning, with all the joy of sharing. The main thing I am trying to do is to share, not to claim credit unjustly. If I seem to do so, it is in complete innocence.

Illus. 1. Variations on a design.

A similar problem arises when it comes to giving credit for someone else's ideas and methods. For the most part, I developed the machine quilting methods I use on my own because I could find so little printed on the subject. Recently, I have occasionally seen a method described which is similar to one I use. I know that the person from whom it came did not get the idea from me because I have not published my methods before. On the other hand, I did not get the idea from her either.

There are, however, some ideas which I have gleaned from reading and study and which I have used or adapted for use in my teaching. Not realizing that I would someday write a book on this subject, I did not keep a record of these instances. I am very sorry about this because I appreciate what I have learned from others and would be glad of this opportunity to express my thanks. I have, nevertheless, enjoyed and appreciated these books and have often found a useful bit of information in them.

SECTION 1
Basic Information

QUILTING TERMS AND EQUIPMENT

Following are two lists of terms you should become familiar with before you begin to work on your quilts. The first is a list of quilting terms, and the second is a list of equipment you will need as you machine quilt.

Definitions

ALL-WHITE QUILT or WHITE WORK. A quilt made entirely of white materials and completely covered with quilting and/or cording as the only design.

APPLIQUÉ. To sew a small piece of fabric to a larger one by either hemming it down or embroidering around the edges or both.

BACK or BACKING. The bottom layer of the quilt.

BASTE. To sew layers or pieces together with long running stitches or pins which are to be removed later.

BATTING or FILL. The fluffy material used between the top and the back to give loft to the quilting and warmth to the quilt.

BINDING. A strip of bias or straight-cut fabric used to enclose the raw edges of the quilt by hemming to both the top and the back. Also the process of attaching this strip.

BLOCK. The unit of quilt pieces which form the quilt pattern and may be repeated to make up the entire top of the quilt. They are usually square, but may be of other shapes.

BORDER. A band of fabric which is sewed to all edges of the quilt and has the effect of a frame for the rest of the top. It can be plain, in which case it may be quilted with a pattern; or it may be pieced and quilted.

COMFORTER. A very thick quilt, 3" or 4" (7.5–10 cm) deep, which may be either tied or quilted.

COVERLET. Originally a quilt not large enough to cover the pillows, it was used primarily for warmth. It was once the most often-made quilt. Today a little larger-size quilt which covers the pillows and is used with dust ruffles to reach the floor is called a coverlet. It is this size for which the yardages in the charts in this book are figured. It is this size, rather than the other, which is more often put to daytime use as a decorative bed covering.

CRAZY QUILT. A quilt without pattern and made of random-size pieces and colors of fabrics over the entire top of the quilt. Blocks or strips of these pieces are sometimes made up and joined together to form the top.

FOUNDATION BLOCK. A plain block or piece of fabric to which pieces are sewed to form the pattern of one block or the entire top of a quilt. These are often used in making Crazy Quilts, Log Cabin Quilts and appliquéd quilts of all types.

LATTICE or SASHING. Strips of fabric used between the blocks to separate them. Squares the width of the strips are sometimes used at the intersections. These can be either plain or pieced. Occasionally the entire lattice is pieced and the block left plain. In this case, quilting skills are usually displayed on the plain blocks.

MASTERPIECE QUILT. A quilt, either pieced or appliquéd, which is made up of thousands of tiny pieces; or else one closely covered with an elaborate pattern of quilting such as the All White Quilt.

MEDALLION QUILT. A quilt with a dominant central area, either pieced, appliquéd, printed or plain, which is surrounded by one or more borders, also either pieced, appliquéd, printed or plain, to complete the top.

MITER. A diagonal seam joining two pieces of fabric to form a corner. For quilts, this is often used on the border.

PATCH. Originally a small piece of fabric sewed over a hole in a larger piece of fabric, the word has come to mean a single piece of fabric which is sewed together with one or more other pieces of fabric to make up a pattern. It is also used to indicate a single shape of fabric piece which is sewed together with other pieces of like shape to make an all-over pattern, such as a one-patch pattern. Both of these are actually a misuse of the word, which may be confusing to some, but is usually understood by quilters. The word may also indicate a piece of fabric which is appliquéd to another piece of fabric. This is a more logical use of the word.

PATCHWORK. This term has come to mean a piece of fabric which has been made up of pieces sewed together to be used as a unit. It usually refers to a quilt but may also indicate the fabric for a garment, such as a patchwork skirt, or that used for any other item made of this fabric, such as a patchwork tote bag, etc.

QUILT. A bed covering of three layers, usually a top and a back with batting in between, which are stitched together to form a single unit.

QUILT TOP. The top layer of the quilt. It may be a single piece of fabric, or it may be pieced, appliquéd or embroidered, etc.

REVERSE APPLIQUÉ. An appliqué technique in which the design is set into the surrounding fabric by hemming this to the design rather than the other way around.

SCRAP QUILT or SCRAP BAG QUILT. A quilt made up of bits of fabric accumulated from other projects, usually garment making. Varieties of fabrics and usually also of colors are used together instead of only a few which were purchased for the purpose. They are more casual but can be equally as lovely as the other kind.

THE SET. The method of joining the blocks together to form the top. The quilt might be "set solid," which would mean that only patterned blocks were used; or it might be set with setting blocks, which would indicate the use of plain pieces of fabric the same size as the blocks to alternate with the blocks. Blocks may also be set with lattice strips.

TEMPLATE. A pattern usually used for marking the parts of a design on fabric. This is used for pieces to be cut for piecing or appliqué as well as for marking quilting designs.

THROW or NAPPING QUILT. A small quilt to be used like an afghan in either the bedroom, family room or living room.

TIED QUILT. One in which the layers are fastened together at regular intervals with single stitches which are then tied. This is usually used for very thick quilts but may also be used for other quilts to save time. The method is much more practical with the availability of polyester batting than it was with other types which would bunch up if not quilted closely.

TRAPUNTO. A type of quilting in which the stitching is done first through two pieces of fabric only and the outlined spaces are then stuffed or corded to raise the design above the surface of the fabric. This type of quilting is extensively used in the All White Quilt.

UTILITY QUILT. One intended for everyday use. When there was a scarcity of time, these might be hurried through the piecing and quilting processes. At other times, they would be done with more attention to good workmanship, though not with the exceptional skills devoted to Presentation, Wedding, Masterpiece or other quilts created to be show pieces.

Equipment

COLOR PENCILS or CRAYONS. These are used for the color diagrams. You can get more for your money if you buy crayons, but the pencils are easier to keep sharp enough for coloring small shapes, especially when you will be making diagrams having blocks made up of a number of small pieces. You might try both to see which you prefer. If you go to an art or office supply store, you can find a wide selection of colors in pencils and you may buy only a few colors at a time as needed, gradually building up a larger collection.

COMPASS. A tool for drawing circles.

CUTTING BOARD. These can be found in fabric shops and departments. If they are not available in your area, one can be made by marking a large piece of thin plywood every inch (25 mm) in both directions. Take care to do this accurately and to see that the lines in one direction are exactly perpendicular to those in the opposite direction (a carpenter's square or a purchased triangle or even a plumb line might be used for this), otherwise, the board is of little use. It is also useful to have occasional diagonal lines marked in one or both directions. Along one or more edges, the inch (25 mm) marks should be numbered and marked off into quarter inches (6 mm). You will find this a very useful piece of equipment for other sewing as well as quilting.

GRAPH PAPER. This can be purchased where school or office supplies are sold. The inexpensive kind is all right for making color diagrams, but the accurately drawn type, which is also more expensive, is needed if you are making templates and want to use the lines in calculating the measurements. This second kind comes in 4, 5, 6, and 8 spaces to the inch (25 mm). One type has heavy ruling evenly spaced in both directions to help you count spaces, etc. The less expensive kind comes in 4 spaces to the inch only. I use all kinds and sizes according to which is most convenient for the purpose. You may want to try them all sooner or later. To begin with, any one will do.

HANDSEWING NEEDLES. One in a medium to small size is occasionally needed. Either sharps or betweens (also known as quilting needles) are all right, so choose the length that is more comfortable to you. A person with small hands often prefers the shorter betweens for all types of sewing rather than just for quilting.

IRONING BOARD. The conventional types are satisfactory for ironing. The ones which have an adjustable height are also convenient to use at the machine to support the bulk of the quilt while you are working on it.

You may also want to make an additional ironing board which is a real help in ironing large, flat items of all kinds, such as laundered fabric, quilt tops and backs, or sections of them, as well as linens and other items. This is made with a base of ½" to ¾" (12–18 mm) plywood at least 2' x 4' (60–120 cm)—or as large as you can handle conveniently. Cover this with pad-ding topped with muslin which has been shrunk. Pull the muslin very snug and tack it to the wrong side of the board securely. The muslin can be marked every inch (25 mm) like a cutting board. This can be used on a table or supported by the backs of two straight chairs (protect the chairs with folded towels to prevent scratching). The table is better if it is not too low for you, however, because it will support the overhanging fabric, which would otherwise fall to the floor.

LIGHT. Good light is a must for all needlework. Try to arrange the best light you can so that you can do your best work without eyestrain.

MACHINE NEEDLES. A size 80 or 90 or a size 14 needle, either sharp or ball-point, is fine for most piecing and quilting. Use a size 90 or a size 16 for a heavier quilt or comforter. Needles must be in good condition. One that has barely tipped a pin in sewing or is even slightly damaged in any way may cause skipped stitches or threads pulled in the fabric. The damage may not be extensive enough to be seen easily. Sometimes a tiny hook on the point can be felt with the thumbnail when it does not show up under a magnifier.

PENCIL. A pencil or ball-point pen is needed for drawing diagrams. A pencil is used for marking pieces on fabric.

PROTRACTOR. An instrument for measuring and laying off angles, a flat semi-circular tool on which are indicated all the degrees of angles from zero degree to 180 degrees. This is used for drafting diamonds and hexagons and other pieces requiring a precise measurement of an angle.

RULER. Many types of rulers are available. Any is satisfactory if it is straight and the markings accurate—not all are.

SCISSORS. For this work, your scissors must be very sharp. Synthetic fibers dull the blades (as well as the points of needles!) more quickly than natural fibers because they are tougher. This toughness is what makes synthetics wear well and resist wrinkles—which is what we like about them. It means, however, that scissors must be sharpened more frequently these days than they used to be. If you are planning to buy new scissors, by all means purchase the very best quality you can afford, even if it means scrimping somewhere else. A good pair of scissors is an investment and will last for many years if properly cared for. It is, therefore, worth its price if you choose wisely. Cheap scissors are more expensive in the long run. They are not as sharp to begin with, do not hold an edge well and cannot be sharpened as well as the quality ones. For all these reasons, less expensive scissors are very frustrating to try to work with and a poor choice.

SEWING MACHINE. You will need a machine which is in good working order, one which is well made and gives you no problems with thread tensions or other mechanical operations. It should be kept oiled frequently enough to prevent wear on the parts and to keep it functioning at its best (about every eight hours or so of actual sewing is often enough). Keep the lint cleared away from the bobbin, feed dogs and needle areas with the little brush provided. A zigzag machine is not required except for some of the embroidery, appliqué and other special processes. Most of the work in this book can be done with a straight stitch machine.

SEWING THREAD. Regular machine sewing thread is the best. Do not use quilting thread. For all cotton fabrics, cotton thread is the best choice. For synthetics and blends, the cotton-wrapped polyester thread works well.

SHRINK ART PLASTIC. One of the plastics used for shrink art which is frosted and has a grain on one side which prevents it from slipping on the fabric. This makes excellent templates because they do not wear on the edges. It is now often available in quilt shops.

STRAIGHT PINS. I like to use two different types. The first is a very fine, extra long pin imported from Switzerland and called "Iris Superfein." They slip through a number of layers of fabric like needles and so are a pleasure to work with. These pins have a very small head, however, so when I am working with batting, I use an extra long, glassheaded pin because it is easier to see and to use for that purpose. Other types of pins are all right, though they may be a little more awkward. Safety pins may be used to hold the layers of the quilt together if you prefer. They do not work their way out of the fabrics and do not prick your hands while you are working. A large number would be required for this, however, so they would be more expensive to start with. On the other hand, you are not so likely to lose them, so they might be

more economical in the long run. They are a little more awkward to pin into place and to remove, so try a few before you invest in them.

WATER-SOLUBLE MARKING PEN. This should be one made especially for marking fabrics. It can be found in some fabric shops. When the marks are no longer needed they can be removed simply by moistening them with cotton, cloth or a fine spray of water. This pen is used for marking quilting patterns and other marks which would show if not removable. A pen with its own liquid "eraser" has recently appeared on the market.

YARDSTICK (METERSTICK). Be sure that the markings are accurate. Some are not.

FABRICS

Generally speaking, the best fabric for making quilts is a cotton or a blended fabric of cotton and dacron or rayon in the weight usually used for blouses, dresses and shirts. A bed sheet can be used and is very economical. However, if you plan to piece by machine and then quilt by hand, a sheet is not necessarily a good choice. If the sheet has been treated to make it permanent press, the hand quilting may be made difficult by this. Other fabrics, such as silk, satin, taffeta, woolens, corduroy, velvets, drapery fabric, and what have you, are sometimes used effectively. Most of these are more easily handled by the person with some experience in sewing them in other projects, and they require the same special treatment and care when quilted that they do when made into garments and other items. They are sometimes used for quilts, but are not the usual choice, nor the best.

One-hundred-per-cent-cotton fabric is soft and is easy to work with. It tends to wrinkle when washed, however. When sewed together in small pieces, this may not be too noticeable, and it gives an authentic, traditional appearance. (Quilts should not be ironed, but may be lightly touched up if necessary.) However, treated cottons and cotton blends do *not* wrinkle, so when they are sewed together with 100 per cent cotton fabric, the difference may sometimes be quite noticeable. For this reason, it is more practical not to mix the two. On the other hand, while 100 per cent cotton prints have become readily available again, solid colors are still hard to find. If you must mix the blends with the all-cotton fabrics—and this is quite acceptable and also commonly done—be careful. If you must use an iron on the cotton, be sure that it is not too hot for the blend. If you cannot find 100 per cent cotton and would like to use it, see the list of sources of supplies at the end of the book.

One decision which often gives a feeling of doubt to a beginning quilter, especially, is choosing the prints and colors for a quilt. Your natural feeling for combining these important elements will grow with experience. Stack the bolts of fabric you are considering and look at the edges together, so that you will see only a small area of fabric at a time as you do in quilt pieces. Rearrange the order of the fabric in the stack to try the different ones side by side. Squint your eyes up tight to get a better comparison of the *value* relationship. This helps you to see the light and dark relationship without being so influenced by color. As a rule of thumb, a good range of values gives a stronger effect.

Look at the street or countryside and notice how the strong lights and darks with various intermediate values define and give character to the scene. The same thing happens with the fabrics in your quilt. Using fabrics of all light colors tends to give a washed-out look, if not handled very carefully. A quilt of all dark values can look drab, lacking in pattern distinction, unless properly combined with an eye for the subtle variations within the fabrics which come from the colors of the prints. When you find a combination that pleases you, you are probably quite safe in your choices. If you still feel insecure and doubtful about what you think you like, then make up a group of four blocks to see how the fabrics actually work together. This can be used as a wall hanging, on a floor pillow or other useful item, so your time and fabrics will not be wasted.

Colorfastness is very important in making quilts. A color that runs into adjoining fabric can ruin the appearance of a quilt. Even good quality fabric, for which you may have paid a high price, may still not have fast color. Usually the darker colors are the ones you have to be cautious about. Wet a corner of the fabric in question in very hot water before putting it into the wash. If the color bleeds at all, it is best to set the color, although a little bleeding in the first washing may not recur after that. You may want to wash the fabric alone and then retest it. To set the color, immerse the fabric in a boiling solution of one cup (240 milliliters) of white vinegar to each gallon (3.8 liters) of water used, and boil for about ten minutes while keeping the fabric pushed down into the solution. Air bubbles form under the wet fabric and lift it out of the water. The best utensil to hold the solution is one of enamel or stainless steel. Aluminum may absorb some of the color and can affect the efficiency of the treatment. I use the insert pan from my electric roaster. When you are sure the color will not run, wash and dry the fabric by machine, using a warm setting to be sure it has shrunk and that all sizing is removed. Iron the fabric if needed. It is now ready for use.

BATTING

Batting is a fluffy "fabric" which comes in large sheets. Batting made of polyester is best to use because cotton must be quilted every inch or two (25–50 mm) to keep it from wadding up in use and washing. Wool batting is the warmest, but it also requires close quilting and it shrinks, so the quilt would need to be dry cleaned or washed in cold water.

Wool gives a nice springy loft to the quilt. Bonded polyester batting can be washed or dry cleaned and holds in place when quilting is done as far as 8" or 9" (20–22.5 cm) apart and even when only tied every 5" or 6" (12.5–15 cm). If very rough use is expected, the quilting or tying should be closer. The best bonded polyester battings have a soft, springy loft and good strength in handling. There are two general types of bonding. One type has a glaze of bonding on each surface with a fluffy layer in between. The other is bonded throughout and looks a little like a sponge. Be sure that the one you choose is soft and pliable like a blanket, not stiff or firm. Unbonded polyester should seldom, if ever, be used because the fibers tend to work through the fabric, especially when blends are used. This will cause an unattractive pilling or linting on the surface of the quilt.

Bonded polyester batting does not require especially careful handling, so it lends itself best to the methods of construction described here and to inexperienced hands when other methods are used. When quilted, the lines of stitching make a more defined indentation, so that the work appears puffier. There is also more contrast between the unquilted area and the closely quilted one than when other types of batting are used. Several sizes of batting are available and some manufacturers make more than one thickness as well. Watch for good softness in the thicker ones. More than one layer of the thin batting can be used to attain the amount of thickness desired. With experience you will become acquainted with the varying effects which can be achieved with different types of batting and you should consider these effects in selecting which to use. Refer to Sources of Supplies listed at the back of this book for any of these items which you cannot find.

THE CARE OF MACHINE-MADE QUILTS

The machine-made quilt is not nearly so fragile as the hand-made one. It can, therefore, be safely laundered in any good washing machine. Since the colors have been set and the fabrics shrunk before they were cut, you can wash them in either warm or cold water. A gentle or a wash-and-wear setting is preferable. Any soap or detergent which is suitable for the fabrics you have used is safe for the quilt. If the dryer does not have a gentle or warm cycle or temperature setting, be sure to remove the quilt before it is thoroughly dry, to prevent the heat from damaging the fabrics.

I share with you this caution, which I learned as a child from my grandmother. The quilt should not always be folded along exactly the same lines or with the same half on the inside. Varying the fold lines will keep it from wearing along the creases. It should be put away with the lining folded to the outside to protect the top.

STANDARD QUILT SIZES

Here is a chart of standard mattress sizes to help you in deciding the size of your quilts.

Crib mattress   27" x 54" (67.5 x 135 cm)
Bunk mattress   30" x 75" (75 x 187.5 cm)
Twin mattress   39" x 75" (97.5 x 187.5 cm)
Extra long
 twin mattress 39" x 80" (97.5 x 200 cm)
Full mattress   54" x 75" (135 x 187.5 cm)
Queen mattress 60" x 80" (150 x 200 cm)
King mattress   76" x 80" (190 x 200 cm)

There are two styles of quilts which are commonly made. The quilt which is like a spread is usually made to reach the floor or come within about an inch (25 mm) of it. The second type of quilt does not soil as quickly along the edges as other types. This style is called a coverlet, which comes in two sizes. One size is used like a blanket and is not long enough to go over the pillows. If this size is to be used for a spread, then pillow shams may be made of one of the fabrics used in the quilt or shams can be pieced or appliquéd, etc., to match the quilt. The other size coverlet is made long enough to cover the pillows. Both of these fall some distance short of the floor. A coverlet should extend down beyond the thickness of the mattress by a full 2" (5 cm) or more. Dust ruffles which hang from just below the mattress to about floor length are used with coverlets for the completed effect that most people prefer today.

The easiest way to make dust ruffles is to attach them to a fitted sheet which is then put on the box springs. Made this way, they will always stay in place without any problem. Make the ruffles as described in Section 5. When they have been hemmed and gathered, place the fitted sheet on the box spring. Lay the ruffle on the spring wrong side up so that the raw, gathered edge lies along the top edge of the spring. Pin it in place all around. Carefully remove the sheet from the spring and sew the ruffle in place as pinned. Replace the sheet on the spring and the ruffle will fall into place to the floor.

Quilts for bunk beds should be made large enough to tuck under the mattress all around and to cover the pillow, or not, as desired. A pillow sham can be used if needed.

A throw or napping quilt should be made long enough to tuck under the toes and cover the shoulders of a sleeping adult. It should be wide enough to cover well along the sides also.

A crib quilt can be made long enough to reach from end to end of the mattress and hang down on each side far enough to cover it. Some are made a little longer than this, some a little shorter, and some are only as wide as the mattress.

SECTION 2

Basic Quilting Methods for the Machine

This is a project in which everyone can begin at the same level. Those who are new to quilting may even be at some advantage here because they have no experience to carry over from hand quilting which may not apply to machine work. If you have had experience in quilting by hand or by machine, try to keep an open mind about the procedures presented in this book, which may be different from those you have used, or which may seem contrary to those you have learned. These methods work very nicely for all my students, so I am sure that they will work for you, also.

Since your primary goal is to learn methods, I have chosen some simple but very pretty patterns for you to work with. This is to keep you from having to struggle with a difficult pattern while you are getting acquainted with the methods. Later on in the book, a number of pattern choices will be suggested for additional practice, and instructions will be given for adapting them to the methods. If you are quite experienced in working with patterns, you may want to use a pattern from this more complicated group in learning the methods. You may, for instance, prefer to make "Trip around the World" (color page E) which has always seemed to be too time consuming in the past, instead of the relatively easy "Patience." A carefully made color diagram will be invaluable to you when working with these alternate patterns. By the time you have learned all the methods, you should be able to make virtually any type of pattern or quilt with your sewing machine.

Follow the procedures in the order given. They are explained in detail to make them quite easy to do. You will find that the work flows smoothly from step to step and that everything has been planned to make the work easy and time saving. Do not try

to hurry. Never sacrifice good workmanship in the hope of saving time, or you will be left with the choice of doing work over or accepting an inferior quilt.

Each method and pattern builds on the previous one and repetition reinforces the learning process. The idea is to use each method often enough to make it feel natural, and to begin to work it into your habits. You know your own skills better than anyone else, so choose a project that will give you the amount of practice required for your own needs. You may not want to make a full-sized quilt of every design used as a learning experience. If you prefer, you may make a crib or a napping-size quilt, or perhaps even a pillow top of the same pattern on a smaller scale.

CONSTRUCTION OF ONE-PATCH PATTERNS OF SQUARES OR RECTANGLES

The most simple quilt pattern, and probably the oldest one, is called "one-patch." Triangles, hexagons or diamonds, as well as the squares with which we will begin, can be made into one-patch designs. (Methods for these other shapes will be found in Section 3.) A one-patch pattern is made up of enough pieces of one shape sewed together to make an entire quilt top, rather than sewing several pieces together to form a block and then sewing repeats of this block together for the top. Surprising as it may seem, a one-patch square can be made into quite a variety of quilt designs. To keep our first design simple, we will start with three colors and/or prints, plus border fabric. We will make a diagonal design called "Patience." (This pattern is actually a nine-patch pattern, as you will see later in Section 2, but it is easier when done as a one-patch.) The following chart will tell you the yardage needed for the various sizes of quilts in this pattern.

Making a Color Diagram

A color diagram is a small-scale picture of the entire quilt. To make one, you will need some graph paper, a ruler, a ball-point pen or a pencil and some color pencils or crayons to indicate the colors or the fabrics you have chosen. See Section 1 for more about these supplies.

When you begin your own planning for a quilt, you may want to make your diagram before buying fabric. It can help you in figuring yardage and can be an inexpensive way to experiment with color. Yardage charts are given to help you with all the patterns used in describing the methods in Section 2. For other patterns, you will find instructions for figuring the yardage in Section 8.

In drawing your quilt top to scale, let one square on the paper equal one inch (25 mm) of the quilt top. Draw a rectangle or a square on the graph paper according to the measurements given for the size quilt you have chosen to make. Count your spaces very carefully to be sure you are accurate. You may need to tape two or more sheets of paper together to have enough room to make a diagram of the larger size quilts. Next, move in enough squares from all sides to indicate the border and draw another rectangle or square inside the original one. Mark off the inside rectangle or square into 3-space squares to indicate the 3" (7.5 cm) square pieces. Any size square could be used for this pattern, but I have figured the yardage for 3" (7.5 cm) finished squares. These are small enough for a pillow top and large enough to work up fairly fast in the quilts. If you prefer a larger or a smaller square, you may use any size you like, but be sure to purchase extra fabric for smaller squares because there will be more seams. At the top or side of the paper, draw square "swatches" of your fabric and label them A, B, C and Border (see Illus. 2).

The next step is to color the squares according to the fabrics you have chosen, placing the colors as shown in the diagram for the "Patience" quilt. Your diagram will be your guide in making the quilt top. It will tell you the number of pieces needed for the length and width of the quilt and show the order in which they are to be sewn together. For a simple pattern such as this, a diagram may seem unnecessary, but it can be a real help and will give you practice before you need to diagram the more complicated patterns.

Yardage Chart for "Patience" Quilts

(Allowances have been made for 3 per cent shrinkage and for straightening fabric carelessly cut from the bolt.)

Twin-size spread: 82" x 109" (22" drop) [205 x 272.5 cm (55 cm drop)] 25 x 34 pieces = 850 pieces, 284 pieces of each of 3 colors 3½" (87 mm) border

Yardage: (44" [110 cm] fabric, selvages trimmed) 9¼ yds. (8 m 32 cm) for back, border and 1 set of pieces 2½ yds. (2 m 25 cm) for each color (2)

Twin-size coverlet: 62" x 98" (155 x 245 cm) 19 x 35 pieces = 665 pieces, 222 of each color 2½" (6 cm) border

Yardage: (44" [110 cm] fabric, selvages trimmed) 6 yds. (meters) for back and border only 2 yds. (meters) for each color

Double bed spread: 98" x 109" (22" drop) [245 x 272.5 cm (55 cm drop)] 31 x 34 pieces = 1,052 pieces, 351 of each color (3) 2½" (6 cm) border

Yardage: (44" [110 cm] fabric, selvages trimmed) 9¼ yds. (8 m 32 cm) for back, borders only 3⅛ yds. (2 m 80 cm) for each color

Double bed coverlet: 77" x 98" (11" drop) [192.5 x 245 cm (27.5 cm drop)] 24 x 31 pieces = 744 pieces, 248 of each color 2½" (6 cm) border

Yardage: (44" [110 cm] fabric, selvages trimmed) 6 yds. (meters) for back, border only 2¼ yds. (2m 2 cm) for each color

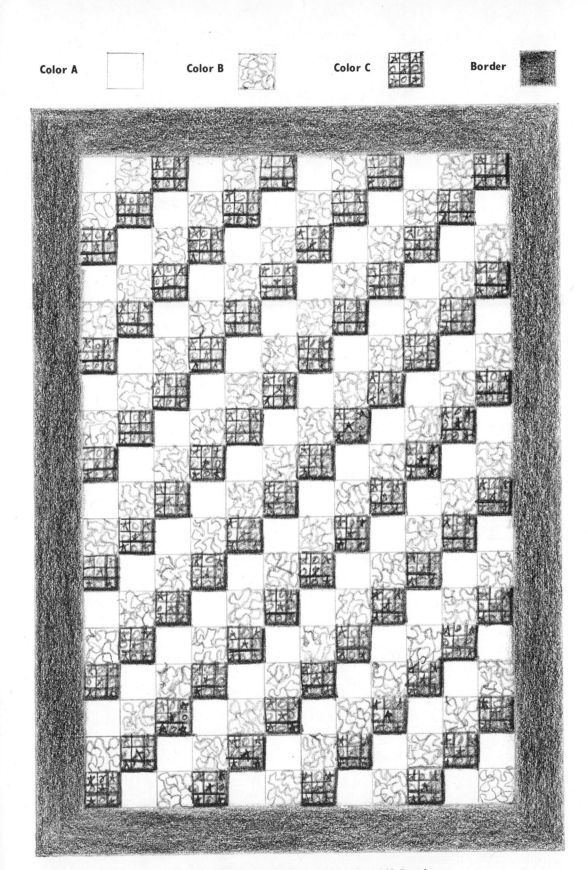

Color A   Color B   Color C   Border

Illus. 2. "Patience." 44″ × 65″ (110 × 162.5 cm).

Queen-size spread: 104″ x 119″ (22″ drop)
[260 x 297.5 cm (55 cm drop)]
32 x 37 pieces = 1,184 pieces, 395 of each color
3½″ (13.7 cm) borders

Yardage: (44″ [110 cm] fabric, selvages trimmed)
11 yds. (meters) for back and border only
3½ yds. (3 m 15 cm) for each color

Queen-size coverlet: 83″ x 92″ (11″ drop)
[207.5 x 230 cm (27.5 cm drop)]
26 x 29 pieces = 754 pieces, 233 of each color

Yardage: (44″ [110 cm] fabric, selvages trimmed)
8¾ yds. (7 m 87 cm) for back, border and one color
2⅜ yds. (2 m 13 cm) for each color

King-size spread: 119″ x 119″ (22″ drop)
[297.5 x 297.5 cm (55 cm drop)]
38 x 38 pieces = 1,424 pieces, 475 of each color
5″ (12.5 cm) border

Yardage: (44″ [110 cm] fabric, selvages trimmed)
14 yds. (meters) for back, border and one color piece
4 yds. (meters) for each color

King-size coverlet: 100″ x 100″ (22″ drop)
[250 x 250 cm (55 cm drop)]
32 x 32 pieces = 1,024 pieces, 342 of each color

Yardage: (44″ [110 cm] fabric, selvages trimmed)
9 yds. (meters) for back and 4″ (10 cm) border only
3 yds. (meters) for each color

NOTE: Cut pieces 3½″ (8.7 cm) square.

Quick and Easy Ways to Mark and Cut Square and Rectangular Pieces

With the diagram completed, you are ready to cut the fabric. Lay out your cutting board on a large table, or on the floor if you prefer. You have, of course, laundered your fabric as described in Section 1. Beginning with the fabric for color A (see Illus. 2), fold the fabric lengthwise, wrong side out, and pin the selvages together carefully. Lay the fabric on the cutting board so that the selvages lie exactly along one lengthwise line near to the side where you will be working. Lay your yardstick (meterstick) along a crossways line of the cutting board near the end of the fabric, and draw a line on the fabric with a pencil to straighten the end, but do not cut the fabric yet (see Illus. 3).

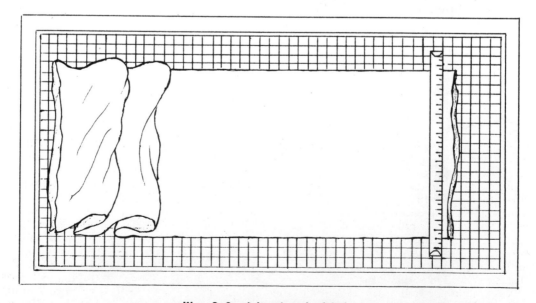

Illus. 3. Straightening the fabric.

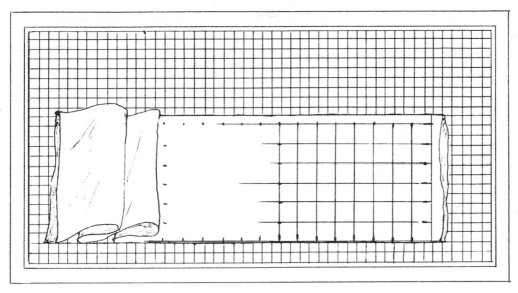

Illus. 4. Marking the pieces.

Never tear a fabric of blended fibers. Cotton *can* be torn, but it is better not to do so when following these methods. If you inspect the torn edge of a piece of fabric, you will find that the threads are broken off irregularly, some perhaps ¼″ (6 mm) from the edge. This weakens the seam allowances. Lengthwise tears often seem to draw up along the tear, making the fabric difficult to work with. If you must have fabric cut right on the grain, pull a thread and cut along it. Most instructions would have you pull a thread and cut along it to straighten the fabric. This method is all right, but it is slow and it may not work well on fabrics of blended fibers. These fabrics are often permanently "set" in the process of winding them on the bolt, so that the threads are warped out of "square."

One-hundred-per-cent-cotton fabric will usually come straight in washing and ironing unless it has a special finish which may prevent this. In either case, marking the fabric as described above gives you a straight line from which to work. If this results in the crossways threads being slightly off grain, it doesn't seem to make any difference, except in the case of woven crossways stripes, plaids and checks. These must be marked and cut separately on the threads, if it is important enough to the appearance of the quilt—and it often is, even though it results in warped pieces. However, the other pieces sewn to these warped pieces usually pull them straight and the quilting holds them in place, so that the result is satisfactory.

Now, make a small mark just inside the selvage, on the line you have drawn to straighten the end of the fabric. The selvage should usually be cut off. (The selvage can be used if needed, but only if it has not shrunk at all in washing.) From this mark, measure off and mark 3½″ (9 cm) spaces along the line. Move the yardstick about 30″ (75 cm) along the fabric and again lay it parallel to a crossways line on the cutting board. *Do not* draw a line here, but mark off the 3½″ (9 cm) spaces as before. Repeat this step as needed until all the necessary fabric is marked. Now join the sets of marks with horizontal lines, so that there will be a number of parallel lines along the length of the fabric. These lines are as far apart as the *width* of the pieces to be cut.

For the *length* of the pieces, start at the original line across the end of the fabric and mark off 3½″ (9 cm) spaces along the lengthwise line near the selvage and along the lengthwise line near the fold. Join these pairs of marks with lines crossways on the fabric (see Illus. 4).

Fold the other pieces of fabric to be cut into squares as you did the first piece and lay the marked fabric (Color A) on top of Color B fabric, with Color C fabric on the bottom, making sure that all layers are smooth. Match and pin all the selvages together carefully. Then place a pin in the lower right and the lower left corners of each square, near the selvage. Place pins in this same position in all the other squares. On the row of squares near the fold, pin both upper corners as well. Pin through all six layers of fabric. All pins should point in the same direction. Pinning in this exact way will hold all the layers together adequately and will save time when removing the pins.

Cut through all layers along the line nearest the fold first and save the long fold-piece for some other quilt such as "Log Cabin" or a string quilt (patterns to be used later). Next, cut along all the crossways lines, and then cut the resulting strips into pieces along the vertical lines. *Do not remove the pins yet.*

Some quilting instructions direct you to cut only the long, lengthwise strips of fabric the width of the pieces plus the seam allowances, then to pin the strips to prevent easing and to sew these strips together in the order in which the pieces are arranged. These long, pieced strips are then cut off into piece or block lengths depending upon the pattern, and the blocks are sewed together in strips which are next joined to complete the quilt top. I am sure that this method is just as accurate as the one I teach, and it would work very well for "Roman Stripe" patterns. It is actually an adaptation of the method used for Seminole piecing, and is a very good method to use when working with patterns requiring very narrow strips of fabric (see Section 7 on Seminole piecing). However, the method I have described saves much more time for several reasons. First, all the

marking is done at one time. Second, the pieces are cut in both directions six or eight layers at a time, so that there is no going back to mark and cut each block one at a time. Third, the pieces are a little easier to sew than the strips, because there is no need to pin them and they are not as awkward to handle as the long strips.

Fold the fabric for the border and straighten the end as before. Measure and mark two strips the width of the cut width of the border along the length of the fabric —the way you marked the first long lines for the squares. You should mark one strip as long as the full length of the quilt (including the end border) plus about 4" (10 cm) for seams and ease in handling. You should mark the other strip as long as the full width of the quilt plus 4" (10 cm). Since the fabric is doubled, when you pin and cut you will have two pieces of each length. These measurements are for the border with mitered corners, which I usually use. Two other types of borders which are used by many quilters will be described later.

"String-Sewing" the Pieces Together

It is very convenient to have a table (or chair, bed, T.V. tray, etc.) to your left (if you are right-handed) while you are working at the sewing machine. Place all the pieces on this table and you are ready to begin sewing. Remove the pins from one set of squares. Place a Color A square right side up in front of the machine needle. (Lay the other A piece aside.) Place a B piece right sides together—no pins are needed—on the first A piece and sew a ¼" (6 mm) seam using 12 stitches to the inch (25 mm). (See Illus. 5.) If the seam puckers, then adjust the tension to prevent this. Be sure to sew accurately, for even a small variation repeated many times will add up to a significant change in the size of the finished quilt top. The side of the presser foot is a good guide for sewing this ¼" (6 mm) seam. *Do not cut the thread.* Now, place the other B piece right sides together with a C piece on top and sew a ¼" (6 mm) seam, but *still do not* cut the thread. Sew the other C piece right sides together with the other A piece on top. Do not cut the thread yet, but continue sewing repeats of these three pairs of squares until you have sewn enough for the *length* of the quilt (consult your diagram). *Now,* cut the thread. This type of sewing is called "string sewing" because the pieces are strung together on threads, like beads.

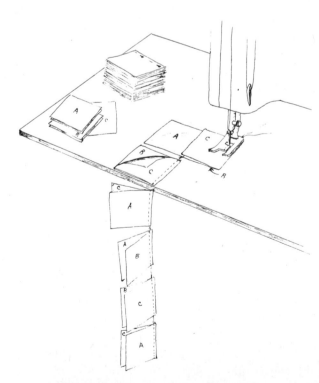

Illus. 5. String-sewing the rows of squares.

When you are ready to string-sew the second row of squares, find the first pair of A and B squares that were sewed. Lay them opened right sides up and sew a C piece right sides together on top of the B piece (see Illus. 5). String-sew an A piece right sides together on the C piece of the next pair of squares on the first string. A B piece is then sewed to the A piece of the following pair of the first string. Sewing long strings of simple pieces is so easy that one is inclined to rush along and to become careless about accurate seam widths and other small errors. This can cause difficulty when setting the blocks together because they may not match in size. You may have to compensate for this by resewing some seams.

Continue to add squares in this order to the pairs of the first string until you have completed a double string of three rows of squares. By now you can see that the diagonal pattern is established. Begin the fourth row by string-sewing an A piece to the C piece of the previous row; then, a B to the next A and a C to the next B, etc. Just follow your diagram, adding row after row of string-sewed pieces until you have the number of rows needed for the *width* of the quilt top. If you are making one of the larger size quilts and feel that the work is becoming a little awkward, you can do a third or a half of the quilt top in sections the length of the quilt, using the same method, and then sew the sections together. If you do this, you must be very careful to keep the pattern accurate when starting a new section and when putting the sections together. It is possible to string-sew even a king size quilt in one piece, however.

At this point, it is fun to spread the top out on the bed or floor to see how the finished top will look, even though you have surely already had at least one sneak preview! Notice that all the pieces are in place. The threads hold the crossways rows in the right position to be sewed together. When this is done and the border is added, the top will be finished! No pressing is necessary at this point, but if you feel that you must do so, press the seam allowances of the first row in one direction, those of the next row in the opposite direction (seam allowances are never pressed open, because the seams are stronger if they are not), and continue alternating in this way so that all the seam allowances will be lying right for sewing.

Match and pin the seams of the pieces in the first crossways row to those of the second crossways row, making sure that the seam allowances in one row lie in opposite directions to those in the other. It is best not to sew over pins, because of the chance of damaging the needle. Either remove the pins just before you reach them, or, if they must remain in place to hold the seams together accurately, "tip-toe" over the pins very carefully, turning the wheel by hand. You may find that the pairs of squares are not exactly the same size due to a slight variation in seam widths. Usually you can compensate for this by stretching the seam between pins as you sew. If not, you may have to adjust the seam width as needed. Sew the seam you have pinned, and continue to pin and sew the other seams in this same way until all are done. Press these seams all in the same direction, letting the short seams lie in the direction in which they were sewed.

The Mitered Border

Mark the middle of one side edge of the quilt top with a pin. Mark the middle of the edge of one long border strip in the same way and pin the two marked places together, right sides together. Lay the quilt top on the cutting board with the border on top and finish pinning the two together, working from the center pin toward each end and measuring off 9″ (22.5 cm) spaces on the border for matching with every third seam on the quilt top. With the border on top, sew the two together, starting exactly ¼″ (6 mm) from the edge of the quilt top (see Illus. 6). The first few and the last few stitches should be sewed with a stitch length of about 20 stitches to the inch (25 mm) to eliminate the need to backstitch or to tie threads. Hold the fabric before and behind the needle to prevent the top layer from easing along ahead of the needle. Repeat this procedure with the other side and the two end borders. Press the seam allowances toward the border.

To make the miter, fold the quilt top right sides together on the diagonal or bias at the corner so that the side border seam lies precisely along its adjoining end seam, and pin it in place. The borders will be lying right sides together also. Lay the yardstick (meterstick) exactly along the bias fold so that it extends across the ends of the borders. Press down on the yardstick (meterstick) where it crosses the borders so that the fabric will not slip, and draw a diagonal line across the border (see Illus. 7). Pin and sew along this line. Sew from the edge of the border just to the beginning stitch of the border seam. Open

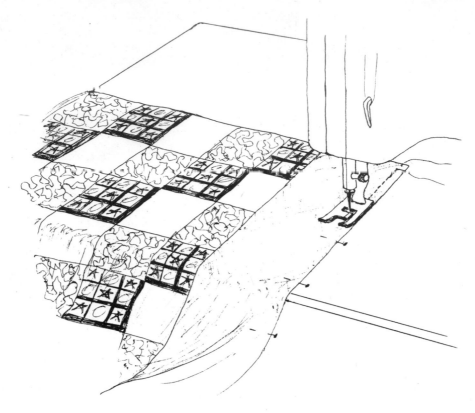

Illus. 6. Sewing the border.

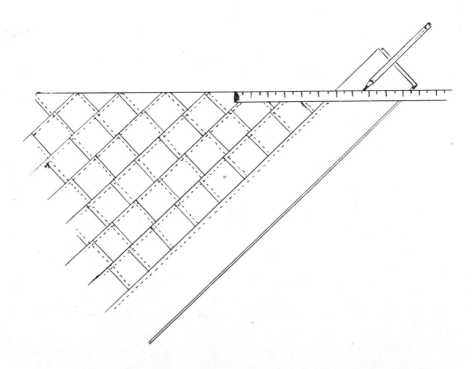

Illus. 7. Marking the mitered border.

the top to be sure that the miter lies flat before cutting off the excess border fabric, leaving a ¼" (6 mm) scam allowance. Mark and sew the other three corners in this same manner. This completes the top.

Skip over to Section 5 and finish the quilt by the "pillowcase method."

TWO ROMAN STRIPE PATTERNS

The second pattern I have chosen, "Roman Stripe," is also an easy one, and makes a very beautiful quilt. We will work with two of the many variations of this pattern: "Rail Fence" and "Windmill." The following yardage chart will tell you how much fabric you will need for the variation you choose. You may even want to make both patterns, since they are quite different in appearance.

Yardage and Cutting Charts for "Rail Fence" and "Windmill"

(All yardage given includes allowance for 3 per cent shrinkage and 4" (10 cm) for straightening fabric that has been carelessly cut from the bolt. All yardage is for 44" (110 cm) fabric. Instructions for cutting the back of the quilt will be found in Section 5.)

RAIL FENCE:

Crib quilt: 30" x 54" (75 x 135 cm)
4 x 8 blocks = 32 6" (15 cm) blocks
2½" (6 cm) borders

Yardage: ½ yd. (½ m) for each stripe for 3-stripe block
(½ yd. [½ m] for each stripe for 4-stripe block)
1⅝ yds. (1 m 45 cm) for back and border

Cutting: For 3-stripe block, cut 32 pieces of each fabric 2½" x 6½" (6 x 16 cm).
Mark 8 pieces across folded color A fabric.
Mark 2 full crossways strips of these pieces.
Stack and cut 3 fabrics together.
(For 4-stripe blocks, cut 32 pieces of each fabric 2" x 6½" [5 x 16 cm].
Mark 10 pieces across folded color A fabric.
Mark 1 full crossways strip of these pieces plus 6 more pieces on 2nd strip.
Stack and cut 4 fabrics together.)
Cut border 3" (7.5 cm) wide.

Napping quilt: 46" x 73" (115 x 182.5 cm)
4 x 7 blocks = 28 9" (22.5 cm) blocks
5" (12.5 cm) border

Yardage: ⅞ yds. (77 cm) for each stripe for 3-stripe block
⅝ yds. (55 cm) for each stripe for 4-stripe block)
4½ yds. (4 m 5 cm) for border

Cutting: For 3-stripe block, cut 28 pieces of each fabric 3½" x 9½" (8.7 x 23.7 cm).
Mark 6 pieces across folded color A fabric.
Mark 2 full crossways strips of these pieces plus 2 more pieces on 3rd strip.
Stack and cut 3 fabrics together.
(For 4-stripe block, cut 28 pieces of each fabric 2¾" x 9½" [7 x 23.7 cm].
Mark 8 pieces across folded color A fabric.
Mark 1 full crossways strip of these pieces plus 6 more on 2nd strip.
Stack and cut 4 fabrics together.)
Cut border 5½" (13.7 cm) wide.

Twin-size spread: 82" x 109" (21" drop) [205 x 272.5 cm (52.5 cm drop)]
8 x 11 blocks = 88 9" (22.5 cm) blocks
5" (12.5 cm) borders

Yardage: 2⅜ yds. (2 m 13 cm) for each stripe for 3-stripe block
(1½ yds. [1 m 35 cm] for each stripe for 4-stripe block)
9⅜ yds. (8 m 32 cm) for back and border

Cutting: For 3-stripe block, cut 88 pieces of each fabric 3½" x 9½" (8.7 x 22.5 cm).
Mark 6 pieces across folded color A fabric.
Mark 7 full crossways strips of these pieces plus 4 more pieces on 8th strip.
Stack and cut 3 fabrics together.
(For 4-stripe blocks cut 88 pieces of each fabric 2¾" x 9½" [7 x 22.5 cm].
Mark 8 pieces across folded color A fabric.
Mark 6 full crossways strips of these pieces plus 4 pieces on 7th strip.
Stack and cut 4 fabrics together.)
Cut border 5½" (13.7 cm) wide.

Twin-size coverlet: 62" x 100" (11½" drop)
[155 x 250 cm (28.7 cm drop)]
6 x 10 blocks = 60 9" (22.5 cm) blocks
4" (10 cm) borders

Yardage: 1½ yds. (1 m 35 cm) for each stripe for 3 stripe block
(1½ yds. [1 m 35 cm] for each stripe for 4-stripe block)
5 yds. (meters) for back and border

Cutting: For 3-stripe block, cut 60 pieces of each fabric 3½" x 9½" (8.7 x 23.7 cm).
Mark 6 pieces across folded color A fabric.
Mark 5 full crossways strips of these pieces.
Stack and cut 3 fabrics together.
(For 4-stripe blocks cut 60 pieces of each fabric 2¾" x 9½" [7 x 23.7 cm].
Mark 8 pieces across folded color A fabric.
Mark 4 full crossways strips of these pieces plus 2 more pieces on 5th strip.
Stack and cut 4 fabrics together.)
Cut border 4½" (11 cm) wide.

Double bed spread: 94" x 103" (20" drop)
[23 x 257.5 cm (50 cm drop)]
10 x 11 blocks = 110 9" (22.5 cm) blocks
2" (5 cm) borders

Yardage: 2⅞ yds. (2 m 77 cm) for each stripe for 3-stripe block
(2 yds. [meters] for each stripe for 4-stripe block)
9 yds. (meters) for back and border

Cutting: For 3-stripe block, cut 110 pieces of each fabric 3½" x 9½" (8.7 x 23.7 cm).
Mark 6 pieces across folded color A fabric.
Mark 9 full crossways strips of these pieces plus 4 more pieces on the 10th strip.
Stack and cut 3 fabrics together.
(For 4-stripe block, cut 110 pieces of each fabric 2¾" x 9½" [7 x 23.7 cm].
Mark 8 pieces across folded color A fabric.
Mark 6 full strips of these pieces plus 7 pieces on the 7th strip.

Stack and cut 4 fabrics together.)
Cut borders 2½" (6 cm) wide.

Double bed coverlet: 79" x 97" (12" drop)
[197.5 x 242.5 cm (30 cm drop)]
8 x 10 blocks = 80 9" (22.5 cm) blocks
3½" (8.7 cm) border

Yardage: 2 yds. (meters) for each stripe for 3-stripe block
1½ yds. (1 m 35 cm) for each stripe for 4-stripe block
7 yds. (meters) for back and border

Cutting: For 3-stripe block, cut 80 pieces of each fabric 3½" x 9½" (8.7 x 23.7 cm).
Mark 6 pieces across folded color A fabric.
Mark 6 full crossways stripes of these pieces plus 4 pieces on 7th strip.
Stack and cut 3 fabrics together.
(For 4-stripe block, cut 80 pieces of each fabric 2¾" x 9½" [7 x 23.7 cm].
Mark 7 full crossways strips of these pieces.
Stack and cut 4 fabrics together.)
Cut border 4" wide.

Queen-size spread: 100" x 109" (20" drop)
[250 x 272.5 cm (50 cm drop)]
10 x 11 blocks = 110 9" (22.5 cm) blocks
5" (12.5 cm) borders

Yardage: Same as for double bed spread.

Cutting: Same as for double bed, *except* cut border 5½" (13.7 cm) wide.

Queen-size coverlet: 82" x 94" (11" drop)
[205 x 235 cm (27.5 cm drop)]
5" (12.5 cm) borders

Yardage: Same as for double bed coverlet, *except* get 8⅜ yds. (7 m 32 cm) for back and border

Cutting: Same as for double bed coverlet, *except* cut border 5½" (13.7 cm) wide.

King-size spread: 120" x 120" (20" drop)
[300 x 300 cm (50 cm drop)]
12 x 12 blocks = 144 9" (22.5 cm) blocks
6" (15 cm) borders

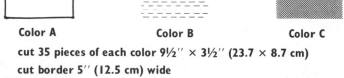

Color A **Color B** **Color C**

cut 35 pieces of each color 9½″ × 3½″ (23.7 × 8.7 cm)
cut border 5″ (12.5 cm) wide

Illus. 8. "Rail Fence." 55″ × 73″ (137.5 × 182.5 cm).

Yardage: 3¼ yds. (2 m 92 cm) for each stripe for 3-stripe block
2⅜ yds. (2 m 35 cm) for each stripe for 4-stripe block)
10 yds. (meters) for back and border

Cutting: For 3-stripe block, cut 120 pieces of each fabric 3½″ x 9½″ (8.7 x 23.7 cm).
Mark 6 pieces across folded color A fabric.
Mark 12 full crossways strips of these pieces.
Stack and cut 3 fabrics together.
(For 4-stripe block, cut 120 pieces of each fabric 2¾″ x 9½″ [7 x 23.7 cm].
Mark 8 pieces across folded color A fabric.
Mark 9 full crossways strips of these pieces.
Stack and cut 4 fabrics together.)
Cut borders 6½″ (16 cm) wide.

King-size coverlet: 102″ x 102″ (11″ drop) [255 x 255 cm (27.5 cm drop)]
10 x 10 blocks = 100 9″ (22.5 cm) blocks
6″ (15 cm) border

Yardage: 2⅞ yds. (2 m 57 cm) for each stripe for 3-stripe block
(2 yds. [meters] for each stripe for 4-stripe block)
8⅞ yds. (7 m 97 cm) for back and border

Cutting: For 3-stripe block, cut 100 pieces of each fabric 3½″ x 9½″ (8.7 x 23.7 cm).
Mark 6 pieces across folded color A fabric.
Mark 8 full crossways strips of these pieces plus 2 more pieces on 9th strip.
Stack and cut 3 fabrics together.
(For 4-stripe block, cut 100 pieces of each fabric 2¾″ x 9½″ [7 x 23.7 cm].
Mark 8 pieces across folded color A fabric.
Mark 6 full crossways strips of these pieces plus 2 more pieces on 7th strip.
Stack and cut 4 fabrics together.)
Cut border 6½″ (16 cm) wide.

WINDMILL:

Crib quilt: 30″ x 54″ (75 x 135 cm)
4 x 8 blocks = 32 6″ (15 cm) blocks
2½″ (6 cm) border

Yardage: ½ yd. (45 cm) for each stripe for 3-stripe block
(½ yd. [45 cm] for each stripe for 4-stripe block)
1⅜ yds. (1 m 22 cm) for back and border

Cutting: For 3-stripe block, cut 32 pieces of each fabric 2½″ x 6½″ (6 x 16 cm).
Mark 8 pieces across folded color A fabric.
Mark 2 full crossways strips of these pieces.
Stack and cut 3 fabrics together.
(For 4-stripe block, cut 32 pieces of each fabric 2″ x 6½″ [5 x 16 cm].
Mark 1 full crossways strip of these pieces plus 6 more pieces on 2nd strip.
Stack and cut 4 fabrics together.)
Cut border 3″ (7.5 cm) wide.

Napping quilt: 48″ x 66″ (120 x 165 cm)
4 x 6 blocks = 24 9″ (22.5 cm) blocks
6″ (15 cm) border

Yardage: ⅝ yd. (55 cm) for each stripe for 3-stripe block
(⅝ yd. [55 cm] for each stripe for 4-stripe block)
5 yds. (meters) for back and border

Cutting: For 3-stripe block, cut 24 pieces of each fabric 3½″ x 9½″ (8.7 x 23.7 cm).
Mark 6 pieces across folded color A fabric.
Mark 2 full crossways strips of these pieces.
Stack and cut 3 fabrics together.
(For 4-stripe block, cut 24 pieces of each fabric 3½″ x 9½″ [8.7 x 23.7 cm].
Mark 10 pieces across folded color A fabric.
Mark 1 full crossways strip of these pieces plus 6 more pieces on 2nd strip.
Stack and cut 4 fabrics together.)
Cut border 3″ (7.5 cm) wide.

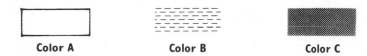

Color A   Color B   Color C

cut 24 pieces of each color 9½'' × 3½'' (23.7 × 8.7 cm)

cut border 5'' (12.5 cm) wide

Illus. 9. "Windmill." 46'' × 63'' (115 × 157.5 cm).

Twin-size spread: 82″ x 118″ (21″ drop) [205 x 295 cm (52.5 cm drop)]
8 x 12 blocks = 96 9″ (22.5 cm) blocks
5″ (12.5 cm) border

Yardage: 2⅜ yds. (2 m 13 cm) for each stripe for 3-stripe block
(1½ yds. [1 m 35 cm] for each stripe for 4-stripe block)
10⅛ yds. (9 m 10 cm) for back and border

Cutting: For 3-stripe block, cut 96 pieces of each fabric 3½″ x 9½″ (8.7 x 23.7 cm).
Mark 6 pieces across folded color A fabric.
Mark 8 crossways strips of these pieces.
Stack and cut 3 fabrics together.
(For 4-stripe blocks, cut 96 pieces of each fabric 2¾″ x 9½″ [7 x 23.7 cm].
Mark 8 pieces across folded color A fabric.
Mark 6 full crossways strips of these pieces.
Stack and cut 4 fabrics together.)
Cut border 5½″ (13.7 cm) wide.

Twin coverlet: 61″ x 97″ (11″ drop) [152.5 x 242.5 cm (27.5 cm drop)]
6 x 12 blocks = 72.9″ (22.5 cm) blocks
3½″ (8.7 cm) border

Yardage: 1⅞ yds. (167 cm) for each stripe for 3-stripe block
1⅝ yds. (145 cm) for each stripe for 4-stripe block
6 yds. (meters) for back and border

Cutting: For 3-stripe block, cut 72 pieces of each fabric 3½″ x 9½″ (8.7 x 23.7 cm).
Mark 6 pieces across folded color A fabric.
Mark 6 crossways strips of these pieces.
Stack and cut 3 fabrics together.
(For 4-stripe block, cut 72 pieces of each fabric 2¾″ x 9½″ [7 x 23.7 cm].
Mark 8 pieces across folded color A fabric.
Mark 4 full crossways strips plus 8 pieces on 5th strip.
Stack and cut 4 fabrics together.)
Cut border 4½″ (11 cm) wide.

Double bed spread: 94″ x 112″ (20″ drop) [235 x 280 cm (50 cm drop)]
10 x 12 blocks = 120 9″ (22.5 cm) blocks
2″ (5 cm) borders

Yardage: 2⅞ yds. (2 m 57 cm) for each stripe for 3-stripe block
(2¾ yds. [2 m 47 cm] for each stripe for 4-stripe block)
9⅞ yds. (8 m 87 cm) for back and border

Cutting: For 3-stripe block, cut 120 pieces of each fabric 3½″ x 9½″ (8.7 x 23.7 cm).
Mark 6 pieces across folded color A fabric.
Mark 10 full crossways strips of these pieces.
Stack and cut 3 fabrics together.
(For 4-stripe block, cut 120 pieces of each fabric 2¾″ x 9½″ [7 x 23.7 cm].
Mark 8 pieces across folded color A fabric.
Mark 8 full crossways strips of these pieces plus 4 pieces on 9th strip.
Stack and cut 4 fabrics together.)
Cut border 2½″ (6 cm) wide.

Double bed coverlet: 76″ x 112″ (11″ drop) [190 x 280 cm (27.5 cm drop)]
8 x 12 blocks = 96 9″ (22.5 cm) blocks
2″ (5 cm) borders

Yardage: 2⅜ yds. (2 m 13 cm) for each stripe of 3-stripe block
(1½ yds. [1 m 35 cm] for each stripe of 4-stripe block)
6½ yds. (5 m 85 cm) for back and border

Cutting: For 3-stripe block, cut 96 pieces of each fabric 3½″ x 9½″ (8.7 x 23.7 cm).
Mark 6 pieces across folded color A fabric.
Mark 8 crossways strips of these pieces.
Stack and cut 3 fabrics together.
(For 4-stripe blocks, cut 96 pieces of each fabric 2¾″ x 9½″ [7 x 23.7 cm].
Mark 8 pieces across folded color A fabric.
Mark 6 full crossways strips of these pieces.
Stack and cut 4 fabrics together.)
Cut borders 2½″ (6 cm) wide.

Queen-size spread: 100" x 118" (20" drop)
[250 x 295 cm (80 cm drop)]
10 x 12 blocks = 120 9" (22.5 cm) blocks
5" (12.5 cm) borders

Yardage: Same as for double bed spread, *except* get 10¼ yds. (9 m 22 cm) for back and border.

Cutting: Same as for double bed spread, *except* cut border 5½" (13.7 cm) wide.

Queen-size coverlet: 82" x 118" (11" drop)
[205 x 295 cm (27.5 cm drop)]
8 x 12 blocks = 96 9" (22.5 cm) blocks
5" (12.5 cm) border

Yardage: Same as for double bed coverlet, *except* cut borders 5½" (13.7 cm) wide.

Cutting: Same as for double bed coverlet, *except* cut borders 5½" (13.7 cm) wide.

King-size spread: Same as for Rail Fence.

King-size coverlet: Same as for Rail Fence.

The "Windmill" pattern requires an even number of blocks across the length and the width of the quilt (see Illus. 9). For this reason, it is sometimes necessary to make the quilt a little longer than usual to complete the design. (The extra length can be tucked under the pillow.) More fabric may be required for this pattern, therefore, than for the "Rail Fence" quilt, which can be made of an uneven number of blocks in either direction (see Illus. 8). For a shorter "Windmill" quilt, an alternative would be to leave off *two* rows of the blocks, which would result in a quilt too short to go over the pillow. Pillow shams made from the same fabrics as the quilt may be used with this type of quilt.

The blocks for "Roman Stripe" patterns are often made up of four stripes (or even more in some variations) instead of the three shown in the illustrations. If you prefer to make them this way and do not mind a little extra work, follow the alternate information in the yardage charts and instructions as you go along. (These alternates will be given in parentheses.) For three stripes, the finished piece will be 9" x 3" (for 4 stripes 9" x 2¼") [22.5 x 7.5 cm (22.5 x 5.6 cm)]. The cut size will be 9½" x

3½" (9½" x 2¾") [23.7 x 9 cm (23.7 x 6.8 cm)] to allow for the ¼" (6 mm) seam allowance.

Prepare the fabric as you have been instructed. Lay it out and straighten the end as you did for "Patience." This time, mark the pieces by the measurements given above. Let the length of the piece—9½" (23.7 cm)—fall along the length of the fabric; and measure off 6 (8) pieces 3½" (2¾") [8.7 cm (6.8 cm)] wide across the folded 44" (110 cm) fabric so that 12 (16) pieces will be cut. Stack the layers of folded fabric as before. (Four fabrics can be cut with a sharp scissors if you pin carefully.) Three pins will be needed along the length of the piece instead of the two you used for "Patience" pieces. Cut the strips and pieces in the same order as before and do not separate them or remove the pins.

String-Sewing the Blocks

Take your stack of pieces to the machine and you are ready to sew. Proceed exactly as you did for one-patch, but sew only repeats of the block, not the entire quilt top. String-sew repeats of a color B piece on top of each color A piece *until all are sewed in pairs*. Next, start at the beginning of the first string and string-sew a color C piece on top of each color B piece. This completes the simple blocks, but they are still strung together with the sewing threads. (For four stripes, string-sew the fourth color D pieces on top of the color C pieces to finish the blocks.) I like to place a card table in front of the sewing machine to catch the pile of pieces as they are sewed.

Pressing and Accordion-Stacking the Blocks

If you have used a card table, just move it to the end of the ironing board and you are ready to press the blocks. Lay a string of three or four blocks wrong side up on the board and press all the seams in one direction. If one of the fabrics is light or thin enough that the seam allowances show through, then you may want to press the seams away from that piece. It is all right if pairs of seams are pressed in opposite directions, but *never* press the seams open. As each group of blocks is pressed, accordion-stack them on the opposite end of the ironing board from the table. Illustration 10 shows the best way to do this. The blocks, still on the strings, will be folded accordion-style with alternating right sides and wrong sides together.

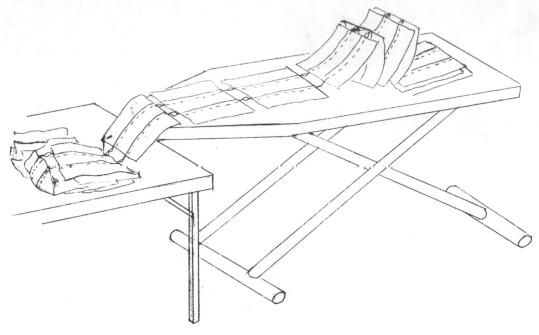

Illus. 10. Pressing and accordion-stacking the blocks.

When all the blocks have been pressed and stacked, take the stack to your work table and you are ready to cut the threads. Beginning at the *bottom* pair in the stack and working toward the top, cut the threads along one end of the blocks only. It is easier to begin at the bottom, and you are less likely to skip threads. Turn the stack and, starting again at the bottom, cut the threads along the other ends of the blocks, but *leave the blocks stacked in the same order as they were.* You will find that they are in just the right order for sewing. Place your stack of blocks beside your sewing machine, with the dominant color C (D) at the top, stripes lying horizontally and the dominant color C (D) stripe farthest from you.

Sewing the Rail Fence Top

If the top block is not right side up, put it on the bottom of the stack right sides or wrong sides together with the bottom block, whichever way it matches. Now the top block is right side up. Place it in front of the needle with the dominant color C (D) stripe nearest the needle. The next block is already wrong side up. Turn it clockwise so that the dominant stripe is on the *right* (crossways to the first block) and sew the two together along this stripe. Refer to your diagram often to check the positioning of the blocks as you sew them. It may be necessary to ease in a slight

difference in the length of the two pieces if the seams in the lower block were not accurately sewed. Do not cut the thread.

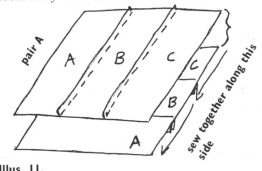

Illus. 11.

Place the next block, which is right side up, in front of the needle with the dominant stripe on the *left* side. Turn the next block so that the dominant stripe is at the top near the needle and place it wrong side up (as you found it) on the other block. Sew a seam along the right edge of the pair of

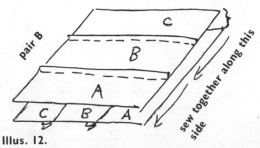

Illus. 12.

(Above) "Patience," an example of one-patch, the simplest quilt pattern (see page 17). (Below) An unquilted section of "Blue Ceramic Tile," a four-patch pattern with lattice (see page 43).

(Above) Close-up of "Primary Arithmetic" shows piecing and the effect of the border, which seems to invade the quilt top and become a part of it (see page 82). (Bottom left) Pillow with folded double ruffle (see page 116).(Bottom right) Construction of Seminole pattern used for pillow shown on page 144.

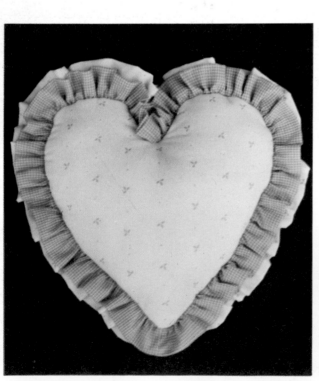

B

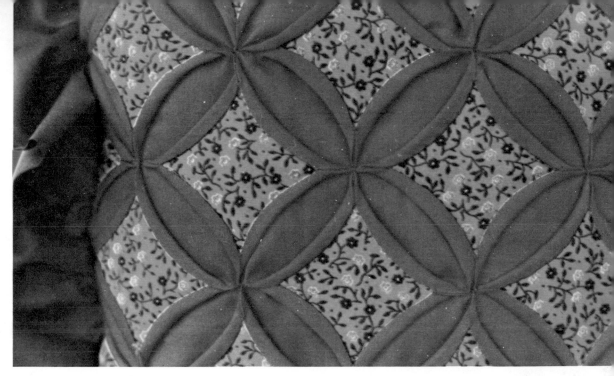

(Above) Close-up of a "Cathedral Window" pillow, showing detail of the four stitched points and of the solid-color fabric folded over the print square and slipstitched (see page 141). (Below) Quilting curves are machine-guided long stitches. Flowers are hand-guided, using a hoop (see page 115).

(Above) A presser foot was used for this work (see page 94). The machine was set for satin stitch. Notice the varying width of the stitching.

(Above) Close-up of sawtooth edge (see page 117).
(Below) Joining of "Cathedral Window" (see page 141) also shows print square covering seam and being stitched into place.

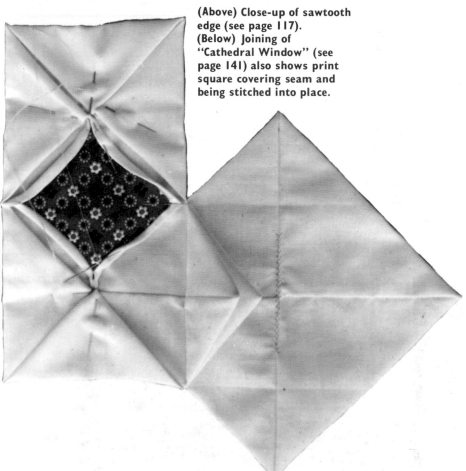

D

blocks. Sew enough repeats of these two pairs of blocks for the length of the quilt. Cut the thread. This completes a vertical two-row section. Make enough of these sections for the width of the quilt. If there are an uneven number of rows across the quilt, string-sew the final row to the last section sewed before sewing the crossways seams. Follow your diagram carefully to be sure that each block is turned to fit the pattern. Now, sew the sections together and the top is ready for the border. You may use the mitered border, described earlier, or the unmitered border described below.

The Unmitered Border

You will see this type of border on both old and new quilts and it is quite easy to do. This border also has the advantage of requiring just a little less fabric, which could be important if you have a limited amount of the fabric you want to use. However, even with these advantages, I still choose the mitered border in most cases because I prefer the way it looks. It is always good to learn all the alternate choices available, however, so keep the unmitered border in mind whether you decide to use it at this time or not.

For the unmitered border, measure the full length of the quilt top you have just finished piecing (do not include any border width). Measure both sides, because there is sometimes a little variation in length. If this variation is only slight, the difference can be eased in or slightly stretched out, as the case may be, to keep the finished quilt as regular in shape as possible. If there is much difference in the length of the two sides, find the seams that were sewed too narrow or too wide and adjust them to correct the difference. Cut two side borders the length of the top plus 2" (5 cm) to allow at the end seams for any slight inaccuracy in measuring. Cut them as wide as the border indicated for your size quilt plus ½" (12 mm) for the two ¼" (6 mm) seam allowances. Starting at the middle and working to the ends, as for the mitered border, pin and then sew these side borders to the sides of the quilt top. Now, measure the full width of the top, including the two borders just sewed, make any necessary adjustments, and cut two end borders as long as the complete width of the quilt plus 2" (5 cm) for the wide seam allowance.

Pin and then sew these strips across the ends of the quilt, sewing off any extra length that is left on the ends of the two side borders. Trim off any extra length that may remain on the two end borders. Lay the quilt top on your cutting board as a guide to keep the corner square when you trim.

If your quilt is to be finished without a border, it may be finished either by the pillowcase method, or bound as described in Section 5.

String-Sewing the Windmill Top

The "Windmill" design is assembled in much the same way as "Rail Fence." The difference occurs in the way that the blocks are turned. As before, if the top block is wrong side up, put it on the bottom of the stack with right sides or wrong sides together to match the bottom block there. Now the top block is right side up, just the way you want it to be. Lay this block right side up in front of the machine needle *with the dominant color C (D) stripe nearest you.* The next block is wrong side up and ready to use. Turn it clockwise so that the dominant stripe is along the *right* side of the block. Sew the two pieces together with a ¼" (6 mm) seam along this right edge. If the two edges of the blocks are not quite the same length, you can ease in or stretch out a small difference. Don't cut the thread.

Place the next block, which is right side up, in front of the needle with the dominant stripe on the *right* side. The next block goes wrong side up (as you found it) on top of the other, with the dominant stripe on top and nearest the needle. String-sew along the right edge. These two pairs of blocks will form a windmill. Sew as many repeats of these two pairs as there are windmills in the length of your quilt— consult your diagram. Sew the crossways seams, joining the windmills, and press. This completes one lengthwise row of windmills. Sew as many lengthwise rows in this manner as are needed for the width of your quilt. Join the rows, press and you are ready for the border. Choose either border described so far.

NINE-PATCH

"Nine-patch" is another of the simple patterns which can be very interesting. It is quite old and especially popular in its basic form, as well as in the virtually unlimited variations that have been, and still are being, developed. You may even design a variation of your own. The fundamental block is made up of small squares, three across and three down, and from this comes the name. First, let us make this basic design and later we will explore some of the variations.

Even with this simple pattern, a great deal of visual variety can be achieved by the use of different colors and prints. This design must be set together with sashing (or lattice) strips or with setting blocks to keep it from looking like a one-patch such as "Patience." To begin with, we will use only two fabrics for the block and one for the sashing or the setting blocks. Later you may explore some other possibilities. The Yardage and Cutting Chart below will tell you the amount of fabric to buy for the size quilt you want to make.

Yardage and Cutting Charts for Nine-Patch Patterns

(All yardage given includes allowance for 3 per cent shrinkage and 4″ (10 cm) for straightening fabric that had been carelessly cut from the bolt. All yardage is for 44″ (110 cm) fabric. Instructions for cutting the back of the quilt will be found in Section 5.)

NINE-PATCH WITH SETTING BLOCKS:

Crib quilt: 32″ x 49″ (80 x 122.5 cm)
    3 x 5 blocks = 8 pieced blocks
    + 7 setting blocks
    2″ (5 cm) border

Yardage: ½ yd. (45 cm) color A
    ⅜ yd. (32.5 cm) color B
    ⅝ yd. (55 cm) color C
    1½ yds. (1 m 35 cm) for back and border

Cutting: Cut 40 pieces of color A + 32 color B 3½″ (8.7 cm) square.
    On folded color A fabric, mark 3 full crossways strips of 6 pieces plus 2 pieces on the 4th strip.
    Lay color A on color B and cut together.
    Cut 7 setting blocks of color C 9½″ (23.7 cm) square.
    On folded fabric, mark and cut 2 full crossways strips of 2 pieces.
    Cut border 2½″ (6 cm) wide.

Napping quilt: 54″ x 72″ (135 x 180 cm)
    5 x 7 blocks = 18 pieced blocks + 17 setting blocks
    4½″ (11 cm) border

Yardage: ⅞ yd. (77 cm) color A
    ¾ yd. (67.5 cm) color B
    1½ yd. (1 m 35 cm) color C
    4½ yds. (4 m 5 cm) for back and border

Cutting: Cut 90 pieces of color A + 72 color B 3½″ (8.7 cm) square.
    On folded color A fabric, mark 7 full crossways strips of 6 pieces plus 5 more pieces on 8th strip.
    Lay color A on color B and cut together.
    Cut 17 setting blocks of color C 9½″ (23.7 cm) square.
    On folded fabric, mark and cut 4 full crossways strips of 2 pieces plus 1 more piece on 5th strip.
    Cut border 5″ (12.5 cm) wide.

Twin-size spread: 82″ x 116″ (20″ drop) [205 x 290 cm (50 cm)]
    7 x 11 blocks = 39 pieced blocks + 38 setting blocks
    8½″ (21 cm) border

Yardage: 1⅞ yds. (1 m 67 cm) of color A
    1½ yds. (1 m 35 cm) of color B
    2⅞ yds. (2 m 57 cm) of color C
    10⅛ yds. (9 m 10 cm) for back and border

Cutting: Cut 195 pieces of color A + 156 of color B 3½″ (8.7 cm) square.
    On folded color A fabric, mark 16 full crossways strips of 6 pieces plus 2 more pieces on 17th strip.
    Lay color A on color B and cut together.
    Cut 38 setting blocks 9½″ (23.7 cm) square.
    On folded fabric, mark and cut 9 full crossways strips of 2 pieces plus 1 more piece on 10th strip.

Twin-size coverlet: 63″ x 99″ (12″ drop) [157.5 x 247.5 cm (30 cm drop)]
    7 x 11 blocks = 39 pieced blocks + 38 setting blocks
    No border

Yardage and Cutting are the same as for twin spread, *except* get 9⅛ yds. (8 m 20 cm) for back.

Double bedspread: 93″ x 112″ (19½″ drop) [232.5 x 280 cm (48.7 drop)]
    9 x 11 blocks = 50 pieced blocks + 49 setting blocks
    6½″ (16 cm) border

Yardage: 2⅛ yds. (1 m 90 cm) of color A
    1⅞ yds. (1 m 67 cm) of color B
    3⅝ yds. (3 m 25 cm) of color C
    9¾ yds. (8 m 77 cm) for back and border

Cutting: Cut 250 pieces of color A + 200 of color B 3½" (8.7 cm) square.
On folded color A fabric, mark 20 full crossways strips of 6 pieces plus 5 more pieces on 21st strip.
Lay color A on color B and cut together.
Cut 49 setting blocks 9½" (23.7 cm) square.
On folded color C fabric, mark and cut 12 crossways strips of 2 pieces plus 1 more piece on 13th strip.
Cut border 7" (17.5 cm) wide.

Double bed coverlet: 76" x 94" (11" drop) [190 x 235 cm (27.5 cm drop)]
7 x 9 blocks = 32 pieced blocks + 31 setting blocks
6½" (16 cm) border

Yardage: 1½ yds. (1 m 35 cm) of color A
1¼ yds. (1 m 22 cm) of color B
2⅜ yds. (2 m 12 cm) of color C
9 yds. (meters) for back and border

Cutting: Cut 160 pieces of color A + 128 of color B 3½" (8.7 cm) square.
On folded color A fabric, mark 13 full crossways strips of 6 pieces plus 2 more pieces on 14th strip.
Lay color A on color B and cut together.
Cut 31 setting blocks of color C 9½" (23.7 cm) square.
On folded fabric, mark and cut 7 full crossways strips of 2 pieces plus 2 more pieces on 8th strip.
Cut border 7" (17.5 cm) wide.

Queen-size spread: 100" x 118" (20" drop) [250 x 295 cm (50 cm drop)]
11 x 13 blocks = 72 pieced blocks + 71 setting blocks
1" (2.5 cm) border (may finish without border if desired)

Yardage: 3⅛ yds. (2 m 80 cm) of color A
2½ yds. (2 m 25 cm) of color B
4⅞ yds. (4 m 37 cm) of color C
10¼ yds. (9 m 22 cm) for back and border

Cutting: Cut 360 pieces of color A + 288 of color B 3½" (8.7 cm) square.
On folded color A fabric, mark 30 full crossways strips of 6 pieces.

Lay color A on color B and cut together.
Cut 71 setting blocks 9½" (23.7 cm) square.
On folded fabric, mark and cut 18 full crossways strips of 2 pieces.
Cut border (if desired) 1½" (3.7 cm) wide.

Queen-size coverlet: 82" x 94" (11" drop) [205 x 235 cm (27.5 cm drop)]
9 x 11 blocks = 50 pieced blocks + 49 setting blocks
1" (2.5 cm) border (if desired)

Yardage: 2⅛ yds. (1 m 90 cm) of color A
1⅞ yds. (1 m 67 cm) of color B
3⅝ yds. (3 m 25 cm) of color C
9 yds. (meters) for back and border

Cutting: Cut 250 pieces of color A + 200 of color B 3½" (8.7 cm) square.
On folded color A fabric, mark 20 full crossways strips of 6 pieces plus 5 more pieces on 21st strip.
Lay color A on color B and cut together.
Cut 49 setting blocks of color C 9½" (23.7 cm) square.
On folded fabric, mark and cut 24 full crossways strips of 2 pieces plus 1 more piece on 25th strip.

King-size spread: 120" x 120" (20" drop) [300 x 300 cm (50 cm drop)]
13 x 13 blocks = 85 pieced blocks + 84 setting blocks
1½" (3.7 cm) border

Yardage: 3⅝ yds. (3 m 25 cm) of color A
3⅛ yds. (2 m 80 cm) of color B
5⅞ yds. (5 m 27 cm) of color C
10½ yds. (meters) for back and border

Cutting: Cut 425 pieces of color A + 360 of color B 3½" (8.7 cm) square.
On folded color A fabric, mark 35 full crossways strips of 6 pieces plus 3 more pieces on 36th strip.
Lay color A on color B and cut together.
Cut 84 setting blocks of color C 9½" (23.7 cm) square.
On folded color C fabric, mark and cut 21 full crossways strips of 2 pieces.
Cut border 2" (5 cm) wide.

King-size spread (alternate number of blocks): 118″ x 118″ (19″ drop [295 x 295 cm (47.5 cm drop)]) 11 x 11 blocks = 61 pieced blocks + 60 setting blocks 9½″ (23.7 cm) border

Yardage: 2⅝ yds. (2 m 35 cm) of color A
2¼ yds. (2 m 2 cm) of color B
4¼ yds. (3 m 82 cm) of color C
10¼ yds. (9 m 22 cm) for back and border

Cutting: Cut 305 pieces of color A + 244 of color B 3½″ (8.7 cm) square.
On folded color A fabric, mark 25 full crossways strips of 6 pieces plus 3 more pieces on 26th strip.
Lay color A on color B and cut.
Cut 60 setting blocks of color C 9½″ (23.7 cm) square.
On folded fabric, mark and cut 15 full crossways strips of 2 pieces.
Cut border 10″ (25 cm) wide.

King-size coverlet: 100″ x 100″ (10″ drop) [250 x 250 cm (25 cm drop)] 9 x 9 blocks = 41 pieced blocks + 40 setting blocks 4½″ (11 cm) border

Yardage: 2 yds. (1 m 80 cm) of color A
1½ yds. (1 m 35 cm) of color B
2⅝ yds. (2 m 35 cm) of color C
8¾ yds. (7 m 87 cm) for back and border

Cutting: Cut 205 pieces of color A + 164 of color B 3½″ (8.7 cm) square.
On folded color A fabric, mark 17 full crossways strips of 6 pieces plus 1 more piece on 18th strip.
Lay color A on color B and cut.
Cut 40 pieces of color C 9½″ (23.7 cm) square.
On folded fabric, mark and cut 10 full crossways strips of 2 pieces.
Cut border 5″ (12.5 cm) wide.

NINE-PATCH WITH LATTICE:

Crib quilt: 34″ x 57″ (85 x 142.5 cm) 3 x 5 blocks = 15 pieced blocks 1½″ (3.7 cm) sashing 1½″ (3.7 cm) borders

Yardage: ¾ yd. (67 cm) of color A
⅝ yd. (55 cm) of color B
3½ yds. (3 m 15 cm) of color C for sashing, back and border

Cutting: Cut 75 pieces of color A + 60 of color B 3½″ (8.7 cm) square.
On folded color A fabric, mark 6 full crossways strips of 6 pieces plus 2 more pieces on 7th strip.
Lay color A on color B and cut together.
Of color C fabric, cut fabric needed for back and lay it aside.
From remaining fabric, cut 4 borders 2″ (5 cm) wide, 2 long sashing strips 2″ (5 cm) wide and 12 short sashing strips 2″ x 9½″ (5 x 23.7 cm).

Napping quilt: 48″ x 77″ (120 x 192.5 cm) 5 x 7 blocks = 35 pieced blocks 2″ (5 cm) sashing 2″ (5 cm) border

Yardage: 1¾ yds. (1 m 57 cm) of color A
1⅜ yds. (1 m 22 cm) of color B
6¾ yds. (6 m 7 cm) of color C for sashing, back and border

Cutting: Cut 185 pieces of color A + 140 of color B 3½″ (8.7 cm) square.
On folded color A fabric, mark 15 full crossways strips of 6 pieces plus 3 more pieces on 16th strip.
Lay color A on color B and cut together.
Of color C fabric, cut and lay aside fabric for back (see Section 5).
On remainder of fabric, mark and cut 4 borders 2½″ (6 cm) wide, 4 long sashing strips 2½″ (6 cm) wide and 30 short sashing strips 2½″ x 9½″ (6 x 23.7 cm).

Twin-size spread: 81″ x 102″ (20″ drop) [202.5 x 255 cm (50 cm drop)] 7 x 9 blocks = 63 pieced blocks 2″ (5 cm) sashing 3″ (7.5 cm) border

Yardage: 2⅝ yds. (2 m 35 cm) of color A
2¼ yds. (2 m 2 cm) of color B
2¾ yds. (2 m 47 cm) of color C for sashing, border and back

Cutting: Cut 315 pieces of color A + 252 of color B 3½″ (8.7 cm) square.
On folded color A fabric, mark 26 full crossways strips of 6 pieces plus 2 more pieces on 27th strip.
Lay color A on color B and cut together.
Of color C fabric, cut amount needed for back and lay aside.

From remainder of fabric, cut 4 borders 3½" (8.7 cm) wide, 4 long sashing strips 2½" (6 cm) wide and 63 short sashing strips 2½" x 9½" (6 x 23.7 cm).

Twin-size coverlet: 60" x 93" (10½" drop) [150 x 232.5 cm (26.2 cm drop)]
5 x 8 blocks = 40 pieced blocks
2" (5 cm) sashing
3½" (8.7 cm) border

Yardage: 1⅞ yds. (1 m 67 cm) of color A
1½ yds. (1 m 35 cm) of color B
8 yds. (meters) of color C for sashing, border and back

Cutting: Cut 200 pieces of color A + 160 of color B 3½" (8.7 cm) square.
On folded color A fabric, mark 16 full crossways strips of 6 pieces plus 4 more pieces on 17th strip.
Lay color A on color B and cut together.
Of color C fabric, cut amount needed for back and lay aside.
Of remainder of fabric, mark and cut 4 borders 4" (10 cm) wide, 4 long sashing strips, 2½" (6 cm) wide and 35 short sashing strips 2½" x 9½" (6 x 23.7 cm).

Double bedspread: 96" x 106" (21" drop) [240 x 265 cm (52.5 cm drop)]
8 x 9 blocks = 72 pieced blocks
2½" (6 cm) sashing
4" (10 cm) border

Yardage: 3⅛ yds. (2 m 80 cm) of color A
2½ yds. (2 m 25 cm) of color B
9¼ yds. (meters) of color C for sashing, border and back

Cutting: Cut 360 pieces of color A + 288 of color B 3½" (8.7 cm) square.
On folded color A fabric, mark 30 full crossways strips of 6 pieces.
Lay color A on color B and cut together.
Of color C fabric, cut and lay aside fabric for back.
From remainder of fabric, mark and cut 4 borders 4½" (11.2 cm) wide, 7 long sashing strips 3" (7.5 cm) wide and 64 short sashing strips 3" x 9½" (7.5 x 23.7 cm).

Double bed coverlet: 76" x 94" (11" drop) [190 x 235 cm (27.5 cm drop)]
7 x 8 blocks = 56 pieced blocks
2½" (6 cm) sashing
3½" (8.7 cm) border

Yardage: 2½ yds. (2 m 25 cm) of color A
2 yds. (1 m 80 cm) of color B
8¼ yds. (7 m 42 cm) of color C for sashing, border and back

Cutting: Cut 280 pieces of color A + 224 of color B 3½" (8.7 cm) square.
On folded color A fabric, mark 24 full crossways strips of 6 pieces plus 2 more pieces on 25th strip.
Lay color A on color B and cut together.
Of color C fabric, cut and lay aside fabric for back.
From remainder of fabric, mark and cut 2 borders 4" (10 cm) wide, 6 long sashing strips 3" wide and 48 short sashing strips 3" x 9¼" (7.5 x 23 cm).

Queen-size spread: 100" x 108" (20" drop) [250 x 270 cm (50 cm drop)]
8 x 9 blocks = 72 pieced blocks
2½" (6 cm) sashing
6" (15 cm) border

Yardage: Same as for double bedspread, *except* get 9¾ yds. (8 m 77 cm) of color C.

Cutting: Same as for double bedspread, *except* cut 4 borders 6½" (16 cm) wide.

Queen-size coverlet: 80" x 98" (10" drop) [200 x 245 cm (25 cm drop)]
7 x 8 blocks = 56 pieced blocks
2½" (6 cm) sashing
5½" (13.7 cm) border

Yardage: Same as for double bed coverlet, *except* get 8½ yds. (7 m 65 cm) of color C.

Cutting: Same as for double bed coverlet, *except* cut border 6" (15 cm) wide.

King-size spread: 102" x 102" (20" drop) [255 x 255 cm (50 cm drop)]
10 x 10 blocks = 100 pieced blocks

2" (5 cm) sashing
6" (15 cm) border

Yardage: 4⅜ yds. (3 m 92 cm) of color A
3½ yds. (3 m 15 cm) of color B
10½ yds. (9 m 45 cm) of color C
for sashing, border and back

Cutting: Cut 500 pieces of color A + 400 pieces of color B 3½" (8.7 cm) square.

On folded color A fabric, mark 41 full crossways strips of 6 pieces plus 4 more pieces on 42nd strip.

Lay color A on color B and cut together.

Of color C fabric, cut and lay aside fabric for back. From remainder, mark and cut 4 borders 6½" (16 cm) wide, 9 long sashing strips 2½" (6 cm) wide and 90 short sashing strips 2½" x 9½" (6 x 23.7 cm).

King-size coverlet: 102" x 102" (11" drop) [255 x 255 cm (27.5 cm drop)]

9 x 9 blocks = 81 pieced blocks
2" (5 cm) sashing
2½" (6 cm) border

Yardage: 3½ yds. (3 m 15 cm) of color A
2¾ yds. (2 m 47 cm) of color B
8⅞ yds. (7 m 97 cm) of color C for sashing, border and back

Cutting: Cut 405 pieces of color A + 324 of color B 3½" (8.7 cm) square.

On folded color A fabric, mark 33 full crossways strips of 6 pieces plus 5 more pieces on 34th strip.

Lay color A on color B and cut together.

Of color C fabric, cut and lay aside fabric for back.

From remainder of fabric, mark and cut 2 borders 3" (7.5 cm) wide, 8 long sashing strips 2½" (6 cm) wide and 72 short sashing strips 3½" x 9½" (8.7 x 23.7 cm).

Illustrations 13 and 14 will help you to choose the version of Nine-patch you wish to make. The best choice, actually, is to make both, if only in small sizes for pillows, because the learning experience is different in each. From these drawings it is easy to see that a great deal of variety is possible with this pattern. If you are an experienced quilter, you are already aware of this, and you may prefer to choose a more involved

version of the block to work with. If so, you will find several versions pictured at the end of this section with instructions for putting them together. (See Section 3, Illus. 34, for more ideas.) Select one that utilizes your present skills. Your learning experience should come from the machine methods rather than from learning a complicated pattern.

Our "Nine-patch" block will be 9" (22.5 cm) square when finished. The pieces for the block will therefore be cut 3½" (8.7 cm) square. Prepare your fabrics as you have become accustomed to doing. Draw a line to straighten the end, and mark off the 3½" (8.7 cm) squares just as you did for "Patience." This time there will be only two different fabrics to fold, pin together and cut. When you have done all this, you are ready to sew. Again, you will start as for "Patience," string-sewing a color B piece on top of a color A piece, then a color A piece on top of color B piece, followed by a color B piece on top of a color A piece (see Illus. 13 for placement of squares).

These three pairs of pieces are for one block—a set of six pieces. Do not cut the thread yet, but continue to string-sew a set of pieces for each block to be made. Now cut the thread. Begin with the first set and add pieces along the right side the same way you added the third row of pieces for earlier patterns. String-sew a color A piece on top of the color B piece that comes first, then a color B piece on top of the following color A piece, and finally a color A piece on top of the color B piece that comes next. You now have enough pieces for one block. Continue to add pieces in this order to each of the sets on the first string. When you have completed all the blocks, cut the thread. Now there are nine pieces to each set, making nine-patch blocks. Press the seams, cut the threads between the sets of nine pieces and stack the sets beside your machine. Each set has three strips of three squares, string-sewed together in pattern order. Pin one strip to its neighbor and sew, carefully matching the seams where they come together. Add the third strip in the same way and you have finished one block. Finish all the other blocks and press the seams.

Illustration 14 is the easier of the two patterns shown, with plain squares or setting blocks alternating with pieced blocks. Fewer pieced blocks are needed for this pattern than for the latticed variation, and the top is easier to put together as well. For these reasons, you may choose to learn to sew lattices later—perhaps when making

 Color A — cut 120 pieces 3½″ × 3½″ (8.7 × 8.7 cm)

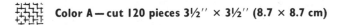 Color B — cut 96 pieces 3½″ × 3½″ (8.7 × 8.7 cm)

Color C — 2″ (50 mm) lattice and 4″ (10 cm) border

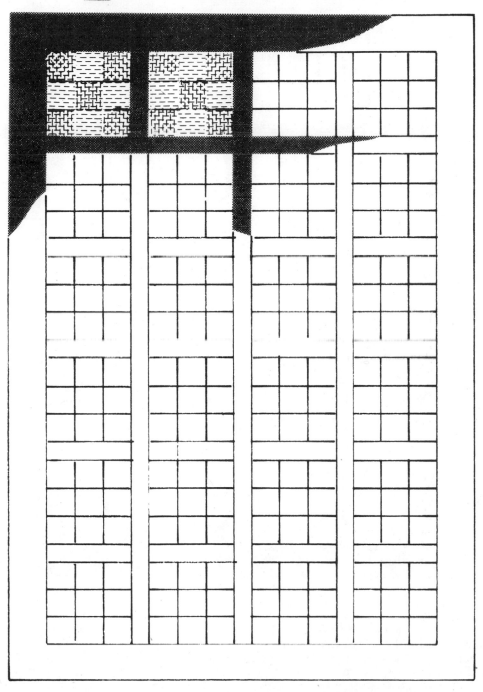

Illus. 13. "Nine-Patch" with Lattice. 50″ × 72″ (125 × 180 cm).

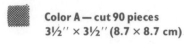 **Color A — cut 90 pieces**
3½″ × 3½″ (8.7 × 8.7 cm)

 Color C — cut 17 pieces
9½″ × 9½″ (23.7 × 23.7 cm)

Color B — cut 96 pieces 3½″ × 3½″ (8.7 × 8.7 cm)

Illus. 14. "Nine-Patch" with Setting Blocks. 63″ × 72″ (157.5 × 180 cm).

one of the patterns shown at the end of this section. For "Nine-patch" with setting blocks it is necessary to have an *odd* number of blocks in width and in length to keep the design balanced. It is sometimes necessary to adjust the width of the borders or the size of the blocks to accommodate this need while keeping the quilt size desired.

Make the number of blocks required for the size quilt you are making (consult your diagram and cutting chart). You will also need to cut the correct number of plain setting blocks 9½" (23.7 cm) square. You will put them together by the method you used when making your "Patience" quilt. Place a pieced block right side up in front of the needle. Place a plain block right side down on it. Sew the two together along the right edge. Without cutting the thread, sew another pair of blocks, this time with the plain one on the bottom and the pieced one on the top. Make enough pairs for the length of the quilt top and cut the thread. Starting with the first pair, string-sew a third row to it. The first block in this row will be pieced, the second plain, and so on. String-sew as many rows as are needed for the top. Sew the crossways seams and you are ready for the border. Choose whichever border you prefer.

Nine-Patch with Lattice

Follow the instructions above to make the number of blocks required in your diagram. Then mark the long lattice strips, first on folded fabric, the same way that you marked the border strips. Remember to mark only half as many as you need because you will cut two at a time. Do not cut yet, but first mark the short lattice pieces. These will be marked on the rest of the fabric width in the same way that the rectangular pieces were marked for the "Roman Stripe" patterns, with the length of the piece along the length of the fabric. When all are marked, pin the two layers together and cut the strips.

The pieced blocks and short lattice strips are now ready to be sewed in lengthwise rows. Sew a strip to a block, then a block to the strip and continue adding strips and blocks until there are enough for the length of the quilt, *ending with a block*. Sew as many additional rows like this as are needed for the top. Refer to Illustration 13 for placement of blocks and lattice.

Add a long lattice strip to one long side of a strip of blocks and lattices. If possible, lay the row of blocks out full length and

pin the strip to it, starting at the middle, just the way you added a border strip to the finished quilt top earlier. Sew this long strip, then lay the row of blocks, with its strip opened flat, right side up, and place another row of blocks right sides together on it so that the blocks in both rows are resting in a line with one another. Pin this row of blocks to the edge of the lattice strip. Check before sewing to make sure that the blocks on either side of the strip are in line, then sew the seam. Continue to add strips and rows in this manner until all are added.

Make a border of the width indicated in the yardage chart for the size quilt you are making. Add it to the quilt top in the same manner as usual. It may be either mitered or not, as you choose. Finish the quilt by one of the methods described in Section 5.

A VARIETY OF PIECED PATTERNS

Now that you have learned a few quick and easy methods for making quilts, try some related patterns using the same methods. Following, you will find a sampling of old and new patterns which will give you practice in the skills you have been learning. These samples should help you to begin learning how to look at a pattern and figure out how to construct it with the procedures you are now familiar with. In Section 3, you will gain even more experience as designs with triangles, diamonds and other shapes are added to your pattern repertoire. The designs in *this* section are patterns which use only squares or rectangles. We will examine the relationship between these new patterns and those you have just made and will explore ways to adapt them to the methods already explained. Instruction for the assembly of the blocks will be given as needed.

You will also be learning something about color and color relationships and how they can affect the design and mood of your quilt, how they can show up a certain piece and make another seem to recede into the distance. A visit to an art museum or a study of books with color prints of paintings will show you how artists use color in this way.

As you work more and more with colors and patterns, you will begin to learn how patterns grow—how the different placement of a color can change a pattern completely; how patterns can be put together to make a new combination; and how a new design can develop out of an old one. You will find that your design will sometimes lead you in a direction you had not intended, but which is interesting or even exciting in its effect. You may, for instance, begin to color the wrong piece on your diagram and find that the color is more effective in that location than in the place you had planned. It is, therefore, important to remain flexible in your planning up to the point of purchasing or even cutting your fabric. It is a good idea to purchase enough extra fabric to make a few sample blocks to see how your prints and solids work best together. If the blocks are set solid, a sample of four blocks may be needed to get the complete effect. Since you may not be able to find the identical color or color value you used in your planning sketches, and because prints of a dominant color may contain bits of other colors which can make a wide visual difference in the way fabrics appear together in any given pattern, these samples can save your making a mistake in your quilt and so are worth the small extra expenditure of time and money. They can be made into sampler quilts, pillows, hot plate mats, pot holders, etc., so that nothing is wasted. Do check your fabric choices by daylight, because artificial lighting can change the appearance of color.

By working with color diagrams you will get practice in figuring the size of blocks, sashing and border needed for the size quilt you want to make. You will also gain some experience in figuring yardage (see Section 8 for help with this). It would be very good practice to work up a number of color diagrams of different patterns and figure the yardage requirements for them, just for the practice of these different skills, even if you do not plan to make up the quilts right away. The experience gained is well worth the time spent, and you can file your diagrams and yardage charts away for future use. Begin your practice with a simple pattern—perhaps even one which has all the information given in this book so you can check your results in figuring yardage. As you gain confidence, try the more involved designs.

When you are ready to make up one of these additional patterns, choose one that you like and that will give you the kind of challenge that you are ready for. The joy of working with patterns and colors that appeal to your personal taste is one of the chief objectives in quilting. Quilts are still very useful items, but they are not made today with the desperate necessity that many were made in the past, when they could literally make the difference between life and death. Today's busy quilter seeks an outlet for personal expression, the development of creative abilities, and the employment of skills that are pleasant to use.

You will find here a variety of patterns to choose from. Some are more complicated than others, but none of them is very difficult to sew because there are no bias seams to work with. Mostly solid colors are used in these diagrams because it is difficult to indicate tiny prints against a colored background, but prints could be used in most places instead. Some solid color does usually create a nice combination with prints, but small and large prints used together can have a similar effect and a combination of all prints can be very effective.

Our first pattern, "Trip Around the World" (color page E), is constructed by the same methods as "Patience." Decide as nearly as possible the arrangement of the pieces while you are working with your diagram. If you are working with more than four different materials, you will need to mark and cut more than one group of squares because it would not be easy to cut through more than four fabrics at once. Follow your diagram carefully in sewing the pieces together. Just follow the steps for "Patience."

There are a number of variations to be found for this pattern. It is usually made without a border, but sometimes it is used as a pieced medallion with several plain or pieced borders. This popular pattern offers you a lot of choice in planning color. Sometimes all solid colors in varying shades are used. At other times it is made of all prints or of a mixture of prints and solids. Usually, the colors are rather bright or have strong contrast. Closely related earth colors are also very effective, however, and more somber or faded colors are sometimes used.

Use the same cutting and piecing methods described earlier and follow your diagram carefully. A paper clip on the page will help you to keep your place.

Next, we have a group of patterns which are variations of "Roman Stripe." The first is the simple block with setting blocks (Illus. 15). The second uses a similar arrangement, but with lattices (Illus. 16). The third is a nine-patch block of "Roman Stripe" squares with a plain block in the center (Illus. 17). It could be used in many of the ways that the basic nine-patch is used. The fourth pattern is "Windmill," put together with sashing (Illus. 18), which creates quite a different effect from the "Windmill" set solid. As always, you can use more than three stripes if you like.

The last pattern in this group is another of my "Roman Stripe" variations which I have named "Foursome" (color page G). The brown pieces become the background, making the lighter colors stand out and seem brighter than they actually are. These dark pieces form a secondary diamond pattern which is brought out by the contrast also. In this quilt, I usually use a block 6″ (15 cm) square. The side pieces for this size block are cut 2″ x 6½″ (5 x 16 cm) and the middle piece is cut 3½″ x 6½″ (8.7 x 16 cm). Another size could be used if you prefer.

We have not discussed four-patch patterns as yet, because they are so closely related to one-patch and to nine-patch. "Checkerboard" (Illus. 19) is actually a four-patch pattern set solid, just as "Patience" is a nine-patch pattern set solid. What makes "Checkerboard" a four-patch pattern instead of a one-patch is that an arrangement of four pieces is required to form the block, which is then repeated for the overall pattern. With one-patch patterns, the overall design cannot be broken down into units of pieces which are repeated. The single pieces are either set without regard to pattern or else the design which is formed covers the entire quilt top as in "Trip Around The World" (color page E).

"Ceramic Tile" (color page A) is a four-patch pattern with lattice. Add the pieced lattice of this type to the blocks, which are then joined together like the basic one-patch patterns to form the quilt top. I chose colors with a happy holiday air for a Christmas quilt, but blues or earth colors would also be very effective for this design.

Now we come to the nine-patch patterns and variations. Illustration 20 is a nine-patch made up of five nine-patch blocks with four setting blocks. The pattern is called "Double Nine-patch," and it can be used in virtually any way that the basic Nine-patch can.

Illustration 21 shows a variation of Nine-patch which is called "Puss In the Corner." There are still nine pieces in this block, though they are no longer of equal size. In Illustration 22 the larger center piece of "Puss In the Corner" has been replaced with a small Nine-patch, thus creating another variation. Illustration 23 is simply the same block with a different placement of the fabrics, showing the change in appearance this can make.

Illustration 26 is another variation of the Nine-patch, this time with the larger pieces at the corners. In Illustration 25 you see it set with sashing. You can see from these samples how a basic pattern can be changed to create a different one. In Illustration 26 this block has been changed by substituting a small four-patch for the corner pieces. Then, in Illustration 27, the block has been set with sashing. Illustration 28 shows the same pattern and sashing with a different placement of solids and prints. What a change this makes in the finished appearance!

In Illustration 29 we have taken "Puss In the Corner" and substituted the block in Illustration 24 for the center piece. The lattice and border are of one color instead of being pieced of mixed fabrics. Notice how this gives visual separation to the blocks, whereas the sashing and borders of pieced mixed fabrics seem to join the blocks into an overall pattern (Illus. 27 and 28).

The block in Illustration 30 is, again, a nine-patch arrangement having tiny nine-patch blocks at the corners, and stripes, pieced after the manner of "Roman Stripe," for the side pieces. The center piece could be a solid color, a picture or flower print, or a pieced block. The arrangement could also be used as a sashing, the stripes being lengthened or shortened if necessary to fit around a center block.

The last two patterns are two old favorites which have always been considered complicated, but are much simplified by these methods. The first is one of the Irish Chain variations called "Double Irish Chain" (Illus. 31). Originally it was made up entirely of little squares, but an easier method has been developed for appliquéing a small square at each corner of a large square (which is used as a setting block) to take the place of the many little squares of a single fabric which were previously used. Much time is saved this way and the effect is almost the same. One reason that many little pieces were popular in the past was that even tiny bits of fabric could be incorporated into the quilt top, thus eliminating their waste.

My method is even easier than the traditional way. It employs two different blocks: one pattern is "Puss in the Corner" (Illus. 31-a); the other is made up of five tiny squares each way, called a five-patch (Illus. 31-b), and put together like a miniature one-patch. The two then alternate in the manner of nine-patch with setting blocks so that they form the lovely old design. The quilt is usually either finished without a border or is bound, but a border would be attractive also. The tiny squares used to be 1″ (25 mm) when finished, but more recently, I have seen them as large as 2″ (5 cm) finished.

"Burgoyne Surrounded" (Illus. 32) dates back almost to the American Revolutionary War and is said to be taken from a battle plan of that period. The British general, Burgoyne, was defeated by the colonists and the quilt design celebrates this victory. The colors used also express patriotism, since the quilt is usually made of reds or blues on white. One very lovely example I have seen was made of deep red with a white-on-blue print for the lighter pieces and set together with white.

Here again, what used to be many small white pieces I now cut as larger rectangles to save time as well as fabric. In this plan, four different blocks are used, three pieced blocks (Illus. 32-a, b & c) and one plain (Illus. 32-d). By studying the diagram, you will see that three different pieced units are put together in the manner of a nine-patch block (as indicated by the dash lines on Illus. 32) and then these are set together with a lattice of a long rectangular strip with a nine-patch variation (Illus. 32-a) at the corners. Mark the smaller squares and cut both colors together. You will find that the same number of dark and light squares, but more of white, are needed. Mark and cut the larger light squares and the large white rectangles separately. The small dark rectangles of Illustration 32-c can be cut with some of the small white rectangles of Illustrations 32-a and c, but many more white ones are needed. Illustration 32-b is made up of a tiny four-patch and a tiny nine-patch pieced together with two small rectangles, which must be cut separately. The medium-sized rectangle used with the smaller pieces in Illustration 32-c must also be cut separately. Illustration 32-a is one of the nine-patch variations you have seen in Illustration 24. Piece as many of each unit as are needed and then assemble them as for nine-patch (refer to the dash lines on Illus. 32) with the lattice type of assembly. There are a few variations of this pattern. The ones I have seen can be adapted to this method of assembly.

In looking through books of quilt patterns you will see a number of other patterns that could have been included in this group. Study each one to see how the methods you have been learning for easy cutting and piecing can be applied to it. Begin to collect a file of these patterns for future reference, with notes for cutting and piecing. Before long, you will automatically think in terms of these methods.

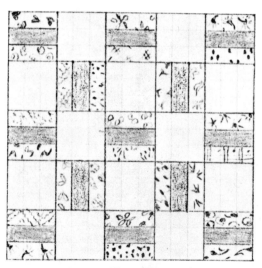

Illus. 15

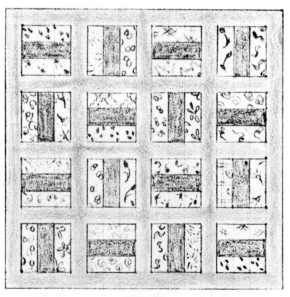

Illus. 16

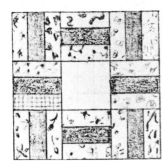

Illus. 17

Illus. 18

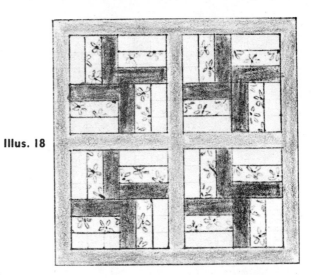

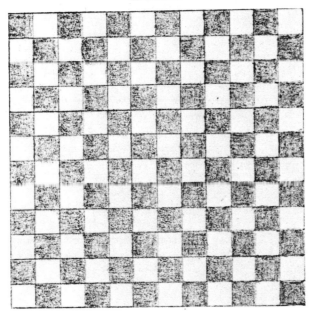

Illus. 19

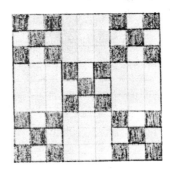

Illus. 20

Illus. 21

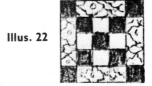

Illus. 22

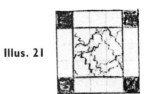

Illus. 23

Illus. 24

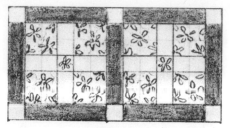

Illus. 25

Illus. 26

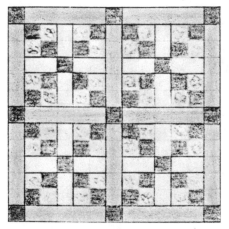

Illus. 27

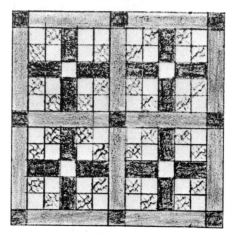

Illus. 28

Illus. 29

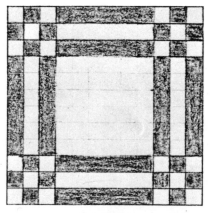

IllIus. 30

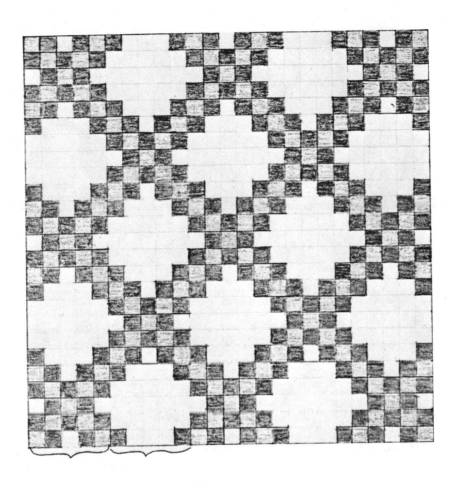

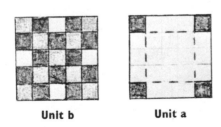

Unit b   Unit a

Illus. 31. "Double Irish Chain."

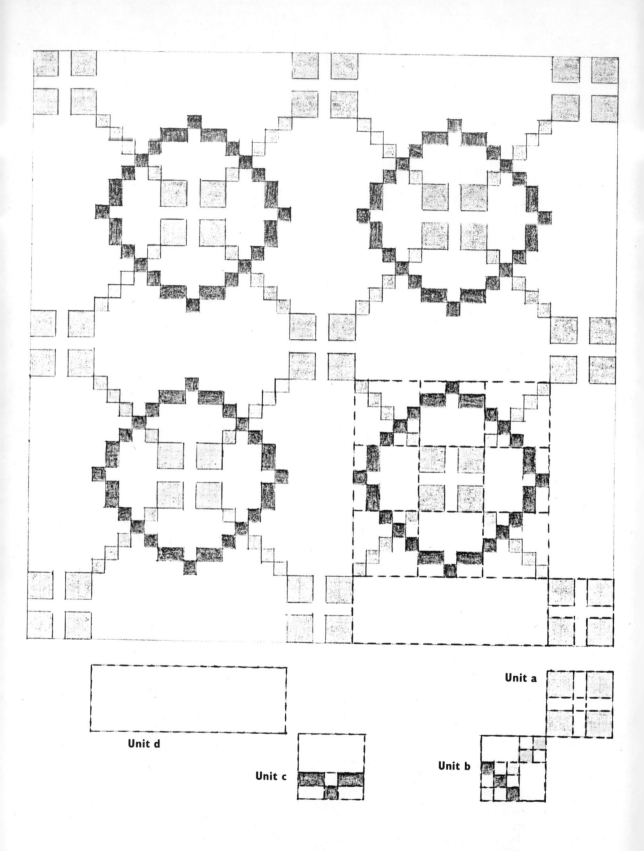

Unit d

Unit c

Unit a

Unit b

Illus. 32. "Burgoyne Surrounded."

SECTION 3
More Machine Piecing

In this section you will find many patterns of different types, grouped according to the shape of the predominant pieces. This time I have not given you the quilt diagrams nor have I worked out the yardages for you. The quilt pattern will be shown and instructions will be given as needed for putting the blocks together. From this, you can plan your own quilt and draw the diagram, choosing the type of setting you want. In Section 8 you will find the necessary information for figuring the amount of fabric you will need. If you are still a beginner at this, start with a simple project. You will gradually gain more confidence as you go through the various processes over and over again.

With each type of pattern, I have included some special methods to make the work go easier and faster. Though some of them may be a little unorthodox, they work well and are more efficient than others I have tried. Even though you may be used to some other method, learn these also. It is always good to know more than one way to do something, and in the process, you may find a method you like better.

For some patterns you will need templates to mark the pieces on the fabric. When you are satisfied with your pattern, draw or trace each different pattern piece on another piece of paper. These must be very accurate. Add ¼″ (6 mm) seam allowances all around. Trace these pieces, with the seam allowances, onto the shrink art plastic described in Section 1, or draw them on stiff, lightweight cardboard (see Illus. 33, and see also the instructions for making quilting templates in Section 5). Cut out the templates just along the inside of the lines. Use these templates to mark the pieces on your fabric—suggestions will be made as needed.

I am presenting the patterns in this way so that you will learn to draft patterns for yourself. This will enable you to take any pattern you see, or even one you have designed yourself, draft the pieces and make the templates, if needed, to mark and cut the fabric for your quilt. If you do not want to draft pieces, you can find many pattern books in which patterns are printed full size. I have also included a few full-size patterns at the end of this section. For hand quilting, seam allowances are not usually included in the pattern pieces. Add them, if they are omitted, because they should be included when you are planning to piece by machine. To make a handle for the template, stick an empty thread spool to it with cellophane tape that is sticky on both sides. The handle can be removed when you store the template.

Whenever looking at quilt patterns, you should take a moment to think about what type of pattern you are studying and which of the methods that you are learning can be used in the construction of the pattern. Soon this information will come to mind automatically when you look at quilts. Then you will know that you have made the methods your own and that they are a part of your thinking just as your observations of color and fabrics, etc.

When planning a design for your own quilt, consider all the piecing and setting alternatives open to you. Work with your diagrams to try out the different possibilities. The position of the lights and darks and medium values can be widely varied to create many different effects with the same shapes. To show you the variety that can

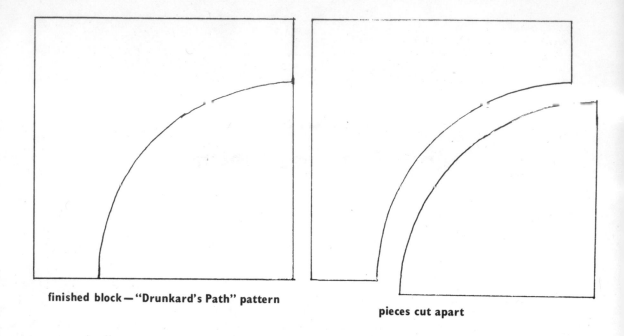

finished block — "Drunkard's Path" pattern

pieces cut apart

make templates of these exact shapes to mark the fabric

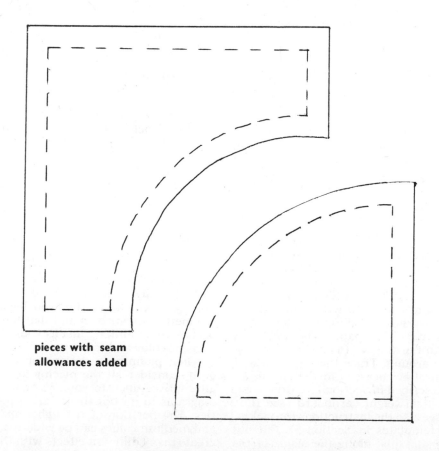

pieces with seam allowances added

Illus. 33. Drafting templates.

be achieved, I started with a nine-patch pattern called "Ohio Star" (see Illus. 34). I began to draw in the dark and medium values, leaving the white paper for the light value, to see how many different arrangements of these values I could find. The basic block is #1. Number 2 through #15 are the more conventional variations. At that point, my ideas began to lead me astray into kindred patterns which are not true "Ohio Star." Some are more closely related than others. By this time I was in unfamiliar territory, not knowing which patterns had been done before and which were new, if any. It is inconceivable that no one else had ever tried some of these variations. For this reason, I have given numbers to all the patterns and names to those that I think may be my own variations.

When exploring a pattern in this manner, we find that the rearrangement of fabrics of different values sometimes results in two pieces of the same fabric coming together. When this happens, the two may be cut as one when it does not make the piecing more difficult. This would work well, for example, in #9, if two of the three dark quarter-squares which fall together were

cut in one piece as a half-square. In such variations as #17, #19, and #25, for instance, some quarter-squares can be cut as half-squares. (This occurs also in #2, #9 and #11, where the star pattern is still distinct.)

In #16, #22, #24, #30, #31 and #32, such a drastic change is made by the coming together of pieces of the same fabric that the entire piecing order would be different, and the design is no longer a nine-patch pattern. Study #30 to understand what happens here. The white center square is joined by four white quarter-squares to become a larger diagonal square. A new corner piece is also formed by a dark square and two dark quarter-squares coming together as the dark pentagon-shaped pieces in the block. Sew a pentagon corner piece to two opposite sides of the diagonal center square to form a middle group. Add two small white quarter-square triangles to each side of the other two corner pieces so that they form two triangles. Sew these two triangles on opposite sides of the middle group to complete the block.

The other patterns mentioned in this connection (#16, #22, #23, #24, and #31) are variations of #30. When piecing these,

basic block

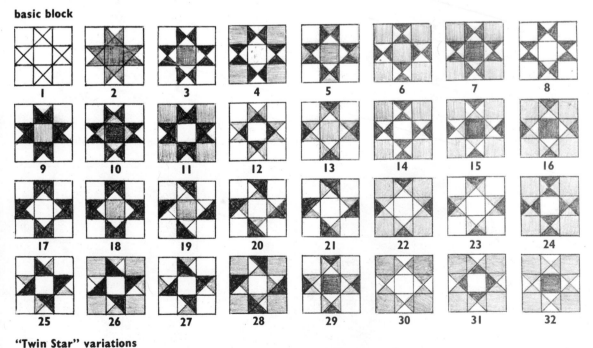

"Twin Star" variations

Illus. 34. Variations on the "Ohio Star" block.

sew four quarter-squares to the center square to form the larger diagonal squares. After that, proceed to piece the block in the same way as for #30.

This type of exploration can be applied to almost any pattern and can lead you to many interesting, and sometimes untried, designs. Another direction to follow in considering the various alternatives in planning your quilt is to experiment with the setting of the block.

The most obvious choice is whether to use lattice or setting blocks, or to set the blocks solid. "Ohio Star" is, again, our example. It is usually set together with lattice or setting blocks, as are most nine-patch patterns. Look at what happens to some of these blocks when they are set solid. An interesting all-over design is formed by this. The first, #33, is a variation of #20. The others are shown among the group of single blocks. In each case it is not easy to see the original block because of what happens to the design when there is nothing to set the blocks apart. In each group the corners of the blocks come to-

gether and look like a single square. This gives the appearance of a pieced lattice around a plain block. This piecing makes these designs different. They are no longer variations of "Ohio Star" or any Nine-patch. I have worked up several other blocks this way also and have given them names (see Illus. 35).

Another setting possibility is to turn the block to different positions. Study the variations of "Kansas Trouble" (Illus. 36) to see how a block can be made to form different designs by placing it in different relationships in the setting.

A third setting alternative is to use two (or more) different patterns together. I have explored several possibilities in combining an eight-pointed star variation of a Nine-patch with a "Roman Stripe" block. This type of thing can be done with other combinations of patterns. Set your imagination and curiosity free to investigate together as you work with your diagrams or when you are just doodling on graph paper. It can be a very exciting experience.

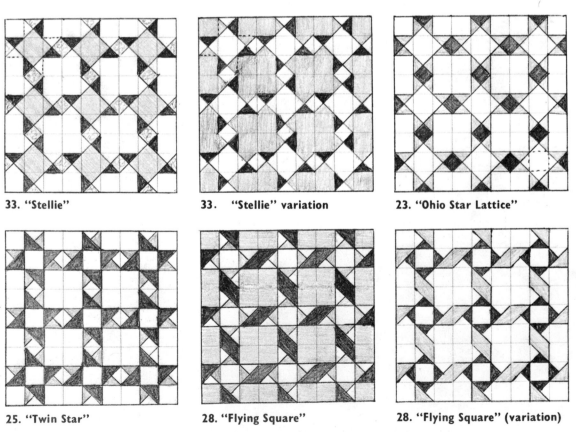

33. "Stellie"   33. "Stellie" variation   23. "Ohio Star Lattice"

25. "Twin Star"   28. "Flying Square"   28. "Flying Square" (variation)

Illus 35. More variations on the "Ohio Star" block.

TRIANGLE PATTERNS

Patterns made up partly or entirely of triangles are not quite as easy to make as those made of squares or rectangles, because of the bias edges of the triangles. Accuracy in measuring, cutting and sewing are particularly important with these patterns in order to make the pieces fit together properly into a block true to measurement. These triangle patterns are found in profusion and are so lovely and varied that no quilter can, or wishes to, avoid them for long. They are well worth the effort of learning to handle the bias seams. A special type of template, which I describe below, will help you with this.

You will soon discover that there are several types of triangles used in piecing. Perhaps the simplest of them is the half-square triangle. A square marked from one corner to the opposite corner on the diagonal will produce this type of triangle. I have sketched a number of patterns using this half-square triangle (see Illus. 36). Choose one to make as you learn to sew triangles.

When your pattern requires that a number of half-square triangles of the same two fabrics be sewed together into squares, the easiest way to do this is to sew the bias seams before cutting them. Lay the laundered fabrics with right sides together (one layer each—not folded) with the lighter fabric on top.

To figure the measurements for half-square triangles, draw a square the size you will use on a piece of plain or accurately drawn graph paper (see Illus. 37). Draw a diagonal line across the square to mark it into two triangles. In another place on your paper, draw this triangle again exactly the same size. Add ¼″ (6 mm) all around for seam allowances. Add the other triangle with its seam allowances to the first, to complete a square of two triangles. Using the measurements of *this* square, mark the fabric into squares by the method learned in Section 1. The squares should be the size of the two triangles *including all seam allowances*. When the squares have all been marked, lay your yardstick (meterstick) along the bias of the fabric and mark diagonal lines from corner to corner in one

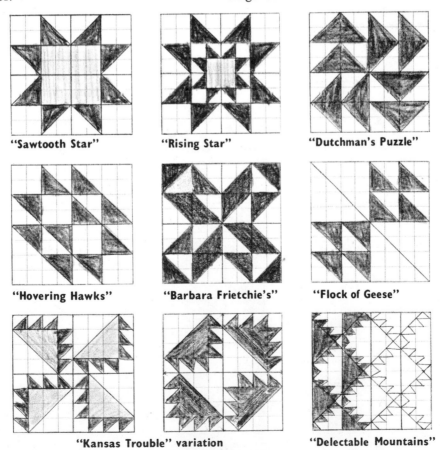

"Sawtooth Star" "Rising Star" "Dutchman's Puzzle"

"Hovering Hawks" "Barbara Frietchie's" "Flock of Geese"

"Kansas Trouble" variation "Delectable Mountains"

Illus. 36. Half-square patterns.

finished size of square

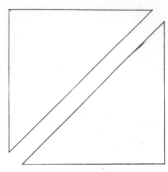

pieces cut apart

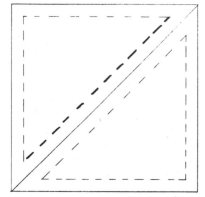

triangles with seam allowances added and then joined into a square

mark this size square on the fabric and draw only one diagonal line — see Illus. 38

Illus. 37. Drafting a half-square.

direction across all the squares. Pin the two layers of fabric together, placing pins along one side of the diagonal lines at the corners of the triangles (see Illus. 38). Point all the pins in the same direction. If the fabric marked and pinned is so large that it will be awkward to handle, cut it into sections along the crossway lines.

Now, sew the bias seams of the triangles. Stitch ¼″ (6 mm) from the diagonal line, first on one side and then on the other. Use twelve stitches to the inch (25 mm). *Do not sew across the right angle corners* of other triangles between the ones being stitched. There is a strong temptation to hurry this sewing, but don't! This seam must be

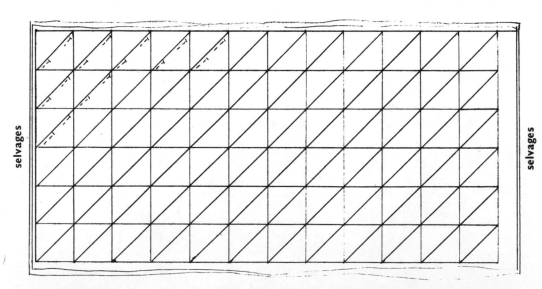

Illus. 38. Marking and sewing half-squares. Two layers of fabric are marked for half-squares.

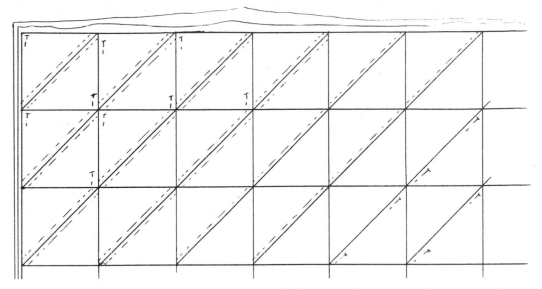

Illus. 39. Marking and sewing half-squares (continued). Pin and stitch two layers of fabric on the diagonal lines only for two half-squares pieced into a square. After doing the diagonal stitching, pin the right-angle corners (as shown at upper left) before cutting the pieces.

accurately sewed or the resulting square will not have the correct measurements.

When all the bias seams have been stitched, pin the two fabrics together at the right angle corners opposite to the seams and then cut along the diagonal lines between the stitching (see Illus. 39). After that, cut each resulting strip along the remaining lines. Now you have a pile of squares made up of two triangles sewed together.

The next step is to make what I call an "ironing template" (see Illus. 40). This is a fabric template for checking the size and shape of the work while ironing, *not* for marking the pieces. Make it of muslin or other firmly woven fabric, which has been shrunk and ironed. The fabric should be several inches (50 cm) larger on all sides than the template drawn on it. In the center of this fabric, draw a square the size of the two triangles sewed together and including the outside seam allowances. *Do not* use a pair of triangles sewed together as a pattern to draw the square for the template. Instead, use the measurements as you drafted them originally. Pin the fabric template to your ironing board. Iron the pairs of triangles over this template. Iron the bias seam allowances to one side. Work carefully so that you do not stretch the seam lengthwise, or shorten it by pressing at right angles to the seam. If you have marked, sewed and cut accurately, the square you have sewed should fit the

square on the ironing-template. If the squares for the quilt are too large, take a little deeper seam. If they are too small, the seam should be a bit narrower. To do this, first sew the new seam, then remove the previous one. The easiest method is to cut every fourth stitch on one side of the fabric and then pull out the uncut thread on the other side. This will not damage the bias seam allowance. Make adjustments as needed so that the pieced squares will fit the template.

Use this method any time you have a pattern which includes half-squares or half-rectangles (see pgs. 53 and 56).

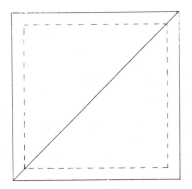

Illus. 40. Half-square ironing template — a drawing on muslin of two half-squares sewed together. Pin this to the ironing board and iron the pieced squares over it to check the size of the squares after piecing.

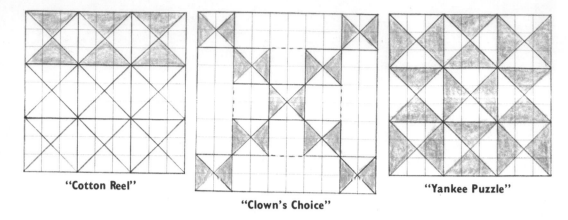

"Cotton Reel"

"Clown's Choice"

"Yankee Puzzle"

Illus. 41. Quarter-square patterns.

Quarter-Square Triangles

Closely related to the half-square patterns are those which include quarter-squares (see Illus. 41). These are just a little more difficult to put together, but you can apply the above methods to them without any worry. Begin by figuring the measurements of the square to be cut for quarter-square triangles, then draw a square of the desired size without seam allowances on paper. Divide it with diagonal lines in both directions (see Illus. 42). Draw one of the resulting triangles exactly the same size in another place on the paper and add ¼″ (6 mm) seam allowances. Add the other three triangles, with their seam allowances, to complete a square. The measurements of *this* square, including the seam allowances, are the ones to use in drawing squares on the fabric using your cutting board and yardstick (meterstick).

When the squares are drawn, draw diaganol lines in *both* directions across all the squares. Pin together the two layers of fabric to be used and sew as before on both sides of the diagonal lines *in one direction only*, stitching ¼″ (6 mm) from the line on each side of it. Cut exactly on the diagonal lines where there was no stitching done and then cut along all the other lines. The result will be quarter-triangles sewed together to make half-triangles. Make an ironing template for use in checking the size of the pieced half-squares as you iron (see Illus. 42). Make seam adjustments as needed to correct any discrepancy in the size of the triangles. These pieced half-triangles may be used with other pieced or unpieced half-triangles in piecing the pattern of the block.

If you have difficulty stitching bias seams without stretching them, pin a piece of tissue paper under the seam to be stitched. This will prevent stretching, and the tissue paper will tear away easily after the sewing is done.

Half-Rectangles

Half-rectangle patterns can be handled in the same way as half-triangles. You will start simply by figuring the measurements of the rectangles you wish to use, drawing them on your fabric, and dividing them by the diagonal lines as you did with the squares. You will sew and cut them by the same methods used for the half-triangles. Ironing templates should be made for checking the measurements while they are being ironed.

A half-square triangle is a right-angled triangle because it has one 90-degree angle. It is an isosceles triangle because it has two equal sides as well. A half-rectangle is *not* an isosceles triangle, though it *is* a right-angled triangle and can be handled by the same methods as half-squares. The 90-degree, or right angle, makes a half-square a special type of isosceles triangle. Other types have two equal sides and two equal angles, but no 90-degree angle. Their third angle can be virtually any size from near 0-degree to near 180-degrees, though the

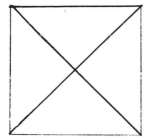

finished size of square

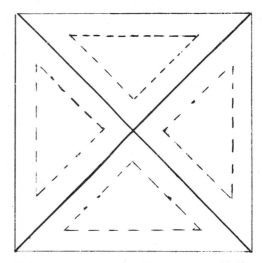

seam allowances added — mark this size square on the fabric and draw solid diagonal lines in both directions

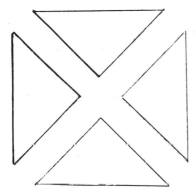

pieces cut apart

make ironing template like this: first check pieced triangles for size while ironing, then check pieced square for size while ironing seam allowance

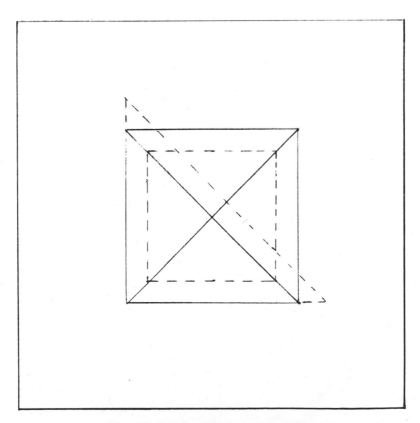

Illus. 42. Constructing a quarter-square.

extreme ones are not practical for quilting. This wide range of possible variations means that the triangle can be either tall or squatty in proportion (see Illus. 43).

You must figure the measurements of the triangle you want to use before marking it on the fabric. To do this, draw on paper a triangle of the finished size and shape desired (see Illus. 44). Add ¼″ (6 mm) seam allowance all around. Measure the height of the triangle, including the seam allowances, from the middle of the base (the unequal side) to the opposite point.

On your unfolded fabric, draw a lengthwise line for cutting off the selvage along one side. Along this line, measure off repeats of the *height* of the triangle and draw crossways lines this distance apart. Starting at the selvage line, measure off repeats of the length of the *base* of the triangle on the first, third and any other odd-numbered line. Then, draw diagonal lines which join the first mark at the far left of the first line, with the second mark on the third line. Draw other lines parallel to the first one, using the next marks along the lines as a guide. Continue this process until all the diagonal lines in this direction have been drawn. Then, in the same way, draw diagonal lines in the opposite direction. Several layers of fabric may be cut at one time.

If only one fabric is to be cut into this size triangle, the fabric may be folded before marking to allow two layers to be cut at once. If quite a lot of triangles of one size are to be cut from only one fabric, the fabric may be folded once crossways and once lengthwise and the triangles marked on only one layer of the fabric. Four triangles can be cut at a time this way. (This method can be used when you are cutting any shape of piece.)

"STRIPEY" QUILTS

"Stripey" quilt is an old-fashioned name for the type of quilt which has pieced stripes which alternate with plain, solid color or print stripes. They can be very striking and interesting, but are not seen as often as quilts made of blocks. I have drawn a diagram to give you an idea of how these quilts can be put together (color page H). This might be a good time for you to start making your own designs. You will find it quite easy to plan some simple pieced stripes joined by plain stripes of various widths. Since little piecing is required, the quilt can be made quickly. The quilting can also be quite easy. You can either quilt in-the-ditch along the seams of the stripes or you can assemble the quilt by the quilt-as-you-go method on a large scale, like the small strips used for string quilts (see "String Patterns" in Section 6).

"Flying Geese," "Ocean Waves," "Birds in the Air,"
"Wild Goose Chase"

"Flying Dutchman"

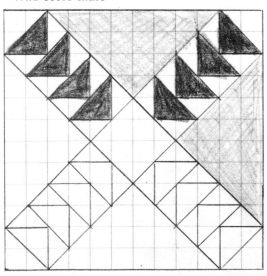
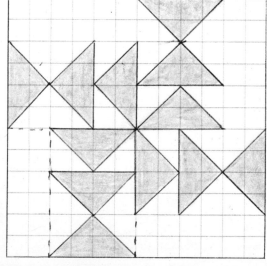

Illus. 43. Isosceles triangle patterns.

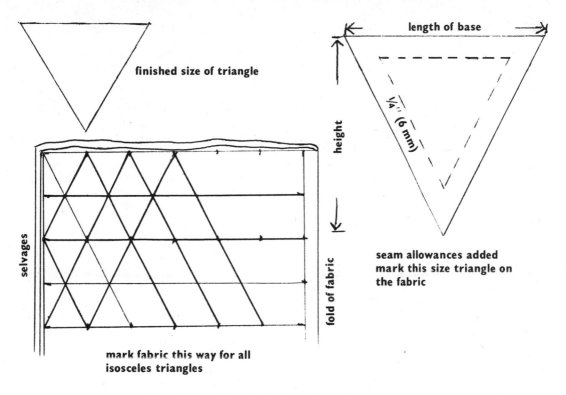

finished size of triangle

length of base

¼" (6 mm)

height

selvages

fold of fabric

seam allowances added
mark this size triangle on
the fabric

mark fabric this way for all
isosceles triangles

Illus. 44. Marking the fabric for isosceles triangles.

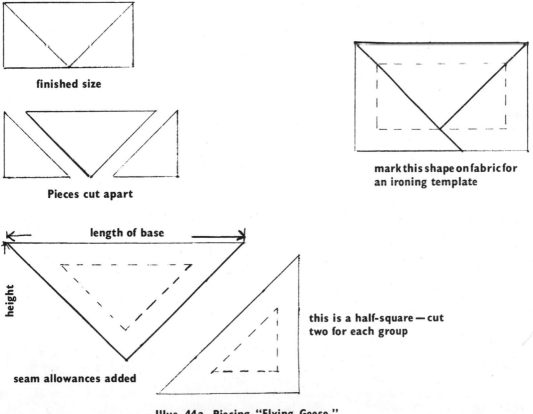

finished size

Pieces cut apart

mark this shape on fabric for
an ironing template

length of base

height

this is a half-square — cut
two for each group

seam allowances added

Illus. 44a. Piecing "Flying Geese."

DIAMOND PATTERNS

Diamond-shaped pieces sewed into lovely star, sunburst and other designs are among the most popular and attractive quilts to be found in any show. A *diamond* is a figure having four equal straight sides and two opposite angles which are larger than the other pair (this excludes the square). It is a type of *parallelogram*, which is a four-sided figure whose opposite sides are parallel and equal. This obviously means that a *square* and a *rectangle* are parallelograms also. The other two types of parallelograms are the *rhombus* and the *rhomboid*. If you were to take a square shape made of wire and push on the two opposite corners, warping the figure out of square, the resulting shape would be a *diamond*, which is the *rhombus* in mathematical terms. If you did the same thing to a *rectangular* shape made of wire, the result would be a *rhomboid*, which is *not* a diamond because the four sides would not be equal. Only the two opposite sides are equal in a rhomboid, as they are in the rectangle.

While diamonds can be either wider or narrower in proportion to their height, only two sizes are generally used in piecing quilt patterns. For one, the two pairs of opposite angles are 60-degrees and 120-degrees. It can be pieced together to form a six-pointed star. Three of these diamonds fit together to form a hexagon, a figure with eight sides (all equal in this case), which is very popular in quilting. More about this later.

The other diamond most often used in quilting has two pairs of opposite angles which are 45-degrees and 135-degrees, and can be pieced together to form an eight-pointed star.

Drafting Diamonds

You can see, by all this, how closely quilting is related to geometry. While a thorough knowledge of this subject is not required, a little understanding of the relationship of shapes is needed when you are drafting or designing patterns.

Perhaps the simplest way to draft diamonds is by folding paper (see Illus. 45). It may not be very accurate, however, unless it is carefully done. The 45-degree diamond is made by folding a square of paper in half on the diagonal, forming a triangle. Cut along the fold. With one piece, make another fold by bringing one short side to the cut side. Draw a line along this fold. Mark the length of the diamond along this line,

starting where the line touches the point. Bring this point to the mark made and fold a crease. Draw a line along this crease. This line touches the sides of the paper at two points. Make marks at these points and draw lines from them to the mark made for the length of the diamond. This completes the diamond shape.

The 60-degree diamond is made by a similar method (see Illus. 45). This time, fold a sheet of rectangular paper into three equal angles, radiating from the middle of one side. Cut off one of these parts and fold it in half lengthwise from the point just cut. Draw a line along this fold. Mark the length of the diamond along this line measuring from the point. Fold the paper so that the point touches the mark for the length of the diamond. Draw a line along this fold. This line will touch the two sides' of the paper. Make marks at these two points and draw lines from them to the mark for the length of the diamond.

The other way to draft diamonds is with a protractor. This method is faster and easier and likely to be more accurate. A protractor is an inexpensive little tool with which angles of various sizes can be drawn with accuracy. Be sure to use a sharp pencil or a fine ballpoint for the drawing because a wide mark can throw the angles off and then the diamonds will not fit together properly. If this happens, the block will not lie flat. If the angles are a bit too narrow, the block will buckle; if they are a bit too wide, the block will ripple. For this reason, it is important to check the diamond (or rhomboid, or any set of pieces, for that matter) before marking the fabric. To do this, draw out the pattern by placing each piece in position and drawing around it (without the seam allowances), or better still, make up a block of pieces cut from scrap fabric. This can be used for a pillow top or some other items, so nothing is wasted.

The process is the same whether you want a 60-degree or a 45-degree angle diamond. Only the angles used are different. The following instructions are for the 60-degree diamond (those for the 45-degree diamond are in parenthesis). Draw a line on paper the exact length you want the finished diamond to be (see Illus. 46 and 47). Label one end of the line A and the other end B. Place your protractor on this line so that point A is at the center of the diameter line. (This is not necessarily the bottom edge of the protractor. If it is not, there will be a tiny hole at the center point of the diameter line.)

FOLDING A 45° DIAMOND

start with square

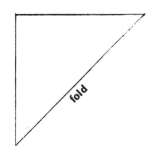

fold on diagonal

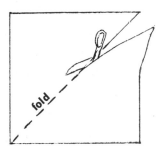

cut apart

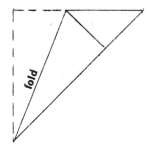

fold side to diagonal

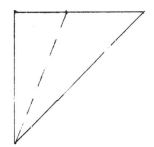

draw fold line

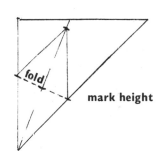

mark height

FOLDING A 60° DIAMOND

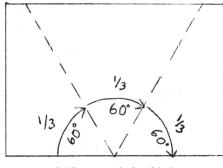

fold rectangle in thirds

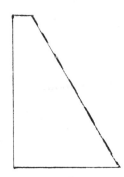

cut off 1/3

for both diamonds, add seam allowances before making templates

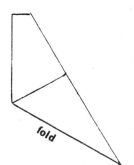

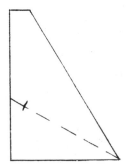

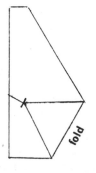

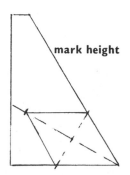

mark height

Illus. 45. Drafting diamonds by folding paper.

61

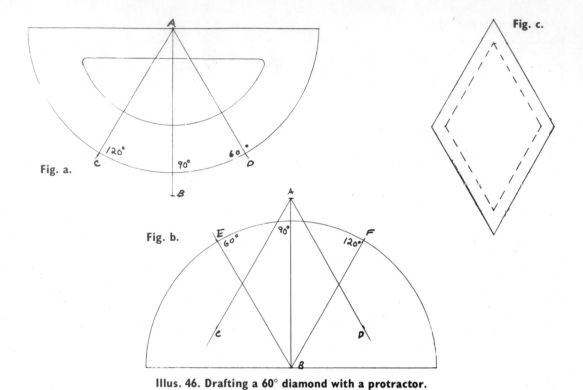

Illus. 46. Drafting a 60° diamond with a protractor.

For either a 60° or a 45° diamond, draw line A-B the finished length of the diamond. With a protractor, draw lines A-C and A-D, then lines A-E and A-F. Add seam allowances to the diamond before making the template.

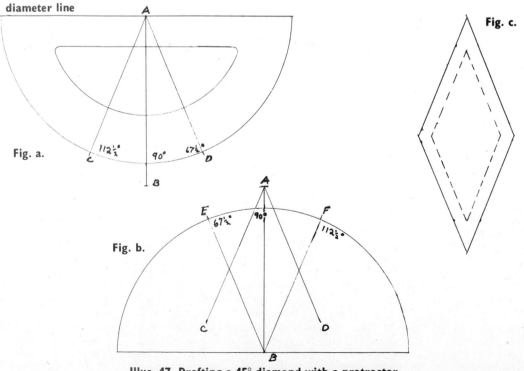

Illus. 47. Drafting a 45° diamond with a protractor.

The mark for 90-degrees must lie on the line AB. If this line is not long enough to reach the 90-degree mark on the curve of the protractor, make a mark at B and then extend the line far enough to reach 90 degrees. Be sure that the position of the protractor is accurate or it will throw the angles off. Make marks at 60 degrees (67½ degrees) and 120 degrees (112½ degrees). Label these points C and D. (See the diagram corresponding to the diamond you are making.) Draw lines from A to C and A to D. Next, place the protractor with the center of the diameter line at point B on the first line drawn. Repeat the process of marking two points at the same angles as before and label these points E and F. Draw lines from B to E and B to F. This will form the diamond. The method can be used to make any size of diamond, though other sizes are not generally used in piecing quilts because their angles do not fit together to form a star, for instance, or other regular shapes.

Whichever method you use to draft the diamonds, be sure to add seam allowances to all sides before marking the fabric. If you merely add ½″ (12 mm) to the length of the diamond before drafting it, the finished size will be much smaller than you intend. The only accurate method is to draft the finished size first and add the seam allowances afterward.

Marking the Fabric for Diamonds

To make just a very few diamonds, make a template using the pattern drafted. Be sure you add the seam allowances. If a large number of diamonds is needed, they can be marked directly on the fabric, using a yardstick (meterstick) and cutting board. In either case, if only one fabric is to be used, mark the *folded* fabric with the template so that two diamonds can be cut at a time (this takes a little more fabric). When more than one fabric is to be used, you can mark either folded or unfolded fabric, depending upon whether you would rather save time or fabric.

On your diamond pattern, draw a line from one side to the opposite side at a right angle to the sides (see Illus. 48). To do this, make this angle on cardboard, using a protractor, or buy a right-angle (90-degree) triangle at an office supply store. Buy the largest you can because it will make a longer line on the fabric. This tends to be more accurate than extending short lines. Measure the length of the line drawn across the diamond and mark the crossways lines on the fabric this distance apart.

Measure the length of one side of the diamond and mark repeats of this length along the first crossways line drawn, using a ruler or a compass. Draw a triangle on cardboard, using a protractor to form the angle accurately, or buy a triangle with either the 60 degrees/30 degrees or 45 degrees of the diamond you are making. This can be on the same triangle with the 90 degrees just used. Place the triangle on the fabric so that the vertical side is parallel to the selvage, and the horizontal side is resting on one of the crossways lines. The side opposite the 90° angle should intersect the first crossways line at one of the points marked on it. Draw a diagonal line on the fabric along this side of the triangle. Make the line as long as you can with the triangle in the position given. From the point that this diagonal line crosses other crossways lines, mark off repeats of the length of the side of the diamond in both directions from the first diagonal line. For example, if the side of the diamond is 3″ (8 cm) long, make a mark every 2″ (5 cm) along the line. It is not necessary to do this on every crossways line, but do it often enough to make an easy reach from one mark to the next with the ruler or yardstick (meterstick) you are using to draw the lines—perhaps every 12″ to 18″ (30–45 cm). (For very small diamonds, mark more often to help assure accuracy when drawing the diagonal lines.) Use these marks to draw additional diagonal lines parallel to the first one, and on both sides of it as needed. This completes the marking of the diamonds.

Rhomboids can be marked on the fabric by this same method (see Illus. 48). Use the narrower width measurement and the longer side length in drawing the lines on the fabric.

Diamonds, like half-squares, have some bias edges to be sewed. To make this easier, you can sew a bias edge to a straight edge, except when the design of the fabric (such as a stripe) would make this undesirable.

The 45-degree diamond can be pieced to form the simple eight-pointed star, which is usually made up into a square block and is known as "Lemoine Star" (Illus. 49). Some people avoid diamond patterns because they feel that it is difficult to sew the corners where the squares are set into the angles formed by the diamonds. I like to do them by the following method which makes the whole procedure quite simple. You have already been following this method when you made a mitered corner on your quilt border. Make a pillow of this

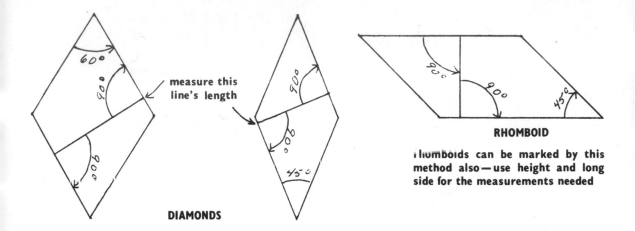

measure this line's length

RHOMBOID

Rhomboids can be marked by this method also—use height and long side for the measurements needed

DIAMONDS

draw a line across the width of the figure and mark the crossways lines on the fabric this distance apart

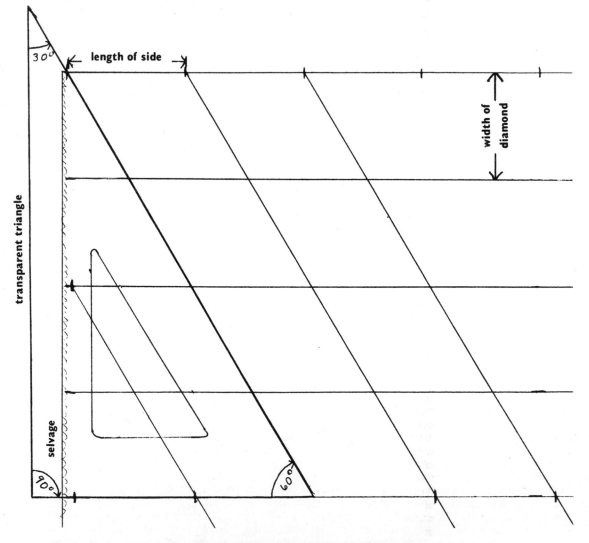

Illus. 48. Marking diamonds and rhomboids on fabrics.

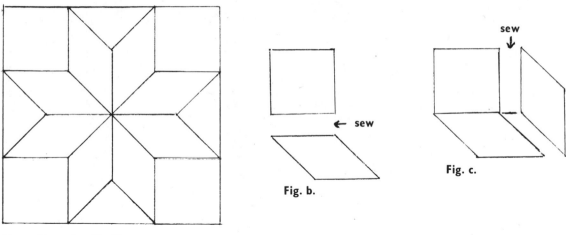

Fig. a. "Lemoine Star"

Fig. b.

sew

Fig. c.

sew

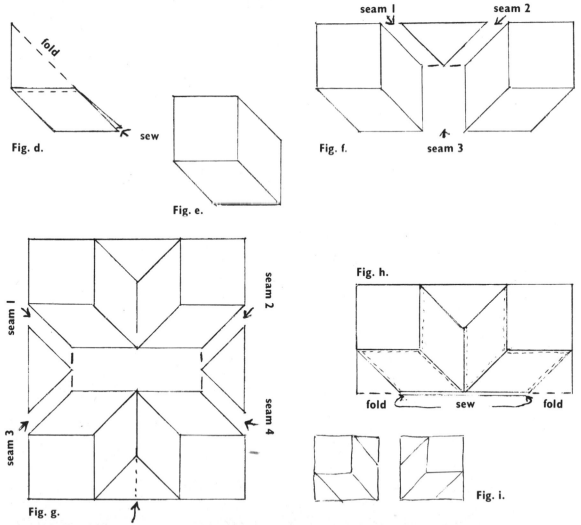

fold

Fig. d.

sew

Fig. e.

seam 1 seam 2

Fig. f. seam 3

seam 1 seam 2

seam 3 seam 4

Fig. g.

Fig. h.

fold sew fold

Fig. i.

note: if the triangles on the sides are cut and half-added to each side of Fig. e., then four pieced squares, like Fig. i., can be made to form the block

Illus. 49. Piecing "Lemoine Star" (45° diamonds).

pattern if you want to practice before you begin your quilt.

Cut eight diamonds in colors of your choice. Draft and cut four squares with finished sides to fit the finished sides of the diamonds. (The cut side of the diamond will be longer than the cut side of the square.) Cut four half-squares, also. You have drafted both of these before. Look now at Illustration 49. Begin sewing by stitching a *bias* edge of one diamond to one side of a square (Fig. b). Start and finish your stitching ¼" (6 mm) from the corner, using tiny stitches at the beginning and end of the seam. Next, sew a *straight* cut edge of another diamond to an adjoining side of the same square (Fig. c). Fold the square in half on the diagonal so that one diamond is lying on the other, and sew the seam from the corners of the diamond to the points where the ends of the seams are (Fig. d). This is a corner group (Fig. e). Make three more corner groups in the same way. Join two of these corner groups to a half-square in exactly the same way, by sewing one diamond from each group to a matching side of a half-square (Fig. f). Repeat this procedure with the remaining two corner groups and another of half-squares. Now you have two half blocks.

Add half squares to the diamonds at the sides (Fig. g) and then sew the pairs of diamonds along the center seam of the block as shown. Be sure to match the cross seams so that all the diamonds will meet in the center properly. This process may seem to be piecing the whole thing rather backwards, but it is really the easiest way. The square blocks, when finished, can be set solid or with setting blocks or with lattice. Add a border, if you choose, and finish the quilt by your favorite method.

When you have mastered this technique, try a "Blazing Star" (Illus. 50), a "Virginia Star" (Illus. 51), or some other variation of eight-pointed star patterns with the larger diamonds of the points made up of many smaller diamonds pieced together. These little diamonds are easily pieced by a method much like the one you used to piece your one-patch squares. You will now sew one-patch diamonds to make a larger diamond (see Illus. 52–53).

Make one color diagram for this larger pieced diamond as well as one for the whole quilt. Follow this diagram carefully to piece the larger diamonds which make up the star.

Start sewing at one point of the large diamond. Lay the first small diamond from

Illus. 50. "Blazing Star."

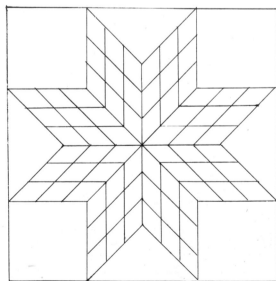

Illus. 51. "Virginia Star."

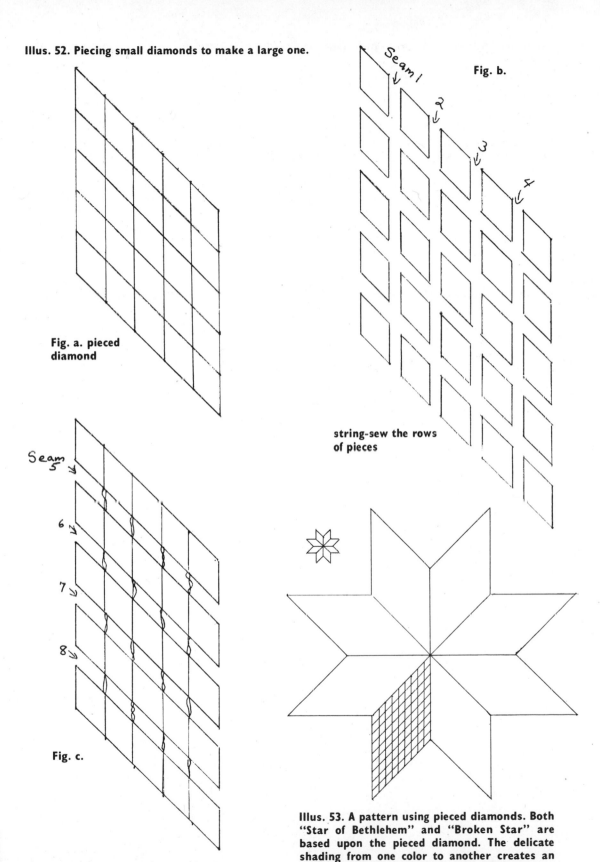

Illus. 52. Piecing small diamonds to make a large one.

Fig. a. pieced diamond

Fig. b.

Seam 1
2
3
4

string-sew the rows of pieces

Seam 5
6
7
8

Fig. c.

Illus. 53. A pattern using pieced diamonds. Both "Star of Bethlehem" and "Broken Star" are based upon the pieced diamond. The delicate shading from one color to another creates an effect of radiant stars which is very effective.

the second row on top of the first diamond in the first row and sew a ¼″ (6 mm) seam. String-sew the next two diamonds from each row and then the next, until all the diamonds in the first two rows have been sewed. String-sew the diamonds for the third row, one at a time, to those of the second row, in the manner that you have done this type of string-sewing before, such as for "Patience." Continue to string-sew rows of diamonds as needed to complete the pattern for one large diamond. "Virginia Star" (Illus. 51) has only three rows of three diamonds each. "Star of Bethlehem" (Illus. 53), also called "Star of the East" and "Lone Star," requires many more rows of diamonds to make up the larger diamond of the star, the number depending upon the size of the diamonds used. If a great many small diamonds are used, the quilt becomes a "Masterpiece Quilt."

A different type of pattern which uses 45-degree diamonds and the same method of sewing them to squares as you have just learned is called "Patience Corners." (I have seen three other patterns by this name!) Begin by sewing diamonds to all four sides of a square set on the diagonal (see Illus. 54). Then join the diamonds in pairs. This forms a small block. Make enough of these blocks for the quilt. The

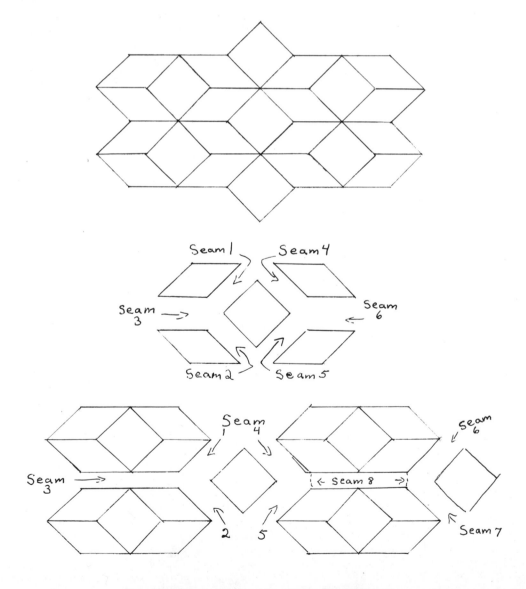

Illus. 54. Piecing "Patience Corners" (45° diamond).

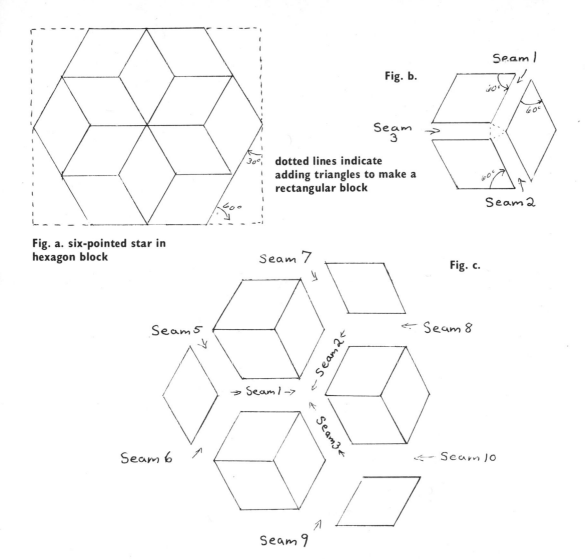

Fig. b.

Seam 1

60°

60°

Seam 3

60°

dotted lines indicate
adding triangles to make a
rectangular block

Seam 2

**Fig. a. six-pointed star in
hexagon block**

30°

60°

Fig. c.

Seam 7

Seam 5

Seam 8

Seam 2

Seam 1

Seam 3

Seam 6

Seam 10

Seam 9

Illus. 55. Piecing a six-pointed star (60° diamond) and "Baby's Blocks."

blocks are then joined by sewing them to more squares (also set on the diagonal) in the order shown in the diagram. This quilt is generally considered a very difficult one to make because of the many set-in corners to be stitched. It, therefore, requires a great deal of patience to piece by hand. This method of piecing diamonds and squares can be applied to any other patterns involving these pieces.

The six-pointed star, with a 60-degree angle at the point, is usually made up into a hexagon block (see Illus. 55). The spaces between the points of the star are filled in with diamonds of the same size and shape as the segments, or points, in the star. The block is assembled by a variation of the method used for the eight-pointed star.

As you can see by the diagrams, the six-pointed star and the pieces between the points are joined together in the same way that the squares are joined to the diamonds of the eight-pointed star. Three sets of three diamonds each are pieced together and the three sets are then joined to form the hexagon block. Either the star itself, or the hexagon block, can be appliquéd to a square or to a whole quilt top, such as a sheet. Triangles can be added to the hexagons, as shown, to make a block instead. Cut the triangular shape with the angles given in the diagram. Adding triangles makes for easier piecing of the blocks. Study the section on small hexagons and hexagon blocks on page 70 to learn how to join them.

RHOMBOID PATTERNS

Rhomboids can be used to replace diamonds in almost any pattern (see pg. 63), just as rectangles can sometimes be used in place of squares. The effect will be a little different, but the methods of construction will be the same. The length of the two longer sides of the rhomboid can be any length needed for the effect desired. The angles at the points can be either 45 degrees or 60 degrees, or any other size required according to the pattern.

The methods for marking the fabric for diamonds also applies to marking it for rhomboids, which have the same angle at the point. The measurement to use for the width is the distance between the longer sides. This can be found in the same way as for diamonds. The measurement to use for marking off the rhomboid along the crossways line is that of the longer side of the rhomboid (see pg. 64).

HEXAGONS

Small hexagon patterns are among the most beautiful of the pieced designs. They are considered to be very difficult to piece, however, because of the many small pieces with short seams and set-in corners. Hexagons need not be small to make the quilt beautiful, though the small ones are considered appropriate for a Masterpiece Quilt.

It is often thought that hexagons are not suitable for piecing on the sewing machine. On the contrary, I find them easy to make, and faster by machine than when sewed by hand. To begin with, be sure that your hexagon template is accurate. The hexagon generally used in quilting has every side and angle exactly the same, though an elongated one could be used instead. Ready-made hexagon templates in various sizes can be purchased from shops or ordered from the sources listed at the end of the book. (Templates in other frequently used shapes are also available.) For machine sewing, the template should include the ¼″ (6 mm) seam allowance.

To draft a hexagon, use a compass and draw a circle with a diameter equal to the width of the desired hexagon from point to point. Do not change the angle of the compass, but use the same radius to mark off six equal segments around the circle. To do this, make a pencil mark anywhere on the circle (see Illus. 56). Place the point of the compass on this mark and make two more marks on the circle line, one on each side of the original point, at the place where the

pencil touches. Move the point of the compass to either of the lines just marked and make a mark farther along the curve of the circle. Repeat this last step to make two more marks (for a total of six pencil marks). Draw a straight line from each point to the next point until six straight lines have been drawn. This completes a hexagon. Add ¼″ (6 mm) seam allowances all around before making a template.

The hexagon pattern can be marked on the fabric with two sides parallel to the lengthwise or the crossways threads of the fabric. Mark the pieces to lie in the direction you want them to lie when pieced (see Illus. 57). They should then be pieced so that the grain is consistent from piece to piece. Variation in the placement of the grain direction will show up on close inspection and may be frowned upon by judges in quilting competition. An exception to this would be in cases when the pieces are turned so that the print on the fabric radiates from the center, as for a stripe or a tiny flower on a stem (color page I). These pieces would have to be cut individually so that the flower or stripe lies in the same position *on each piece*. A special template should be made for this. A hole the size of the hexagon plus the seam allowances is cut out of the template (cut just *outside* the line), and the hole is used to mark the piece. This allows you to see the design on the fabric as it is marked.

Hexagon pieces which do not need to be cut from scattered places on the fabric in order to include a certain printed design or stripe, can be marked side by side on the

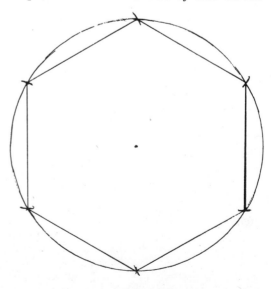

Illus. 56. Drafting a hexagon.

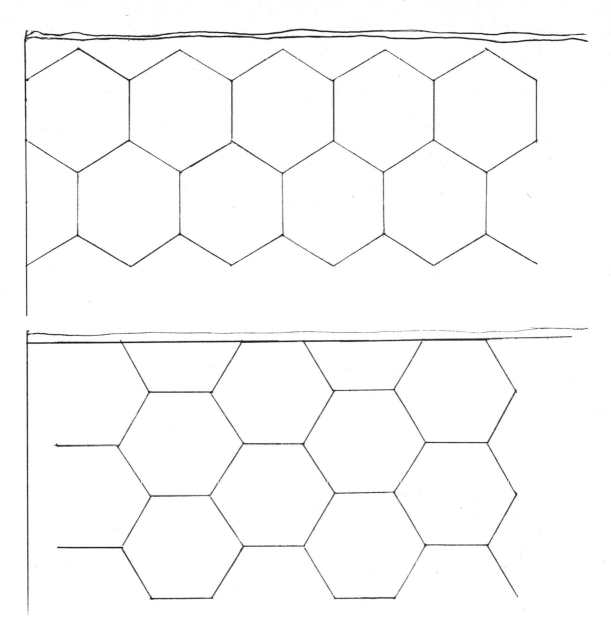

Illus. 57. Marking hexagons on the fabric. Turn the template so that the grain line of the fabric lies in the direction you want to cut the template.

material, one at a time. If several layers of fabric are to be cut, mark only one layer and stack the others. Use plenty of pins at the corners (and along the sides also, if the pieces are large). Cut carefully with sharp scissors. This is not the time to hurry!

Grandmother's Flower Garden

The best known hexagon pattern is called "Grandmother's Flower Garden." The flowers have one hexagon in the center with one or more circles of hexagons around it (color page I). Sometimes an additional ring of green print or solid color is used to represent the foliage. This group of hexagons make up a block. They are set together with one or more rows of hexagons, traditionally of unbleached muslin, to represent the garden path. One or more rows of hexagons are sometimes used to form a border around the whole quilt (see Illus. 58).

For hand piecing, most teachers instruct you to make a paper template for each fabric hexagon cut, and to baste the seam allowances in place over this paper pattern before joining them into blocks. When sewing by machine, this is not done.

Lay out the pieces of the block in the order in which they are to be sewed. First, sew the pieces of the *outside* ring of hexagons together along the one side where they touch. Begin and end every seam in this block ¼″ (6 mm) from the edge and sew a ¼″ (6 mm) seam allowance. The first and last few stitches should be tiny ones to take the place of backstitching because *no seam will be sewed across any other seam*, thus keeping the stitching from pulling out. When the outside ring has been put together, lay it aside and sew the next ring and then any others, depending upon your pattern. Last, sew the center hexagon to the inside of the smallest ring. Begin at one of the two hexagons in the ring that does not have bias seam allowances exposed. In the case, mentioned before, when the first ring of pieces is sewed with a design that radiates from the center, stitch the center piece so that its grain will conform to that of the other rings of the pattern. Stitch with the center hexagon on the *bottom* and the ring on the top. Stitch only between the two seams on the pieces of the ring. Next, match the adjoining side of the center hexagon to the next hexagon in the ring and sew this seam as you did the last. Continue around the ring in this manner until all the short seams are sewed. Add the next ring in this same way, and then add any other rings.

Piece partial rings of the pieces for the "path" as indicated in Illustration 58 and add them to the blocks in a way similar to adding complete rings before joining the blocks. Join the blocks by sewing the short seams of hexagons as they come together. The pieces for the border can be joined together in sections and added to the outside blocks before they are joined to the top.

Innumerable patterns can be created by piecing hexagons of various prints and colors. Paper printed with a hexagon grid is available from Quilts and Other Comforts in Wheat Ridge, Colorado, and is very helpful when making designs with this shape. (Paper printed with diamonds can also be bought.)

A larger hexagon can be divided into pieces and become a hexagon block (color page F). Three diamonds are sometimes used this way (see "Baby's Blocks" on the front cover). Other attractive designs might also form a hexagon block. They can be set solid like small hexagons, or they can be pieced with setting blocks of the same size.

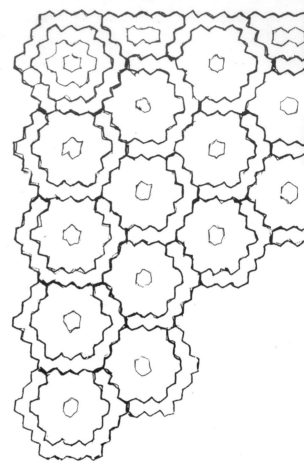

Illus. 58. Adding a path and border to "Grandmother's Flower Garden."

OCTAGONS

Octagons do not fit together evenly. They require a square setting block to fill in the space left when they are joined. This square is often divided diagonally into quarter-square triangles, which are then sewed to the sides of the octagons to form a square block. This arrangement makes the blocks very easy to set together. The octagon used in quilting usually has all eight sides the same length, but an elongated octagon could also be used.

The only pattern of octagons I have been able to find to include in this unit is an English two-patch which is sometimes pieced as a "Rob Peter To Pay Paul" pattern (see Illus. 59).

Octagon-shaped blocks can be very pretty. Illustrations 60–61 will give you a few ideas for designing your own octagon patterns.

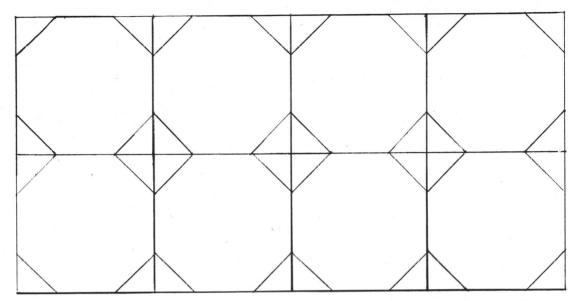

Illus. 59. An Old English octagon pattern. This is a two-patch pattern of octagons and triangles. It is often pieced as a "Rob Peter to Pay Paul" pattern, as in the four blocks in Illus. 60.

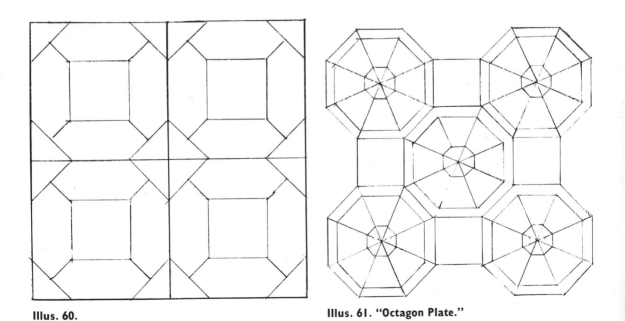

Illus. 60.

Illus. 61. "Octagon Plate."

In these patterns, the octagonal shapes are formed by piecing other shapes together.

Illus. 59, 60, 61. Octagon patterns.

PATTERNS WITH PIECED CURVES

Patterns with curved pieces are often reserved for hand piecing. This has always seemed strange to me because few people who sew would hesitate to sew curved seams on the machine. Quilt pieces are of course, usually much smaller than those for garments, but the construction is similar and is not difficult for someone with average sewing skills. If you are new to piecing curves by machine, start with a pattern which has gentle curves, such as "Dolly Madison's Workbox" (see Illus. 63). Make one or more blocks for practice before you begin the pieces for your quilt.

You will need templates for these patterns. First draw the design on graph paper the same size that the finished block will be. Carefully cut out one piece of each shape, fold the curved edge in half and mark the fold at the edge. Make templates of the pieces and transfer the middle mark of the curves to the template. Use the template to mark the fabric. See the sketch for the lay-out of the pieces in Section 8. Pin the marked pieces at the corners and cut them out. Before removing any pins, mark each piece along the edge at the middle of

the curves with the special marking pen referred to in the list of supplies. If this is not available, use a pencil or some other type of marker that is absolutely waterproof so that it will not run in washing.

Sew with the convex curved piece on the bottom and the concave curved piece on the top (see Illus. 62). Place no more than one pin in the middle of the curve at the marked place and one pin at the start and at the end of the seams, to hold the pieces in place as you begin to stitch. As you sew, the feed dogs pulling at the bottom fabric will help ease it to fit the top piece. Remember that the *edge* of the convex curve is a little larger than the curve at the *stitching line*, while the edge of the concave curve is smaller. Stitch slowly, letting the edges ease along together. The piecing diagrams with the patterns will help you to put the pieces together in the easiest order. In some cases it will be necessary to sew a seam to the middle and then start at the other end and sew to the middle from that direction in order to keep the concave curve on the top. A few patterns using curved pieces are shown on the following pages and on color page J.

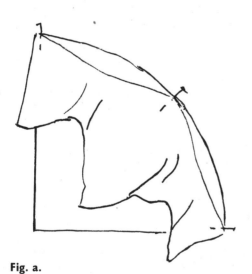

Fig. a.

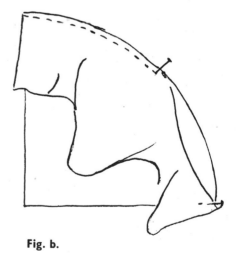

Fig. b.

Illus. 62. Sewing curved seams. "Drunkard's Path" pieces are shown (see page 80). (Fig. a.) Pin the concave edge to the convex edge. (Fig. b.) As you stitch, ease the edges together. The bias cut of the fabric will permit them to fit together smoothly.

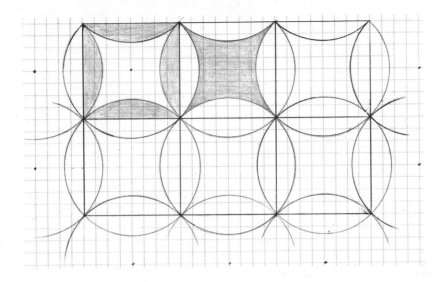

Illus. 63. "Dolly Madison's Workbox." This design is drawn with a compass. The distance between the point of the compass and the pencil is equal to the distance from the middle of the square block to the corner, either on the diagram or when making a full scale pattern for a block. Place the point of the compass in the middle of each square and draw a circle around it which touches each corner. Cut the full scale pattern apart and make a template of each square, adding ¼" (6 mm) seam allowances all around. This pattern is often pieced as a "Rob Peter to Pay Paul" design. Assemble this pattern by adding the curved sides to the central pieces.

NOTE: To complete curves on the outside edges of the blocks, place the point of the compass in the middle of imaginary squares beyond the edge of the quilt.

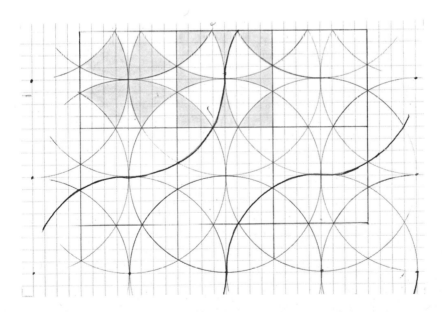

Illus. 64. "Winding Ways" is another interesting design drawn with a compass and pieced as a "Rob Peter to Pay Paul" pattern. The radius of the circle is equal to the width of the square block. Place the point of the compass in the middle of each square and draw a circle which touches the middle of each square which has a common side. The overlapping circles form the graceful pieces. After completing the diagram, draw a full scale block. Cut the pieces apart and add ¼" (6 mm) seam allowances when making the templates. This is a difficult pattern to piece because of the sharply point ● pieces, but the result can be well worth the care required to do it (see also color page J).

"Double Wedding Ring" (see Illus. 65) has the most involved piecing order of the group shown. Originally, the rings were pieced and then appliquéd to a square block. Squares of fabric were appliquéd where the rings seem to cross. Sometimes a piece of fabric was used to cover the seam of the block. The pattern can be all pieced, however (see Illus. 66–68). First, stitch all the little pieces (6 pieces of D with 1 of C at each end) for the segments of the rings, adding piece E to the same end (not both ends) of each segment. Join the segments by joining piece E of one segment to piece C of another segment. Then join the other ends of the two segments in the same way. Piece B is stitched to fill the space between the two. This completes a unit of pieces. Make enough of these units for the entire quilt. Four of the units are set together with a plain diamond-shaped piece, to form a round block. Make all the blocks needed for the quilt. Another dia-mond-shaped piece, like the one used as the center of the block, is used as a setting piece.

Start by adding one group to each setting piece needed for the first (and last) length-wise row of the quilt. These units will be along the left and right sides of the quilt. Now add a block to the top of each setting piece in the row. To the last setting piece in the row, add a block to the bottom also. If there are an *odd* number of blocks in the lengthwise rows, the odd-numbered rows will begin and end with a block and the even-numbered rows will begin and end with a setting piece. Add a unit to each end with the setting piece to complete the de-sign at the edge. If there are an even num-ber of blocks in a lengthwise row, make all rows begin with a block and end with a setting piece and a unit. Then turn every other row so that they alternate, with a block and then a setting piece and unit at the top, when the rows are joined.

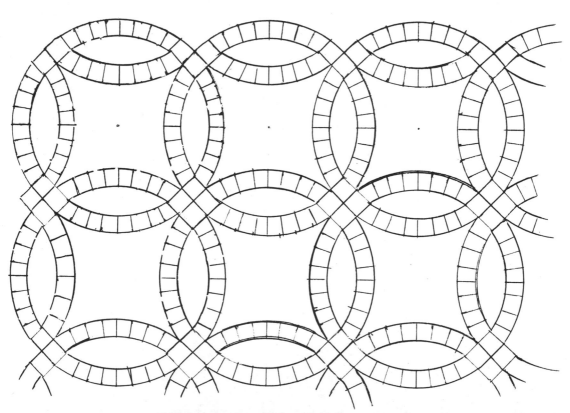

Illus. 65. "Double Wedding Ring" pattern. This pattern is formed by interlocking circles of small pieces. The pattern given here is a true circle. The four small pieces at the intersection of the circle are true squares. The circular "blocks" are set together with setting pieces, which are the same size and shape as the middle of the block. A piecing diagram and a set of pieces drawn full scale are given for this pattern since it is quite difficult to draft. (Note the resemblance to "Dolly Madison's Work-box" on page 75.)

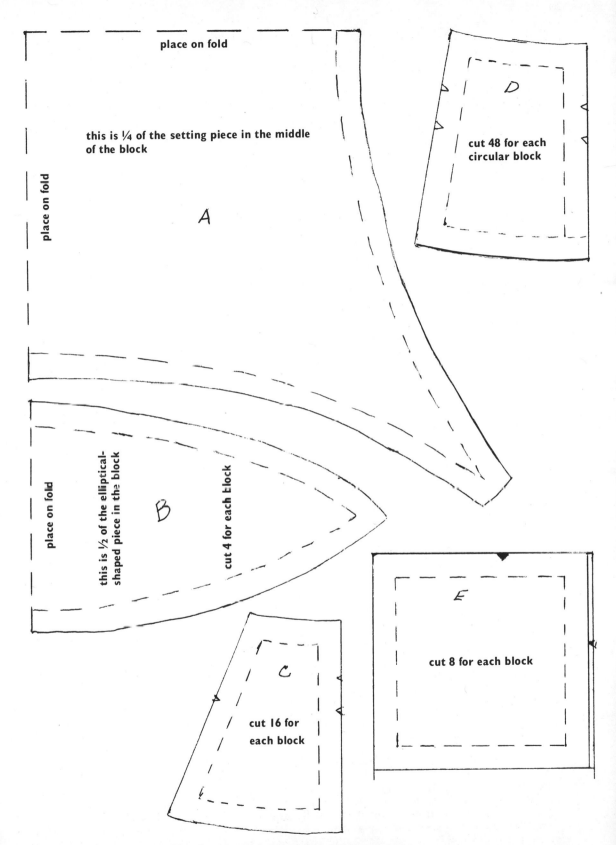

place on fold

this is ¼ of the setting piece in the middle of the block

place on fold

A

D

cut 48 for each circular block

place on fold

this is ½ of the elliptical-shaped piece in the block

B

cut 4 for each block

E

cut 8 for each block

C

cut 16 for each block

Illus. 66. Pattern for "Double Wedding Ring."

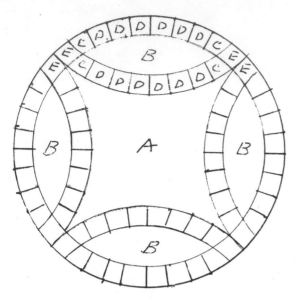

Fig. a. circular block

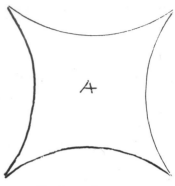

Fig. b. setting piece

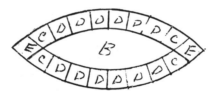

Fig. c. elliptical-shaped
group

Illus. 67. Piecing "Double Wedding Ring." Piece all the elliptical-shaped groups needed for the quilt. Add four of these groups to a setting piece to form the circular block. Piece enough of these blocks for the quilt top. Add elliptical-shaped groups to setting pieces as needed to fill out the curves of the setting pieces used in the outside rows of the quilt. Consult your diagram for the numbers needed for each of these combinations. Join blocks and setting pieces to form enough lengthwise rows for the quilt. Examples of rows are shown in Illus. 68.

All the rows should now have serpentine curves along the sides to be joined to another row. Match the second row to the first, pinning all the seams which must be matched (see Illus. 68). Then sew each segment of curved pieces, making sure that it is pinned in the middle and that you stitch with the concave side of the seam on the top. This means that you will sew every other segment, then turn the work over and sew the ones in between. Sew each lengthwise seam in this same way to complete the quilt top.

The quilt may be finished by the pillowcase method or with a bound edge. Quilt around the rings. A quilting design may also be done in the setting piece and block centers if desired. The easiest type would be a trapunto design which should be done *before* the pieces are cut out. Work and stuff or cord the trapunto on a square of fabric, then mark and cut the piece. This will allow for shrinkage or easing in of the fabric created by stuffing the trapunto.

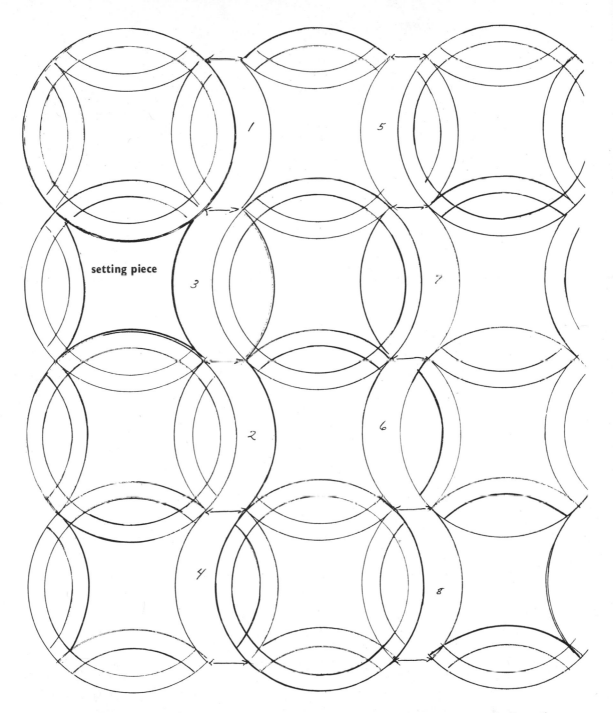

Illus. 68. Joining rows for "Double Wedding Ring." Pin the rows together at the arrows and sew the curved seams in the order given, keeping the concave curve on top as you stitch. Sew segments 1 and 2, then turn the work over and sew segments 3 and 4. Sew all segments in this way.

ROB PETER TO PAY PAUL PATTERNS

Many beautiful patterns are included under the interesting group name of "Rob Peter to Pay Paul" (see Illus. 69–71). This name indicates a method of combining the fabrics rather than the piecing design. Two different blocks of the same design are made so that the light piece or pieces in one block becomes the dark ones in the other block and vice versa. Very interesting effects are created in this way. Some blocks, such as one by the very colorful name of "Drunkard's Path," can be put together in several ways to create entirely different designs. Each design has its own name, though the block is nearly always referred to as "Drunkard's Path." The pieces of this pattern have quarter-circle edges, but they can be machine sewed by the method described earlier. This pattern is a little more involved than some, since there are two larger blocks, each of four two-piece squares, which alternate to form the pattern. With some other variations the two-piece square is set together in different combinations to form an all-over pattern.

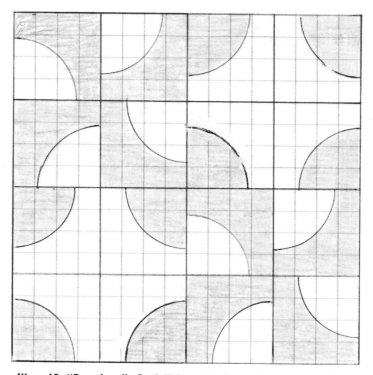

Illus. 69. "Drunkard's Path." (See full-size pattern on page 90.)

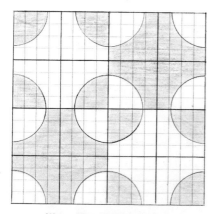

Illus. 69a. "Mill Wheel"

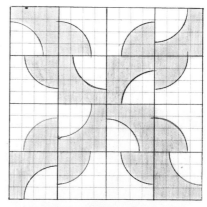

Illus. 69b. "Solomon's Puzzle"

Illus. 69, 70, 71. "Rob Peter to Pay Paul" patterns.

Illus. 70. "Around the World."

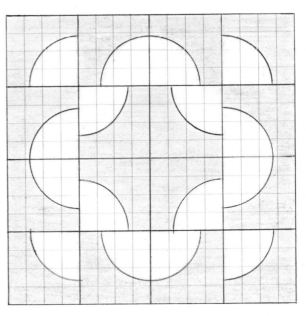

Illus. 71. "Baby Bunting."

PIECED CIRCLES AND SET-IN RINGS

Patterns with circles and rings are virtually always restricted to appliqué because of the difficulty encountered in piecing them. I developed a method of piecing circles when I was making Christmas-wreath placemats (see front cover), and it works just as well for quilt blocks. It also lends itself well to the "quilt-as-you-go" method of making a quilt because the rings are added one after the other from the center out. (This quilting method will be discussed on page 120.)

If there is to be a circle in the middle of the block (or somewhere else), pin the fabric circle to a piece of paper the size and shape of the block. On the piece which fits around the circle, stay-stitch just within the seam allowance that is to be sewed to the circle. (To do this, sew a line of tiny straight stitches, just barely within the seam allowance.) Slash the seam allowance about every 1/3" (8 mm), cutting *just* to the stay-stitching. Turn under the seam allowance and press. Place the round hole of the ring in position over the circle. Pin *only* the seam allowance to the circle, using enough pins to hold the piece firmly in place. Lift one side of the piece and begin to sew the piece to the circle along the stitching line. Sew all around the circular seam, lifting the top piece out of the way as you go, but do not disturb the pinned seam allowance. You can remove the pins just before you stitch over them. This is really quite easy, though it may sound a bit involved at first. If there are concentric circular pieces, add each successive one in this same way.

Since I have found no patterns with pieced circles, I have made a few for you (see Illus. 72–74).

Illus. 72. "Infinity" (author's pattern).

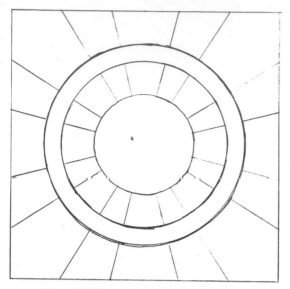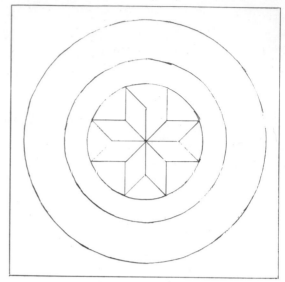

Illus. 73, 74. Patterns with pieced circles and rings. (Left) "Bright New Day." (Right) "Ann's Star." (Both are author's patterns.)

THE BORDER AND THE LATTICE

A whole book could be written on this subject alone if a truly representative selection of possible variations were included in the instructions, for there are as many possibilities for piecing and appliquéing these parts of the quilts as there are for the blocks themselves.

Besides cutting the border and the lattice into block-length segments to be set together at the corners of the blocks with corner squares (or setting squares), extensive piecing of these segments can be done. The corner squares themselves are frequently pieced into a four-patch or a nine-patch or some other pattern. The strips may be made up of triangles, diamonds, etc., which are pieced together.

The border, especially, is often pieced or appliquéd to match the pattern of the quilt by adapting a segment of the design of the block or overall pattern for this purpose. A quilt of a much-used pattern will often be made quite distinctive by what is done with the lattice or border (see color page B).

A pieced lattice may even be used with only plain blocks, so that all the design is in the lattice. This is one instance where a wide lattice is attractive (see Illus. 75).

"Arrowhead Collection" (Illus. 75-b) is a variation of "Flying Geese." The matching block (75-c) was designed before the lattice and could be used without it, just as the lattice could be used with a plain block.

Many of the variations of "Ohio Star" form lattice-like patterns when the block is set solid. They are more easily pieced as lattice with plain blocks and become a different pattern when done that way.

The hexagon with the star "lattice" (see Illus. 76) is an old pattern I found long ago in a book. I do not know the name of it. This star lattice is pieced by a method similar to that for "Patience Corners" among the 45-degree diamond patterns. In this case, sew a 60-degree diamond to each of the four sides of a *diamond* of the same size instead of to a *square* (which is the shape of the piece used in this position for "Patience Corners"). Join three of these units to form a six-pointed star. Join six of these stars in a ring to form the lattice. Add the hexagon center as you did the center hexagon of the "Grandmother's Flower Garden" block. To the first ring of stars, add enough stars to make another ring and add the hexagon to the center. Continue in this way for the entire top, or make sections to join later for easier handling. A few diamonds may be used to fill in along the shaped edge, or to fill in before adding the border.

A variation of this pattern would be to piece the large hexagons into a star pattern. This star with the diamonds which radiate within the "lattice" from its points makes a pattern called "Flaming Star" (see Illus. 77).

Fig. a. "Flying Geese" lattice

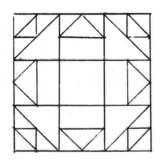

two coordinating blocks

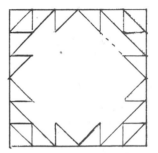

Fig. b. "Arrowhead" collection

Fig. c.

Illus. 75. Lattice patterns.

block

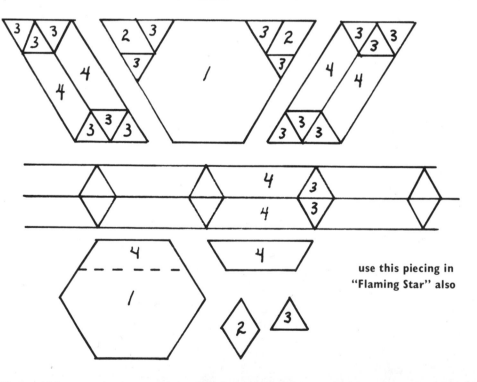

use this piecing in
"Flaming Star" also

Illus. 76. An old hexagon and star pattern (like a lattice). At upper right you see the conventional piecing of this design. The left half of the design shows the shaded areas divided in a different way. The same number of pieces are involved, but only straight seams are required for this piecing. (Piece #4 is made by drawing a line from the middle of one side of the hexagon to the middle of the side across from it, as shown. Add seam allowances.)

Illus. 77. "Flaming Star."

INTERCHANGEABLE PATTERNS

Squares and rectangles can easily be marked directly on the fabric by the methods given in Section 2. Instructions for drafting and marking other shapes have also been given. Since many people do not wish to draft patterns, however, sets of pieces of various shapes are printed here in several sizes (see Illus. 78–84).

The measurement given on each piece is for the *finished* size. That is, the measurement is taken along the stitching line or between two stitching lines. In each case this is clearly stated with the drawings. This will help you to select the right size in each shape you need for your pattern.

In most groups, each piece has one or two common sides and is increased on the other side or sides. To enlarge these shapes, make your increases in the same way. Measure from the stitching (dash) line of the largest piece given, and then add the ¼″ (6 mm) seam allowance beyond that.

Hexagons and octagons are drawn like concentric circles. To enlarge them, increase all sides. The set of octagons (Illus. 81) is too large for the page. Trace the half figure in the desired size, including the fold line. Fold the paper exactly on the fold line and cut out the piece. Unfold the paper to a full size pattern for the piece or for making a template.

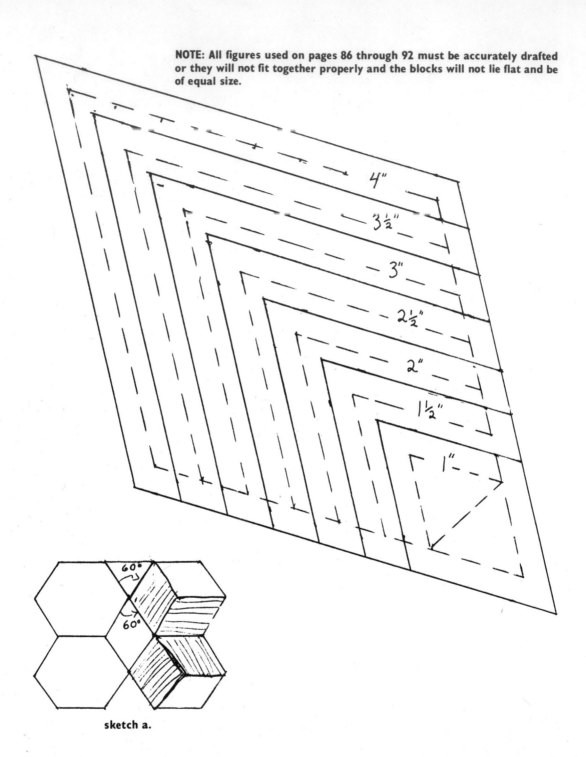

4"

3½"

3"

2½"

2"

1½"

1"

60°

60°

sketch a.

Illus. 78. 60° diamonds. Measurements given indicate finished length of each side. For triangles to fit this shape, draw a stitching line from corner to corner of the stitching line of the size piece you want to match. Add ¼" (6 mm) seam allowance along this new stitching line before making a template for the diamond. Three of these diamonds can be pieced together to form a hexagon. It can also be used with many hexagon patterns (see sketch a. above).

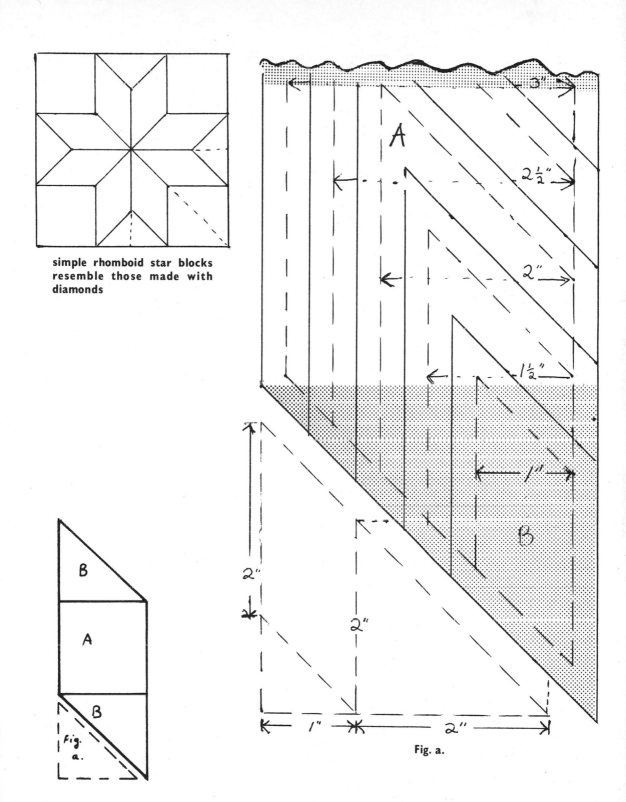

simple rhomboid star blocks resemble those made with diamonds

Fig. a.

Illus. 79. 45° rhomboid. The measurements given are for the finished width of the piece. The stitching line of the short side can be matched to the stitching line of the diagonal side of a half-square of the same width. The length is twice the width. A square or half-square of that measurement can be pieced to it (see fig. a.).

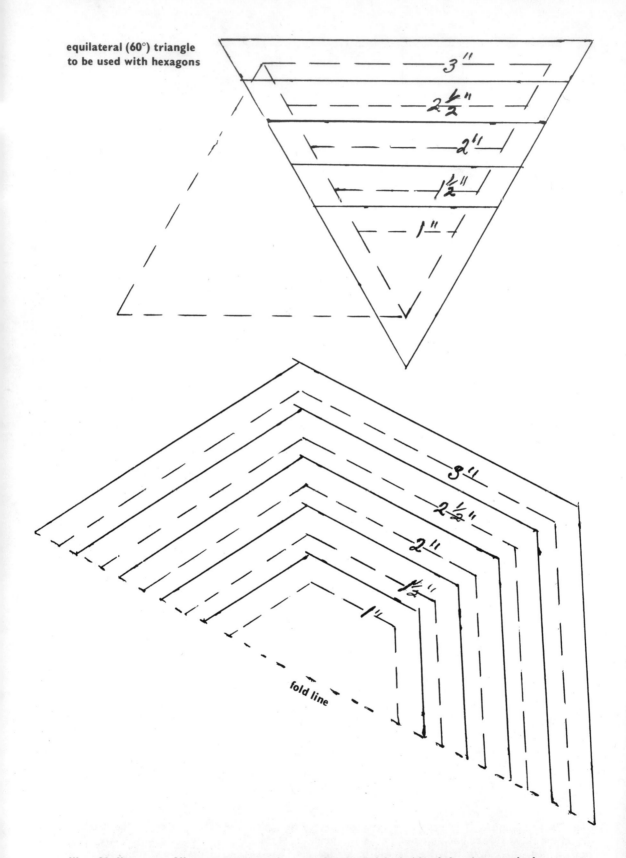

equilateral (60°) triangle to be used with hexagons

3"

2½"

2"

1½"

1"

3"

2½"

2"

1½"

1"

fold line

Illus. 80. Hexagons. All measurements given are for the finished side of the piece marked.

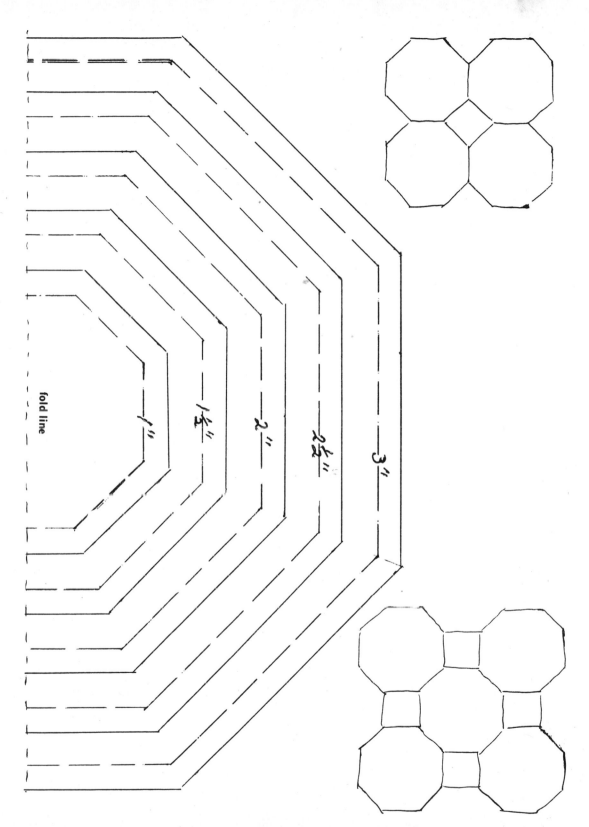

fold line

1″

1½″

2″

2½″

3″

Illus. 81. Octagons. Octagons must be pieced with squares. Measure the stitching line of the octagon you have chosen, add ½″ (12 mm) for two seam allowances, and mark the fabric with squares of that size (see Section 2).

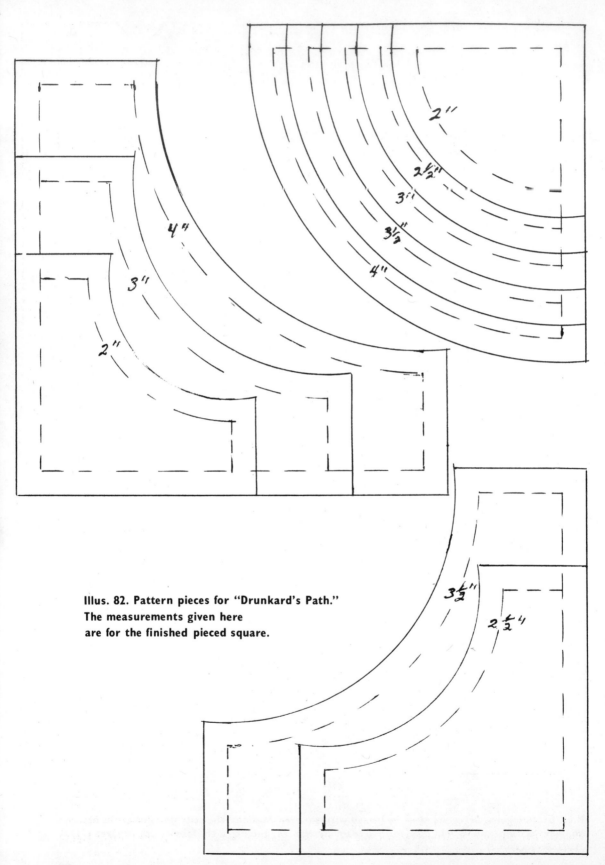

Illus. 82. Pattern pieces for "Drunkard's Path."
The measurements given here
are for the finished pieced square.

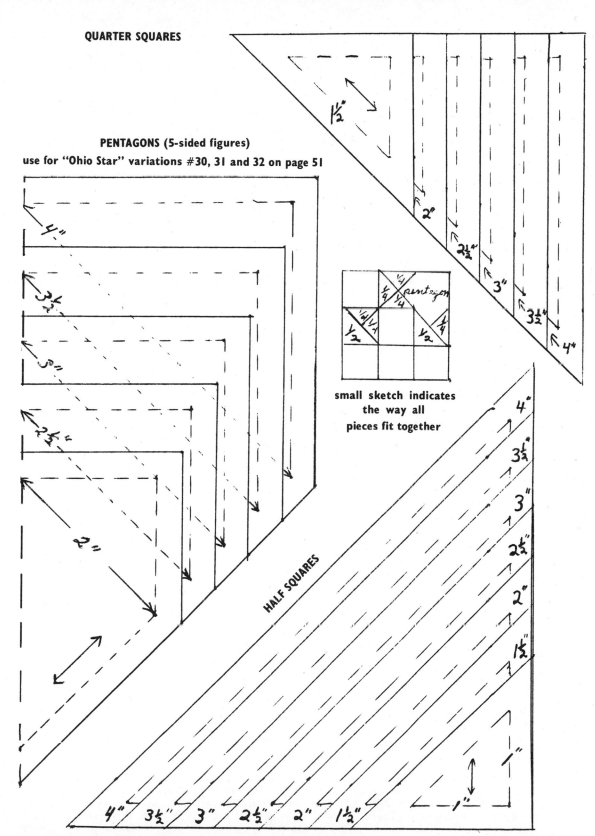

QUARTER SQUARES

PENTAGONS (5-sided figures)
use for "Ohio Star" variations #30, 31 and 32 on page 51

small sketch indicates
the way all
pieces fit together

HALF SQUARES

Illus. 83. Half-squares, quarter-squares, and pentagons. All measurements are for the finished length of the side parallel to the grain line arrows.

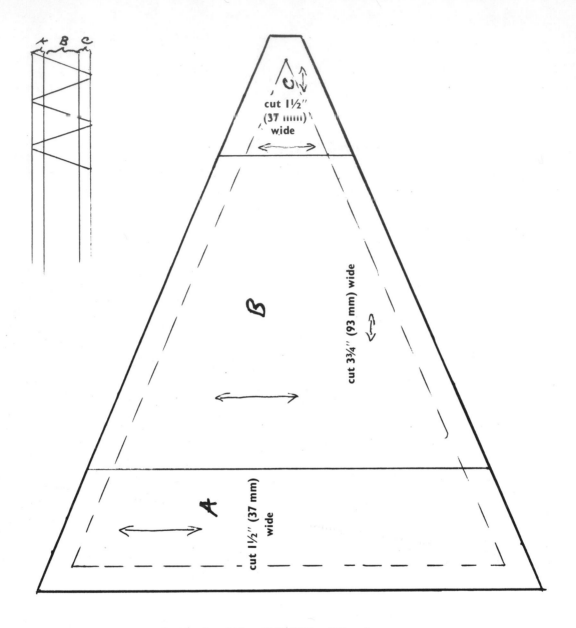

double size: 94" × 108" (235 × 270 cm)
will have 6 × 7 10½" (26 cm) octagonal blocks
4" (10 cm) border

twin size: 99 × 108" (247 × 270 cm)
will have 5 × 7 10½" (26 cm) octagonal blocks
4" (10 cm) border

Illus. 84. Piecing instructions and patterns for "Octagon Plate" on page 73. This pattern can be pieced by the Seminole method (Section 7). For a 10½" (26 cm) octagonal block, cut strips A and C 1½" (37 mm) wide and strip B 3¾" (93 mm) wide, with the grain or acrosswise grain. Sew strips together. Make one template exactly the size of the heavy lines of the pattern, and mark the pieced strips as shown. If A and C are the same fabric, all the plates will be alike. If they are different, half the plates will be bordered in one fabric and half in the other. Join the wedges into octagonal blocks and set them together with pieces cut 5" (12.5 cm) square.

SECTION 4
Some Other Types of Patterns

Embroidery, appliqué and trapunto are sometimes used as part of the design of a quilt. I have grouped these methods together in one section, partly because they are not pieced designs and so do not belong with the previous patterns, and partly because they are somewhat related to each other by the way they are made. These sewing methods are sometimes used in combination with one another, as well as with pieced patterns. Very beautiful work in these areas can be done by machine, so they are well worth exploring.

EMBROIDERY

Embroidered quilt blocks are sometimes used with plain or printed setting blocks and sometimes with blocks of a simple pieced pattern. Several books have been devoted exclusively to the art of embroidering by machine. Obviously, a comprehensive coverage of the subject is not possible here, but some of the basic methods will be explained to get you started. Some types can be done without a zigzag machine. If you become especially interested in making this type of quilt, you can find books on the subject of machine embroiderery in book stores, libraries or from sewing machine agencies.

Patterns to be used for machine embroidery are easy to find. You can use the usual embroidery transfer patterns, or you can draw your own designs, if you are so inclined. Designs for embroidery can be traced from coloring books, seed catalogues, greeting cards, wallpaper books, magazines, and even fabrics. If the picture you want to trace does not show through your tracing paper well enough, it may help to tape the picture, with the tracing paper over it, to a window glass, so the light will show up the pattern more vividly. Some-times the printed matter on the wrong side of your chosen picture confuses the lines you want to trace, but you can usually get enough of the pattern for your purpose.

Special transfer pencils are available for transferring patterns to fabric. Draw your pattern on paper just the way you want it to appear on the fabric. Then, using the transfer pencil, trace the lines on the *wrong* side of the paper. Place the design in position on the fabric with the wrong side down. Pin it securely and press (do not move the iron) with a dry iron and a heat suitable for the fabric used. These lines can be washed out of the fabric when the work is finished. The pattern can be used repeatedly by renewing the transfer lines after each pressing.

Whenever learning something new, one is naturally inclined to feel anxious about one's ability to accomplish what is to be done, and this tends to produce tightened muscles. You will learn faster when you are rested and relaxed. Remember that this is something you are doing for pleasure. Try to have an attitude of exploring an exciting new art—which you are—*not* one of being tested on your abilities. You have not had a chance to develop these abilities yet, so no test is involved. You are learning, and learning can be one of life's greatest joys.

The use of a hoop is usually necessary to keep the fabric to be embroidered taut enough to take the stitches well (the machine will sometimes not make stitches if the fabric is too loose). A hoop will also prevent puckering or stretching of the fabric as the stitching is being done. You should use a narrow wooden hoop especially made for use with a sewing machine. It should have a screw on the side for tightening the outer ring on the inner ring. I have several sized hoops, but I usually

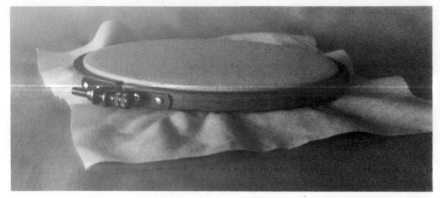

use one which is 8″ (20 cm) in diameter. If the fabric to be embroidered is too small for the hoop, machine-sew it to a piece of muslin, using about six stitches to the inch (25 mm). Trim away the muslin under the fabric to be embroidered but do not cut so close to the stitching that the fabric will pull apart under the stress of being tightened into the hoop. Place the *larger* ring under the fabric. Push the fabric firmly into it with the *smaller* ring so that the fabric is held smooth and flat against the machine needle plate while the stitching is being done. After tightening the screw, push the inner ring down about ⅛″ (3 mm) beyond the bottom of the outer ring to tighten the fabric just a little more and to help the hoop move smoothly on the machine bed (see Illus. 85).

The stitching used for the design may be simple or elaborate, depending upon the effect desired. If you have no experience with this type of embroidery, you should practice the different methods until you can do them with some confidence. For some people this is easy, while others require a little more time, depending partly upon the amount of hand control they have already learned by doing other types of hand work.

A sharp (not ballpoint) needle should be used for embroidery. A size #70, or a #9 or #11 is best, depending on the number range you use. Lower the feed dogs or cover them with the special plate provided. If you can do neither, cover the feed dogs by fastening a piece of smooth heavy paper or light-weight plastic or cardboard over them with tape. Remove the presser foot, but be sure to *lower the presser foot lever when you stitch* in order to engage the tension on the top thread. If you forget to do this you will make loops of top thread on the back side of the work and the stitching will not look very nice on the right side, nor will it wear well.

Some of the embroidery stitching is done with the feed dogs up and using a presser foot. If at all possible, use a special embroidery foot for this stitching, especially if any satin stitching is involved. The closely stitched zigzag required to make a really nice satin stitch lies thicker on the fabric than ordinary stitches. A regular stitching foot will not move easily, if at all, over this raised stitching, so close "satiny" stitching cannot be done with it. An embroidery foot has a raised area on the bottom to allow the thick stitching to move under it easily (see Illus. 86). With it, the stitches can be worked closely and will have a nice sheen (see color page D).

Two types of embroidery feet are available with some machines (see Illus. 86). Both are indented on the bottom to allow for the thickness of the embroidery. One is called a "cut-out" embroidery foot. It has the bar between the "toes" removed so that you can see the approaching line to be embroidered, as well as the work as it is being done. This is a great help. The other foot sometimes has a small hole in the bar. This can be threaded with some type of cording such as pearl cotton (a very glossy one), or the heavier crochet cotton used for bedspreads. Both come in a variety of colors. When satin stitch is done over this cording, it is more raised and "satiny" in appearance. The corded satin stitch is very

Illus. 86. Various machine feet mentioned in the text. Top row: cut-out embroidery foot; zigzag sewing foot; blind hem foot. Bottom row: yarn or wool-darning foot; darning foot.

effective around appliqué, also. If the zig-zag stitch is set longer so that the cording shows, a couching-type of embroidery can be done.

Several companies make special fine cotton thread for embroidery by machine, and it gives a nice sheen to the stitches. I have, at times, used regular sewing thread when this special thread was not available, but with only fair results. A needle one size larger is needed if you must use regular thread. You will find that the satin stitch is not so smooth as it is with the special thread because the larger threads show up more than the fine embroidery threads. Experiment with the different brands of embroidery thread available in your stores to see which works best in your machine. If you are going to be changing from one color to another frequently, you can use white thread in the bobbin since bobbin thread should never be seen on the top of the fabric.

The tension must be adjusted so that the bobbin thread is a bit tighter than the top thread. There are two ways to do this. First, and easier, is to thread the little hole in the finger on the bobbin (see Illus. 87). The other way is to loosen the top thread slightly. (Read your machine manual to learn how to do this.) This makes the bobbin thread tighter by comparison.

Before you begin to practice, learn the most comfortable working position for you so that you will not become tired easily and develop aching muscles from a poor posture. Sit up straight but relaxed in a chair that is the right height for you. Your eyes should be a comfortable distance from your work in this position. If they are not, try a different chair. Relax in this upright position and let your forearms rest on the edge of the machine bed. This allows your hands to move the hoop freely as you guide the fabric under the needle. Do not push yourself. It is not necessary to learn everything in one sitting. If you become tired or tense, stop and relax for awhile before going on, or wait until another time. The important thing is to enjoy what you are doing. Otherwise, don't do it.

Now for some practice. If your machine has two ranges of speed, set it for the slower range. Raise the needle and place the hoop with the fabric in position for sewing. Lower the threaded needle through the fabric and bring up the bobbin thread. Wrap the two threads around the left index finger and lower the needle again. Make three or four tiny stitches in the same place

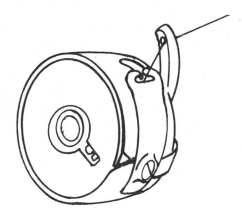

Illus. 87. Adjust the tension on the bobbin by threading the hole in the finger on the bobbin.

to tie the thread. The ends may then be cut to get them out of the way, so at least you do not need to continue to hold them. Work first with a straight stitch setting and later with various widths of zigzag.

Since the feed dogs are down, your hands must move the fabric under the needle. What you are working toward is evenly spaced stitches, both long and short. To achieve this, the relationship of the speed of the machine needle and the speed of the movement of the hands must be coordinated and steady. A fast needle makes a shorter stitch, while a faster hand movement makes a longer stitch. With a little practice, you will begin to feel the relationship needed for the stitch length desired. With straight stitches you can make outline stitches of various types (see Illus. 90). This stitch can also be used for filling in an area with either rows of straight stitching or with a meandering stitch. The hoop can be moved in any direction, but does not need to be rotated.

The zigzag stitch is also very versatile. Hold the hoop the same as before. It can still be moved in any direction. If the hoop is not rotated as it is moved, one type of stitch can be created, while rotating the hoop creates a different appearance. After you have practiced different ways of moving the hoop, try changing the width of the zigzag as you stitch by slowly or rapidly moving the stitch width control with the right hand while you control the direction and movement of the hoop with the left hand. This will give you a tapering of the zigzag. It is all right to go over the work done to fill in spaces or to build up a raised effect. No way of placing the stitches is wrong, so long as it achieves the effect you want, and corrections can often be made.

Illus. 88. Zigzag stitch used as an outline.

The conventional way to do the zigzag embroidery, with the use of built-in or cam-regulated stitches when the feed dogs are up and the presser foot is in place, can also be used on a quilt. No hoop is required for this. Just follow the instructions in the book that came with your machine.

Zigzag stitches can be used in two other ways for embroidery. One is for outlining (see Illus. 88) and the other is for filling in an area. For this work, the hoop is moved from side to side and is rotated, as needed, to keep the stitches in line with the desired flow of the work. The stitches follow along the lines of the pattern rather than across them. For outlining, a medium width stitch usually works best. Try various widths of zigzag stitches for filling in and for shading. Move the hoop from side to side, gradually easing it backwards to form row after row of closely placed stitches which fill in the area solidly like long and short stitches by hand (see Illus. 89). You can work back over a sparsely covered area (unless this was the intended effect) and you can build up the work if you want to. By changing thread colors and working some stitches of one area back into the previously worked area, a beautiful shaded effect can be created.

Too much close or layered stitching stiffens the piece. This is not always desir-able in embroidery for quilts and quilted projects. For these items, it is usually best to use the heavily embroidered areas sparingly as accents, rather than over a large proportion of the surface.

Illus. 89. An example of long and short stitches.

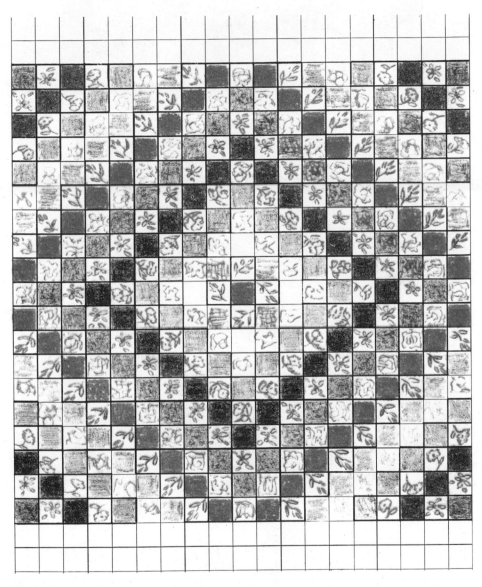

"Trip Around the World," a popular pattern constructed in the same manner as "Patience" (see page 42).

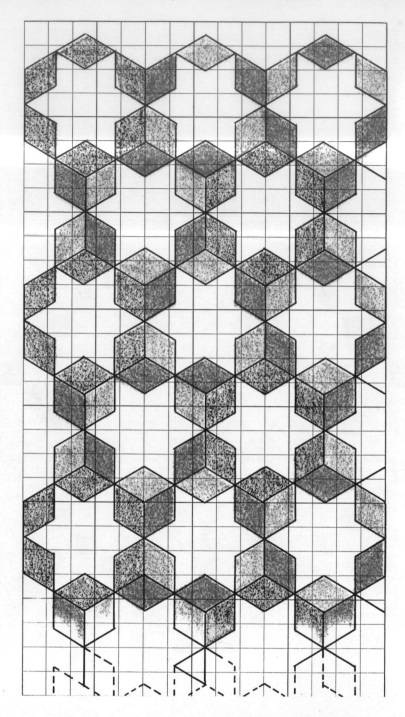

An old hexagon block pattern, "Tumbling Blocks," which would make a lovely baby quilt (see page 72).

F

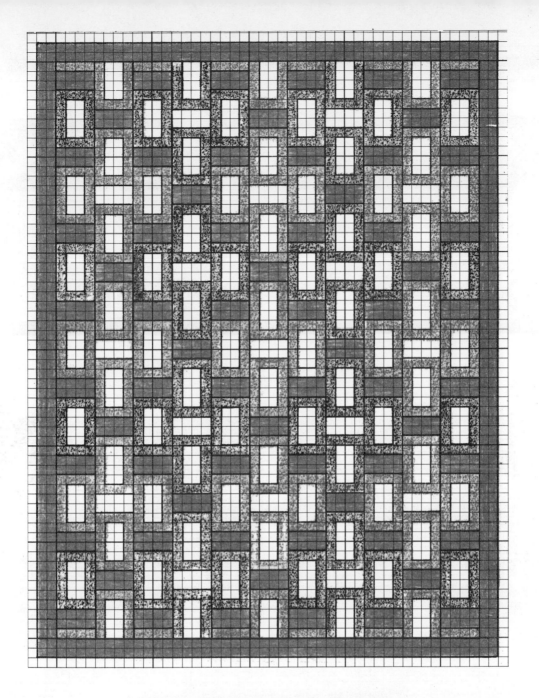

"Foursome," a Roman Stripe variation (see page 42).

Diagram for a "Stripey" quilt (see page 58). This one is called "Autumn Glory." The design was planned for the stripes to run the length of the quilt, but they would be just as attractive going across it. It would be necessary to change the spacing for this, or to repeat the pattern. Seminole patterns are especially suited for this type of quilt.

H

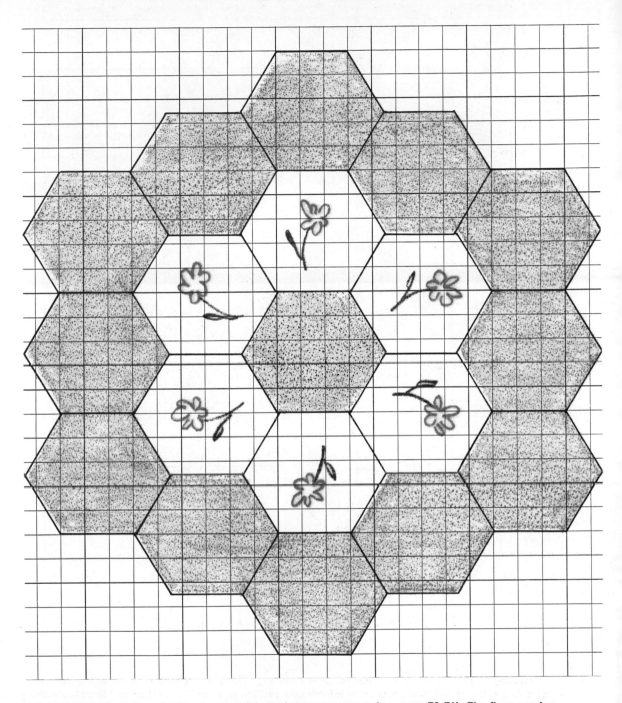

"Grandmother's Flower Garden," a well-known hexagon pattern (see pages 70-71). The flower print has been cut in the same position on each hexagon so that they can be placed with each flower radiating from the middle. Each of these hexagons must be marked and cut separately, but the effect is well worth the effort.

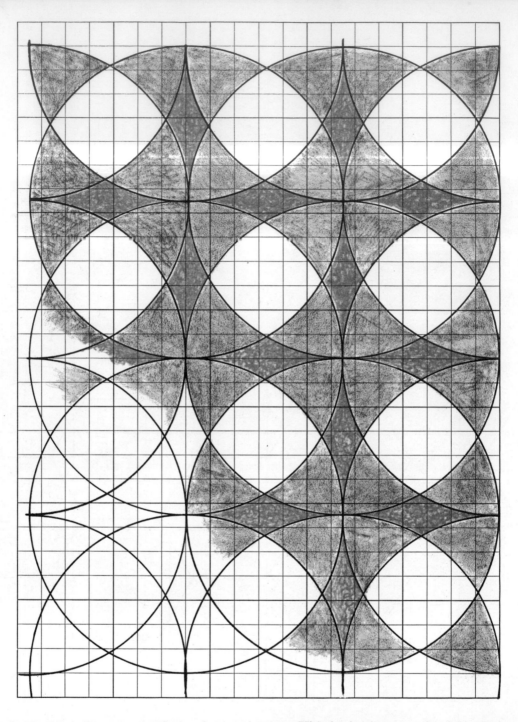

"Winding Ways," a pattern with pieced curves (see page 75) is fascinating even when it is not pieced as a Rob Peter to Pay Paul pattern. Assemble this pattern in a similar method to "Double Wedding Ring" on page 76.

J

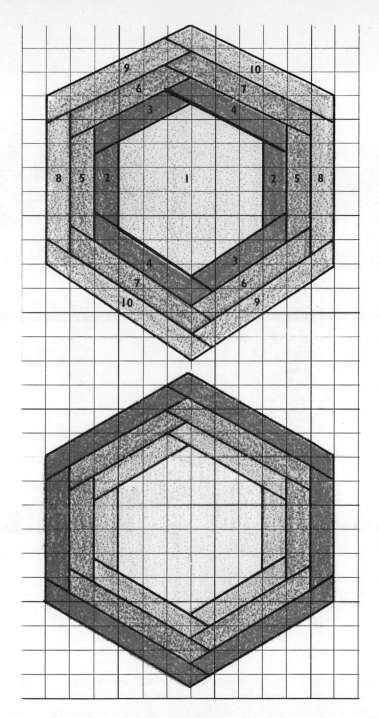

Two of the author's variations of a "Courthouse Steps" type of construction (see page 131). If seven or more rounds are used and the colors on opposite sides are alike (3 color groups), the design is called "Six-Way Pineapple." If the colors are added in rings, as shown above, it is called "Stadium."

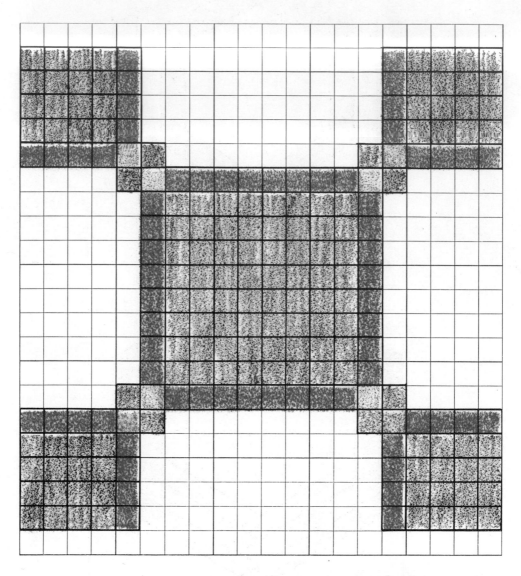

A Seminole design adapted for quiltmaking (see page 147). This arrangement is very orderly and symmetrical, giving a feeling of tradition, but with a fresh approach.

L

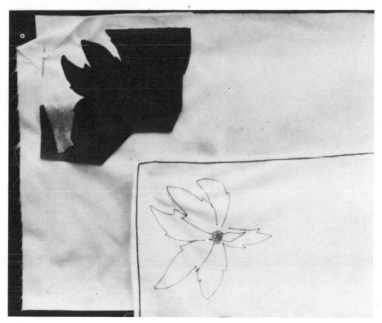

Illus. 90. Steps in appliqué: the poinsettia appliqué patch with press-on interfacing on the back; the three petals on the right have only the first stitching done; the middle petal is being trimmed; the satin stitch on the left petal was machine-guided; the second petal from the left was corded as well. Bottom right pattern shows outline stitch.

APPLIQUÉ

Appliqué is more often found in quilts than embroidery or trapunto are. It can either be padded or not, as you prefer. I have given instructions for padded appliqué. If you want the unpadded type, simply leave the padding out as you proceed from step to step. A group of small pieces can share a single piece of padding. First, I will give instructions for a simple appliqué of a single piece. Afterward, you will find the additional information for an appliqué of more than one piece.

The fabric used for appliqué may be either a print or solid color. A printed design, such as a flower or a bird, may also be used. Pieced designs are also sometimes appliquéd to a background fabric (see Illus. 91). Pieced star patterns are occasionally appliquéd to a large sheet of fabric instead of being made into blocks.

The appliqué is generally stitched to a plain background fabric, such as fabric used for setting blocks. At other times, an all over pattern is appliquéd to a large sheet of fabric. An elaborate appliqué medallion

Illus. 91. The finished placemat, with hand-quilted "frame." The middle of the poinsettia is a group of French knots made with six-strand embroidery thread.

may form the center of the quilt with one or more borders surrounding it. These borders may themselves be an appliquéd design or they may be pieced or plain. Even though the appliqué stitching may double as the quilting in some instances, it is generally much better to do all the appliqué before the layers of the quilt are put together. One reason for this is that the wrong side of the work is often not attractive and is, therefore, better hidden by the batting and the back of the quilt.

Cut out the pieces to be appliquéd, in-

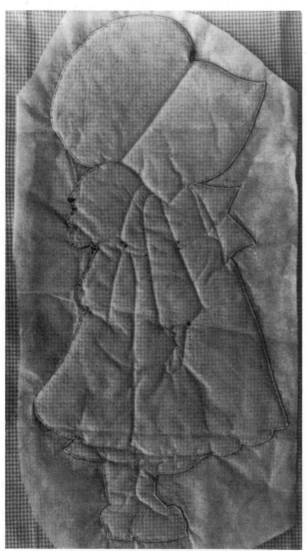

The Holly Hobbie® design used as an example is reproduced through the courtesy and with the permission of American Greetings Corporation. All Holly Hobbie® designs are the copyright of American Greetings Corporation.

Illus. 92. When padding is used, quilting within the appliqué itself can bring out printed detail or create a quilted pattern on the piece. Wrong side of pattern is shown.

cluding the seam allowance. The width of the seam allowance is not important since it will be trimmed away later. Cut out a layer of batting—or a half layer, if you prefer less padding (some batting can be separated in half)—and place it between the piece to be appliquéd and the fabric for the block or the top. (Leave the batting out if you prefer.) Place a piece of stiff, non-woven interfacing under the block of top fabric to back the work and to prevent stretching the fabric on the bias. Pin the layers together securely so that there will be no slipping as you work. It is not usually necessary to use a hoop when the interfacing is used. A piece of typing paper may be used in addition to the interfacing if it is needed. It will tear away easily when the work is completed. If you have never done any of this type of work, practice first on a scrap of fabric.

Begin by stitching all around the appliqué, using a narrow zigzag to hold the piece in place and to secure the fabric along the stitching line. Trim away the extra fabric and batting (if any) that is outside the stitching. Be careful not to cut the fabric to which the appliqué is stitched.

The next step is to go over the same zigzag stitching with satin stitch embroidery. Use the special embroidery foot for this work. The embroidery should be smooth and closely stitched so that no gaps appear between the stitches. If a stitch or two have been skipped, go back over that small area to cover it. If the entire line of stitching seems sparse, go all around it again. This may not be quite as good as making the stitches close enough in the first place, but it is better than having the stitches look skimpy. At the corners, the stitches must be overlapped. Stitch clear to the corner and stop with the needle down. If the piece is to be turned *clockwise*, stop the needle on the *left* side. If it is to be turned *counterclockwise*, stop the needle on the *right* side. Lift the presser foot only and pivot the piece to sew in the next direction. Lower the presser foot and continue to stitch. If you stop with the needle down on the wrong side, there will be a gap in the stitching at the corner. Trim off the extra interfacing which extends beyond the appliqué on the back of the work.

When padding has been used, some quilting may be done within the appliqué itself, to bring out a printed detail or to create a quilted pattern on the piece (see Illus. 92). This is done in the method described for machine quilting in Section 5, using small straight stitches.

Appliqué designs are often created with several overlapping pieces. Each should be cut with a seam allowance. Padding can be used here also. Place a single piece of batting under the whole area or use it only under certain pieces. Begin with the bottom-most piece and zigzag it in place along all the edges that are not to be covered with another piece. Trim away the seam allowance. Then add each succeeding piece by this same method in the order of its position, finishing with the top-most piece. Zigzag each piece along all edges not to be covered by another piece and trim away the seam allowances before adding the next piece. When all the pieces are in place, do the satin stitching around the pieces in the same order as they were added. Cover only the zigzag stitches for each piece, so that the satin stitching of each succeeding piece will slightly overlap the ends of the satin stitching of the previous piece.

There is a way to appliqué without having to cut out any pieces before stitching. Start by drawing the entire pattern on the interfacing or back of the fabric to which the appliqué is to be stitched. The first piece to be appliquéd will be the one on the bottom. Pin a piece of fabric for this piece over the area where it is to appear. *On the back side*, where the pattern is drawn, do the first zigzag stitching as before. Trim the extra fabric from around the piece. Pin the fabric for the next piece and repeat the process. Continue to add any other pieces for the design, always using the lines of the pattern on the back as a stitching guide. When all of the appliqué is in place, turn the work to the right side and do the satin stitching as before. This method is easy and time-saving, but may not save fabric.

Satin stitching may be all of one color which matches the piece, or may be a little deeper in hue, or may be in contrast to the piece or pieces. If more than one piece is used in the appliqué, more than one color may be used if desired. Some machines have an embroidery pattern which resembles a buttonhole stitch. It makes about four narrow zigzag stitches followed by about two wider ones. This might be used to cover the edges of the appliqué. There may be other stitches on your machine which could be used, but a satin-type stitch is necessary to cover the raw edges of the fabric. If the seam allowances are turned under, other types of stitches are a possibility, even a short straight stitch.

The width of the satin stitch used for appliqué can be adjusted somewhat according to the effect desired, but it must be wide enough to cover the first row of zigzag stitches. Aside from that restriction, any other width can be used. One very attractive choice is to vary the width of the stitch. The appearance this creates is a little like that of a brush stroke beginning narrow, then becoming wide, and then going back to narrow. A little practice is needed to achieve this. The work must be guided with the left hand while the width of the stitching is controlled by the right hand.

If you want your appliqué to resemble pieces that are slipstitched by hand, this can be done with the blind hem pattern. Turn under the seam allowance on the pieces and baste them in place. Set your machine for the blind hem pattern. If you have a special blind hem foot, be sure to use it. Set the stitch width very narrow. You want the straight stitches to follow right along the edge of the piece. The occasional zigzag stitch must be only wide enough to catch the very edge of the turned-under seam allowance. The stitch length should be rather short so that the zigzag stitches which catch the appliqué will be about 3/16″ (5 mm) apart. (On some machines, the blind hem pattern has so many straight stitches between the zigzags that it is not adaptable for this method.) When this method is properly done, it is virtually invisible and hard to distinguish from hand work.

TRAPUNTO

There is some disagreement among needleworkers as to the exact definition of trapunto. For our purpose, we will say that it is a decorative type of quilting which is produced by raising an outlined design by filling the area from the underside with stuffing or yarn. We will work with three different methods of doing this.

The first method is to outline the design to be stuffed with a straight stitch (see Illus. 93). This may be done by stitching around it, using the regular sewing foot in the usual manner. It may also be done by the hand-guided embroidery method already described. The stitches should be small and even. In either case, two layers of fabric are required. The top layer will be the fabric you use for the quilt top or pillow.

What you use for the under layer will depend upon the size of the area and the method you plan to use for inserting the stuffing. The easiest method is to make a slit in the bottom fabric large enough to insert the stuffing (see Illus. 94–95). The slit is then closed with loose stitches which

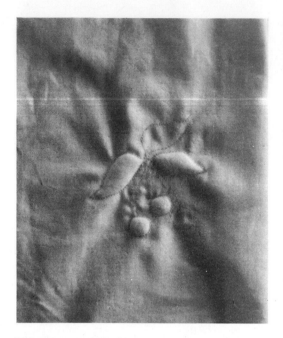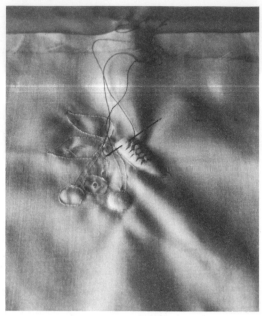

Illus. 93 and 94. (Left) Sample of trapunto—right side of work. (Right) Leaf on the left is slit; leaf on the right is stuffed and closed. The cherry in the middle has threads separated for stuffing; the cherry on the right has been stuffed and the threads replaced.

catch into the stuffing as well as the two sides of the slit. Since a quilt batting and back will hide these stitches, no particular care must be taken to make the stitches attractive or even. They should, of course, be done in such a way as to hold the slit closed, whatever use the quilt may have. For this method, the bottom fabric may be almost any type that will not show through the top fabric—even used material.

The other method must be used only if the area to be stuffed is so small that a slit in the bottom fabric will ravel out because it comes too close to the stitching which outlines the design. For these small areas, a thin, loosely woven fabric is required. A hole is made in the fabric by spreading the threads apart with a pointed tool (see Illus. 96). The bits of stuffing are then pushed through the hole with a blunt instrument

Illus. 95. Stuffing a slit opening.

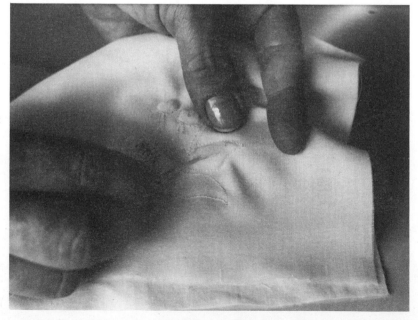

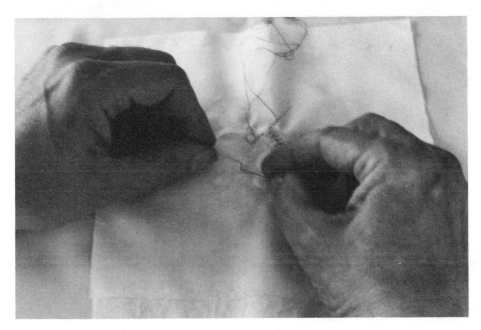

Illus. 96. Separating threads so that a cherry can be stuffed. Two blunt tapestry needles are used.

such as a tapestry needle or a toothpick (see Illus. 97). The hole is then closed by working the threads back into place.

The best stuffing material is the polyester fluff used for stuffing pillows. Cotton tends to pack. Wool will shrink. Both have been used traditionally and are a second choice if the polyester fluff is not available.

The second type of trapunto is called cording or Italian quilting. For this, two parallel lines of stitching are sewn and then yarn or cording is drawn between the lines with a tapestry needle. Again, two layers of fabric are used. Use the presser foot and make the first row of small stitches. The second row can be guided with the edge of the presser foot to be exactly parallel to the first. A change in the needle position can give you a variation in the distance between the two rows, even though the edge of the presser foot is still used along a previous line. An alternative to the two parallel rows is to make a narrow tapering space between the two rows.

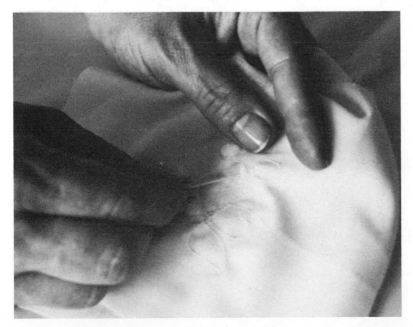

Illus. 97. Stuffing a cherry using a toothpick.

Various types of cording, yarn (wool must be pre-shrunk), twine, candlewick, etc., may be used to raise the design. Cording should be untwisted into single strands and then several may be used in the needle as needed to fill the space. Otherwise, the twist might show through the fabric. Experiment to find out how many strands are required to raise the design the desired amount. Work on the wrong side, pulling the yarn or cording along the little paths made by the stitching. If the lines are straight, the needle may be worked from one end to the other, leaving little ends of cording at each end of the line. For curved lines, the needle must be pushed out at one or more points along the curve. It is then re-inserted in the same place, leaving little loops of the cording to prevent puckering. With both straight and curved lines, gently but firmly pull and stretch the fabric from different angles to work the cording and the fabric smooth after each stitch.

Sometimes when cording is done by hand, the parallel rows of stitches are made in only one layer of the fabric. Cross-over backstitch is used to form the backing for the cording. On the right side of the fabric this looks like straight stitching. On the back side it looks like the catch stitching done when sewing clothing. I have devised a way to do this type of parallel stitching on the sewing machine. Here, too, only one layer of fabric is used and the threads on the back support the cording as

they do in handmade cross-over back-stitching.

You will need a double needle, which is a pair of needles fastened to a single shank so that it can be attached to the machine in the same way as a single needle would be attached. This type of needle comes in various sizes. Size 4.0/100 and size 3.0/90 work well on the cotton fabrics usually used for making quilts, as well as on many other fabrics. (Size 2.0/70 might be better for silks, but the space between the two needles is very narrow.) The first number indicates the width between the two needles in centimeters. The second number is the size of the needle. Two threads are used on the top, one leading to each needle. Each spool must be placed on a separate holder while in use, but the two may go through the tension disks together. Continue threading the two threads as one until you come to the needles. Thread one thread through each needle. Only one bobbin thread will be used. Thread the hole in the bobbin finger also. Stitch in the usual manner, guiding the needles according to the design, which may be either straight or curved. On curves, take care to keep the fabric lying flat as you stitch. When the stitching is completed you will see that some raising has already occurred between the rows of stitching.

Turn the piece to the wrong side and you will find that the bobbin thread has pulled the two top threads slightly to the back and

 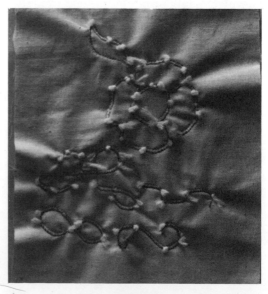

Illus. 98 and 99. (Left) Trapunto cording sample. A double needle was used for this.
(Right) Wrong side of cording. The movement of the hoop was similar to that used in embroidery.

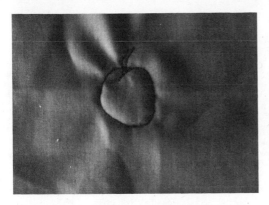

Illus. 100 and 101. (Left) Padded trapunto sample. (Right) Wrong side of padded trapunto.

that the three have formed a loose backing for the slight rise which has occurred on the top of the fabric (see Illus. 98). The cording is pulled under these threads on the back side so that they fill out the fabric and raise the design on the right side. This is by far the easier method for doing the cording type of trapunto and the raise of the design is higher also than when two layers of fabric are used (see Illus. 99). On some machines, the cording can be fed through a hole in the needle plate. It will then be caught between the bottom thread and the underside of the fabric as the stitching is done.

Some designs lend themselves to a third type of trapunto, which is similar to the padded appliqué and might be called padded trapunto (see Illus. 100–101). Put a layer of batting under the top fabric. Place the bottom fabric upon which the design has been drawn on the batting. Pin the layers together and stitch around the outline of the design. Pull or trim (very carefully!) the extra batting away from the outside of the stitching. Extra bottom fabric can also be trimmed away, leaving a ¼″ (6 mm) seam allowance. Additional stitching may be done as needed within the design if desired. This method makes a less distinct raise between two adjoining areas which share the same piece of batting than can be achieved if the two areas were stuffed or padded separately. Both effects are good—only different. If more raise is needed than is achieved by the batting, extra stuffing may be added by the cut-back method.

Trapunto can be done on larger single pieces of a pattern before cutting, or on setting blocks, also before cutting (because the work "shrinks" the fabric), or on smaller pieces after they have been sewed into blocks for easier handling. All trapunto work is better done before the layers of the quilt are assembled. After it is done, proceed to join the blocks or the whole quilt top in the usual way. Then put the layers of the quilt together and quilt it. No quilting is used around the trapunto design as this would depress the design instead of raising it above the surface as it should be.

A great deal of variety is possible both in the size and the form of trapunto patterns, as well as in the unlimited combinations of them. Individual blocks are easier to handle on the machine, but working with a full top is made less difficult by the fact that no batting or stuffing is involved until all the stitching is completed.

Some antique quilts having no other work except the elaborate and closely worked types of trapunto, which is known as "white work," often had no other back than the loosely woven fabric which held the stuffing and cording in place. The slightly disarranged threads of this fabric show how the work was done. Such quilts required untold hours of intricate and painstaking work. Other items such as christening robes and bonnets were also decorated in this way.

Any quilt which has this much trapunto should not have any other batting added. It would not add to the beauty of the quilt, but it *would* add bulk, which would detract from the effectiveness of the trapunto.

SECTION 5
Finishing Quilts and Pillows

FINISHING QUILTS

When you have completed the quilt top, you are ready to put the layers together, finish the edges and do the quilting. There are several ways to do these things. We will explore each one in detail.

Read through the various methods to decide which ones best suit your needs for any given project. Don't learn just one method and then limit yourself to that, though most of us do have our favorite ways of doing things. It is better to have a choice, because sometimes an alternate method is needed.

The Quilt Back

After the quilt top, the quilt back is the next layer of the quilt to be made. If the quilting is to be done by hand, it is necessary to make the back and the batting larger than the top to allow for the easing in of the back and the batting which occurs during hand quilting. Information for quilting by hand is available in numerous books on the subject. Consult one of them if you need help.

When quilting by machine, easing in during quilting does not occur, so you don't need to cut extra fabric to compensate for it. If you have planned to use the fabric left over from the back in piecing the top of the quilt, the back must be cut first. In this case, cut the fabric for the back, adding 2" (5 cm) in both directions. This allows for a possible difference from the size planned, due to any slight variation in sewing the seam allowances while piecing the top.

It is more accurate to cut the back after the top is completed, so it can be cut to fit the finished top. Unless the quilt is quite narrow, more than one width of fabric will be needed to make the back wide enough. If two widths are needed to make the back wide enough, sew the two pieces together along the length of the fabric, sewing ¼"

(6 mm) within the selvages. Trim off the selvages. With the layers of the fabric still lying together as sewed, measure from the stitching and mark half the width of the back, including the side seam allowances, and cut off the extra fabric. The seam will then go down the lengthwise middle of the back. For example: if the back is to be 60" (150 cm) wide, measure 30" (75 cm) plus ¼" (6 mm) side seam allowance, totalling 30¼" (75.5 cm). Draw a line 30¼" (75.5 cm) from the stitching line. Pin and cut along this line. The fabric which is cut away can be used in another quilting project.

Sometimes the back for a small quilt can be pieced along the crossways middle instead of the lengthwise middle. This is acceptable and may require less fabric. Quilt backs may also be made of strips of various congenial fabrics pieced together to make the size needed. Occasionally, a quilt back is pieced in a different pattern (or different color combinations of the same pattern) from the top so that the quilt is reversible. When considering this option, give careful thought to how the quilting is to be done. Tying might be a good choice in this case.

Many quilt backs require more than two widths of fabric. For these, cut off one piece of fabric the length needed for the quilt back and lay it aside for the center back. Cut off two more lengths and pin them right sides together along one side. Trim off the selvages. Measure the width needed for the quilt back, including the side seams. Subtract the number of inches (millimeters) of the width of the fabric with the selvages cut off. (This is for the piece which was cut first and laid aside.) Divide the remaining inches (millimeters) needed by two. Add the width of the seam allowances for sewing the side pieces to the center piece (½") [12 mm] and the sum is the width to mark and cut the two lengths you have pinned together. For example: If the size of the quilt back is to be 94½" x 108½" (236 x 271 cm), cut one piece of fabric 108½" (271 cm) long, cut off the selvages and lay it aside. Cut two more pieces the same length, pin them together along one side and trim off the selvages. Now figure the cutting of the side-back pieces:

The cut width of the
quilt back is to be .. 94½" (236 cm)
Subtract the width
of the center back
piece .... − 43½" (109 cm)
                          51" (127.5 cm)

Half of 51 is .... 25½" (63.7 cm)
+ two seam allow-
ances for sewing
the side pieces to
the center piece .... ½" (12 mm)
+ one side seam
allowance .... ¼" (6 mm)
Width to cut the
side back pieces .... 26¼" (65 cm 6 mm)

Draw a line 26¼" (65 cm 6 mm) from the trimmed edges on the length of the pieces of fabric which are pinned together, and cut along this line. Sew one of these pieces to each side of the center piece (see Illus. 102).

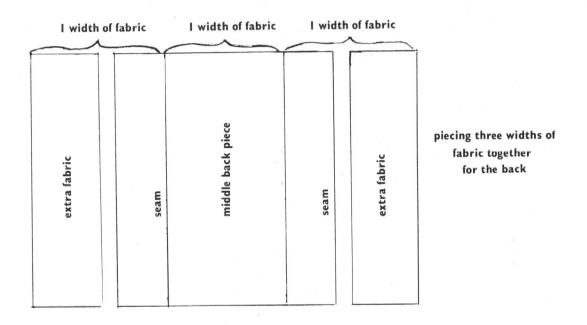

I width of fabric   I width of fabric   I width of fabric

extra fabric   seam   middle back piece   seam   extra fabric

piecing three widths of
fabric together
for the back

I width of fabric   I width of fabric

piecing two widths of fabric
together for the back

extra fabric   middle seam   extra fabric

Illus. 102. Diagram of piecing back.

For some types of machine quilting, the marking for the quilting should be done before putting the layers together. Read the various quilting instructions to find out which ones must be marked before assembling the quilt. Do the marking first where it is suggested.

Some type of trim is occasionally sewed into the edge of the quilt. This should be done before the layers are put together. Ruffles, cording or fabric folded to a point and stitched into a sawtooth effect along the edge of the quilt are sometimes used very effectively as an edge trim. Directions for adding these are given in the section on finishing pillows (see pg. 116).

Putting It All Together

After finishing the top and back of the quilt, you are ready to put the layers together. The third layer of the quilt which is needed is the batting. This must be the same size as the top and the back. If you cannot find batting as large as you need, it can be pieced out to that size by sewing two or more pieces together. There are several ways to do this.

You can lap the two edges and machine stitch them with a long stitch. The lap should be about ½″ to 1″ (12–25 mm) wide, or as narrow as you can sew it easily. Do not stretch the batting in the process of sewing it. Some types of batting do not lend themselves well to machine stitching. The types that do are those that have a glazed finish on both sides, or those which are fused in such a way that they do not catch on the presser foot so they can be sewed like fabric.

Another way to piece batting is to lay the two edges with no overlap and sew them together loosely by hand using a 1″ (25 mm) long whipstitch. A large darning needle is easiest to use for this.

A third method is to lap the edges and sew them together loosely with a long diagonal or tailor's basting stitch. Take 1″ (25 mm) long stitches through both layers of the batting at right angles to the edges. The result is crossways stitches on the bottom.

The Pillowcase Method

The easiest way to put the three layers of the quilt together is known as the "pillowcase method." Bonded or fused batting is necessary for this method. Lay the batting out smoothly on a large surface, such as the floor. Lay the quilt top right side up on the batting, making sure that it is smooth. Lay

the back *wrong* side up on top of the quilt top, smoothing it carefully.

Start at the middle of one end of the quilt and pin all the layers together, working toward the corners. I prefer to use extra-long, glass-headed pins for this because they do not catch in the batting as much as other pins. Quite a lot of pins are required for this process. If you want to avoid being pricked by them, you may prefer to use large safety pins which can be closed and which also have the advantage of not working out of the quilt in the process of handling. Pin about every 4″ (10 cm) all around the edge of the quilt. Now you are ready to sew the layers together.

If you can possibly do so, place your sewing machine (on its own table) beside a large table, with the table on your left and the machine alongside the middle of the long side of the table. Place a card table in front of the machine, touching the table, so that a large L-shaped work surface is formed to receive the quilt as it is being stitched (see Illus. 103). The card table may

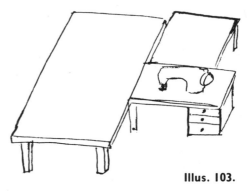

Illus. 103.

not be quite as high as the other table, but that is all right. If you do not have a card table, you might use an ironing board. The idea is to form a large surface to support the quilt so that it will be easier to handle and so that the weight of it does not pull against the area being sewed. Do your best to set up this type of working area, for it will be a real help as you finish the quilt.

When you have everything ready, take your quilt to the machine. Begin sewing about two-thirds of the distance along one end of the quilt and sew to the corner. Make one or two diagonal stitches at the corner. This, surprisingly enough, makes a more pointed corner than if you stitched it to a square point. Sew along the side, then continue to sew around all the other edges. Sew a ¼″ (6 mm) seam, using about eight stitches to the inch (25 mm). When you come to the end on which you began, sew only about one-third of the way across. The few beginning and finishing stitches should be about twenty stitches to the inch (25 mm) to prevent unraveling in handling. There will be an unstitched space of about one-third of this quilt end left open. Lift the edge of the quilt back and sew the *top only* to the batting in this area, using just under ¼″ (6 mm) seam. This is to secure the batting firmly so that it will be held in place along the edge. This is much easier to do now by machine than to try to do later by hand.

Trim away any extra batting. Trim off the extra materials at the corners to eliminate bulk. Now, put your hand through the opening you left at the end and reach between the back and the top to one far corner of the quilt. Pull it through the opening and continue to turn the quilt right side out, like turning a pillowcase, until the right side is all out. Work gently so as not to damage the batting. Work the corners out square using a heavy needle or a seam ripper.

Place your card table with your quilt on it before a comfortable chair and you are ready for the next step. One of the smaller quilts could be held in your lap. Working with the top toward you, pin about every 4″ (10 cm) along the edge of the quilt, hand pressing the seam as you go. When you come to the open area, turn under a ¼″ (6 mm) seam allowance on both edges, pin and slipstitch the seam, using about eight stitches to the inch (25 mm). The quilt is now ready for machine quilting. The instructions for this will be given later.

The Bound Quilt

Another easy method of joining the layers is to bind the edges. The binding may be cut either on the straight grain of the fabric or on the bias. If all the edges to be bound are straight, it is easier to use the straight-cut binding. Where there are curved edges, however, the bias binding must be used. The fabric for the binding may match the back, the border, or one of the pieces in the top, or it may be entirely different from any of these, according to the effect you want. Both bias and straight binding are cut at least 1½″ (37 mm) wide, and enough pieces must be cut to go all around the edges of the quilt when they are joined together. Trim off the selvages, if any, and sew the ends right sides together with a ¼″ (6 mm) seam. Join all the pieces before beginning to sew the binding to the quilt.

At least nine yards (meters) of 1½″ (37 mm) wide bias binding can be cut from ½ yard (45 cm) of 44″ (110 cm) fabric. Here is the easiest way I know to mark it. Most cutting boards have a true bias line drawn several places on the board. Lay a long straight edge of the fabric (single layer) along one of these lines; draw lines across the fabric every 3″ (7.5 cm) by laying your yardstick (meterstick) along the crossways or lengthwise lines on the board (see Illus. 104). Next, measure half way between each of these lines, mark two places and draw a line between each pair of the first lines. Trim off the selvages before cutting along the lines.

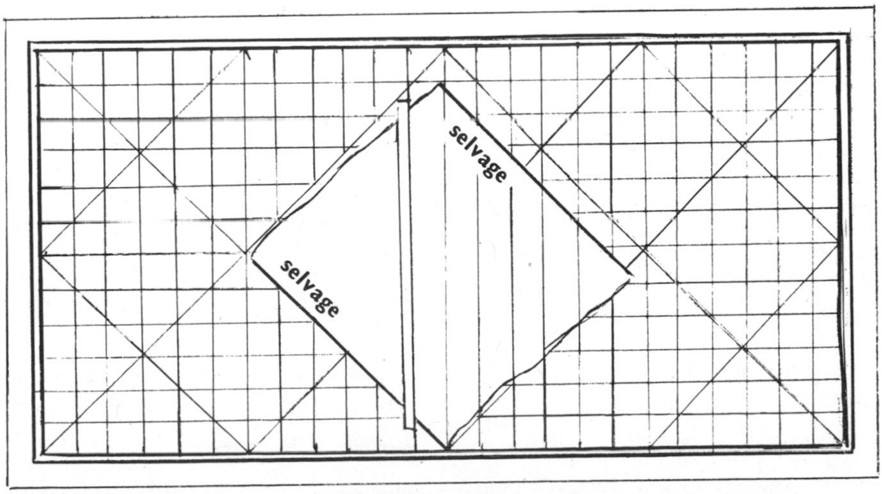

Illus. 104. Marking bias binding. Lay one selvage of the fabric along a diagonal line on the cutting board. Use straight lines on the board to mark fabric on the bias, since these occur every inch (25 mm), while diagonal lines are infrequent.

Illustration 105 shows the correct way to place the ends together in order to join them. Pressing is not necessary, but if you wish to press, be careful not to stretch the bias fabric.

To prepare the layers of the quilt for binding, lay out the quilt back wrong side up. Lay the batting on top of it, and then add the quilt top, right side up. Be sure that all layers are smooth. The reason for stacking them in this order is that the quilting will be done with the top right side up, so you want the pins on the top. Pin all the layers together the same way as for the pillowcase method.

Turn one end of the binding at right angles to the edges, making a ½″ (12 mm) fold to the wrong side on this end of the binding. Start the binding along the top end of the quilt which will be tucked behind the pillow. Sew the binding through all layers with a ¼″ (6 mm) seam, using about eight stitches to the inch (25 mm). The corners must be mitered. To do this, sew to a point ¼″ (6 mm) from the corner. The last few stitches should be tiny ones to prevent raveling. Cut the thread. Turn the quilt so that you are ready to sew down the side. Hold the binding right at the very corner of the quilt with a ripper point or a long needle to keep it in place, and turn the binding to lie along the side of the quilt ready to be sewed (see Illus. 106). Set the machine needle into the work ¼″ (6 mm) down from the end edge and ¼″ (6 mm) in

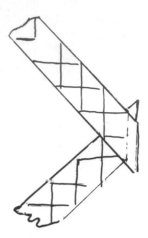

Illus. 105. Joining bias binding. Lay bias strips along the straight threads (either direction) of the fabric. Sew along the straight grain.

from the side edge. Begin sewing with tiny stitches and then finish sewing the binding along the side of the quilt. Repeat this procedure at each corner and edge until you come to the beginning of the binding. Overlap the start of the binding by ⅝″ (16 mm) and cut off any remaining binding. The ½″ (12 mm) fold at the beginning will make a finished joining on the outside and the ⅝″ (16 mm) lap should eliminate the need for hand stitching the folded end, but you may do this if you prefer. Trim off any excess fabric or batting. Turn under a ¼″ (6 mm) seam along the free edge of the

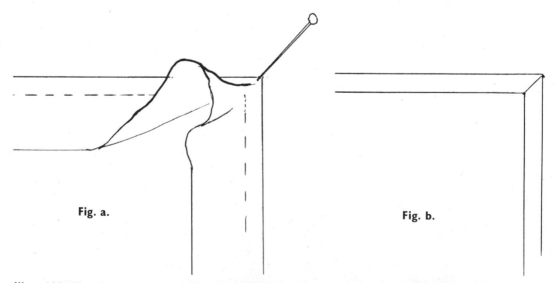

Fig. a.

Fig. b.

Illus. 106. The mitered binding. (Fig. a.) When turning the corner with the binding, stitch to ¼″ (6 mm) from corner on cut thread. Hold binding at corner with a large pin. Lay binding so that it continues along right edge, and begin stitching ¼″ (6 mm) from the corner. (Fig. b.) Turn the binding to the back, making a diagonal lap at the corner on front and back sides as shown.

binding and slipstitch it to the back along the stitching just finished. The mitered corners should also be slipstitched.

A variation of this method is to cut the bias or straight binding 2″ (5 cm) wide, sew as directed, turn under ⅜″ (9 mm) seam allowance along the unstitched edge of the binding and baste it to the back, covering the stitches just made by ⅛″ (3 mm). On the top, stitch through all layers right against the binding, into the seam that joins the binding to the top, but do not stitch on the binding. These stitches will be almost unnoticeable. This type of stitching is called "stitching-in-the-ditch" or "quilting-in-the-ditch."

A cording foot or a zipper foot that can be adjusted from side to side can be a help in stitching in just the right place. The adjustable zipper foot should be set so that the needle is exactly parallel with the right edge of the foot. This way, the stitching will go right beside the binding but not into it. If the needle is too far out of the curve indented into the foot (to protect the needle from damage by a zipper or other hard material), the stitches will go into the binding. If the needle is within the indented curve, the edge of the foot will push against the binding too much, forcing the stitches out away from it a little and making them conspicuous. Experiment a little with scraps to get the adjustment just right, and practice until you can guide accurately; then stitch the binding.

A blind hem foot obtainable for some sewing machines can also be used for stitching-in-the-ditch. These feet have a little metal guide which rests in the seam and guides the stitching in the right place. If this metal guide has a curve to protect the needle, stitch so that the binding is on the opposite side to this curve, or it will prevent the needle from stitching near enough to the binding. This "stitch-in-the-ditch" method of finishing the binding eliminates a great deal of hand work. It is strong and it looks attractive.

Someone has suggested to me that an occasional stitch-in-the-ditch may damage one of the seam stitches. I feel, however, that these machine stitches are so much stronger than hand stitches that even if one is weakened now and then, they will *still* be at least as strong as hand stitching.

"Binding" with the Back or the Border

A third method of finishing the edges of the quilt is to create a "binding" of the quilt back (see Illus. 107). Machine stitch

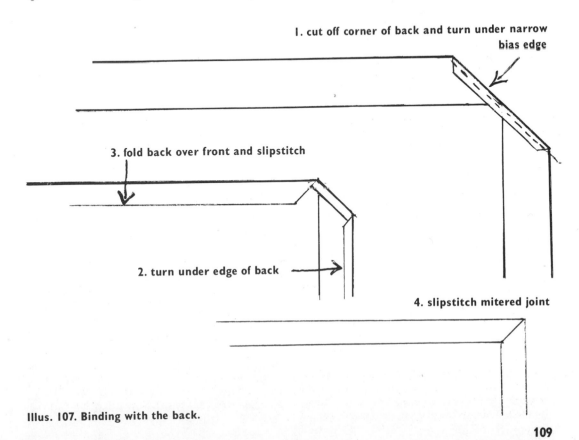

1. cut off corner of back and turn under narrow bias edge

3. fold back over front and slipstitch

2. turn under edge of back

4. slipstitch mitered joint

Illus. 107. Binding with the back.

the batting to the quilt top within the ¼" (6 mm) seam allowance. Cut the back ¾" to 1" (18–25 mm) larger all around. Turn under ¼" (6 mm) along the edge of the quilt back, then fold the edge of the back over onto the top of the quilt and slipstitch it down, creating the appearance of a binding. The top, especially if there is a border, can be turned to the back of the quilt and finished in the same way. In this case, about ¾" to 1" (18–25 mm) should be added to the width of the top or border and the batting should be machine stitched to the back within the seam allowance. In either case, the corners should be mitered to create a neat finish. To do this, before turning the edge over onto the quilt, fold over the corner fabric with a bias fold exactly where the finished corner is to be. Trim off this triangular part to leave about a ⅜" (9 mm) seam allowance along this fold. Baste the seam allowance in place. Fold the edges over onto the quilt like a binding, and the ⅜" (9 mm) seam allowance will come together to form a miter at the corner. This miter should be slipstitched to hold it together.

Yet another method is sometimes used to finish the edge of the quilt. The seam allowances of the top and back edges are turned in and slipstitched together. The batting should first be machine stitched to the top within the seam allowance in order to fasten it to the edge of the quilt. Sometimes a row of straight or zigzag stitches is sewed all around the edge, about ½" (12 mm) from the edge, to hold the batting in place. However, the result does not look nearly as nice as the method described above.

Quilting by Machine

Quilting has two purposes. First, the layers of the quilt must be secured in place to prevent the shifting of the fabrics and the bunching of the batting. Cotton batting must be quilted every inch or two (25–50 mm) to accomplish this. Polyester batting holds its shape much better than cotton and, therefore, much less quilting is necessary. With polyester batting, the intended use of the quilt will influence the amount of quilting needed to insure the long life of the quilt. A comforter which is rarely used and seldom needs washing might be tied every 5" (12.5 cm) or quilted every 9" (22.5 cm) and still wear a long time. A quilted spread for a child's bed, where use is likely to be comparatively hard, might be quilted every 3" to 5" (7.5–12.5 cm). More quilting generally means longer wear. However, too much quilting packs the batting and thus decreases the warmth of the quilt. An area of close quilting makes an attractive contrast to less quilted areas.

The other reason for quilting is to enhance the pattern and add to the beauty of the quilt. This will also influence the amount of quilting to be done. Many of the traditional quilting designs can be done by machine. Fine workmanship is valued in this, as in other types of needlework. As always, practice increases your skills. Remember that accuracy and neatness are to be desired over speed, so work unhurriedly and patiently and speed will come as your skills develop. Try for an even stitch length wherever it will show on the quilt top or back.

When deciding the type or the amount of quilting you will do on your quilt, study your pattern to see what effect you wish to create. Think about the design or parts of the pattern you want to emphasize or to have catch the eye. Consider the possible ways you might achieve this, using one or more types of quilting. With many patterns, the choice is obvious. With others, more alternatives are possible. As you become acquainted with the various methods, you will be able to be more flexible in your choices, or at least more adept at seeing what will work best in a given situation. A wide variety of effects can be achieved with the different methods described here. It is fun to experiment with each method until you have gained enough skill to employ it when you choose.

General Instructions

Some general instructions for machine quilting will be helpful. When quilting, *do not* hold the fabric taut by pulling gently in front of or behind the needle. This does *not* prevent the layers of the fabric from easing in front of the presser foot. On some machines the pressure on the presser foot may be eased up a little to help with this problem. Even if you do this, however, also place the hands, palms down, on the fabric on either side of the needle and stretch the fabric by *pushing the hands in opposite directions*. To understand how this works, take a piece of fabric and pull it on the bias (see Illus. 108). Notice how this makes the fabric draw together at right angles to the direction of the pull. Though you will often be quilting straight along the fabric, as well as on the bias, to pull at right angles to the line of stitching still has just enough effect to prevent at least most of the easing of the fabric in front of the needle. You will, of

course, be pushing toward the needle at the same time, so this will help, too. If you still have a problem, try lifting the presser foot (but not the needle at the same time) often enough to release the buildup before it becomes a tuck as you stitch or at the end of a row of stitching. With a little practice on scrap fabric and batting, you will get the feel of this.

Use regular machine sewing thread for the stitching. Cotton is best for all-cotton fabric. Cotton-wrapped polyester thread works well with blended fabrics. All-polyester thread can also be used. The most important requirement is that the thread must work well in your machine. If what is suggested does not work well for you, then find one that does. If you prefer stitches that show as little as possible, choose a color that blends in well with the fabrics. Thread of a contrasting color is sometimes used for special effects. White thread is traditional.

Usually, all quilting should begin and end with a few tiny stitches to prevent unraveling of the threads. Instead of this, long ends of thread may be left and later tied in a square knot on the back of the quilt. Better yet, thread a needle with the ends one at a time and take a long stitch. Tighten the thread as you cut it off next to the fabric and the end will slip back under the fabric. It is all right to backstitch at the beginning and end of the stitching, but be sure that the thread take-up lever is at the highest position before changing direction, to prevent the pucker that would otherwise occur. Tiny stitches, threads knotted on the back, and backstitching may not gain you any points in judging, but they are not usually noticeable to others. If your quilt is to be judged, work the untied ends of

threads under the surface of the fabric. Fine needlework requires that no knots show and that all the visible stitching be as even as possible.

Arranging the Work Area for Quilting

Quilting in sections will be discussed in Section 6. Whether your quilt is small or large, however, you can quilt it in one piece. When quilting, it is important to be sure that the quilt is well supported. Place your machine so that a large table is to the right. Place a card table or lowered ironing board in front of the machine to receive the quilt as it is stitched. Most of the time, at least some of the quilt will be resting in your lap. If your chair is of regular height, you will find yourself reaching over the rolled layers to guide the work through the machine. This can be very tiring and can cause pains. The best solution I have found for this problem is to sit on a tall kitchen stool or a bar stool. If a stool is not available, build up the seat of your chair with books, folded blankets, or anything which will raise you enough so that your arms extend slightly down to the sewing area instead of up over the quilt.

Work only when you are rested. If you should become tired or tense, take a break or stop, for it is not pleasant to work under these conditions and, besides, you will not be able to do your best work at such a time.

Quilting around the Border

If your quilt has a border, this is the first place to quilt. After the layers of the quilt have been sewed together by one of the methods given, pin all around the edge of the quilt, about every 4″ (10 cm), finger pressing as you go. It is important to do this first. Then pin the seam line where the border is sewed to the top. The pins along the edge can be removed as this seam line is pinned. Be sure that the seam allowance is turned toward the border as you place the pins in the seam to hold it in place. Next, stitch almost into this seam by quilting-in-the-ditch. This should be done before the rest of the quilting because it helps to hold all the layers in place during the rest of the work.

Using the Pattern Pieces as a Quilting Guide

One of the oldest ways to quilt is to follow the seams of the pieces. This does not require marking before quilting. When quilting by hand, the lines of stitching are usually done about ⅛" (3 mm) from the seam line, on one or both sides of the seam. Sometimes, however, the stitching is done into the seam (quilting-in-the-ditch). Either method can be done by machine, but I think quilting-in-the-ditch is more attractive. Even tiny pieces can be quilted in the seam if you wish. This method is especially good for larger pieces, such as the size used in the "Rail Fence" and "Windmill" or even "Nine-patch" quilts described in Section 2. You may not want to quilt all the seams, however. To bring out the pattern, you might quilt along the seams of the dominant-color pieces of "Rail Fence."

For "Windmill," quilt all the seams of the larger four-square block and then quilt the outside seams of the dominant windmill. This is enough in both cases to create an interesting pattern on the back if you want a reversible quilt. Other patterns can also be quilted by this method, and it can be combined with other ways of quilting.

When quilting-in-the-ditch around pieces on a quilt, do not follow the seams around the piece. It is much easier to stitch all the lines that go in one direction, then turn the quilt and stitch in the direction crossways to the first stitching. To prevent the stitching from unraveling, begin and finish each segment of the quilting with tiny stitches or with backstitching, or leave ends to be tied on the back of the quilt and/or pulled under the back with a needle (to hide the ends).

First, assemble the quilt layers and finish the edge by one of the methods described earlier. Then, lay the quilt out flat and be sure that all the layers are lying smoothly. Starting at the middle of one end of the quilt, and working to left and right, pin the corner of each block or piece where the quilting is to begin and to end. If the stitching is to be more than a few inches (50 mm) long, pin every 3" or 4" (7.5–10 cm) along the seam to be stitched. Move up one row of blocks at a time, repeating the pinning process until the entire top has been pinned. As you crawl across the quilt in doing this, it is very easy to pull threads in knit garments, so wear some other type of clothing or else wear something you do not mind having pulled from the pins.

When the top has been pinned, roll half the quilt from one end to the middle. Take the quilt to the machine and place this roll on the right so that it will unroll and move under the arm of the machine as you quilt. Begin to stitch at or near the edge or border (which has already been quilted). Stitch along the crossways seams you want to quilt. If you are quilting along blocks, you may need to quilt an unbroken line from edge to edge. If you are quilting along pieces, however, you will likely be doing short pieces of stitching across the quilt. When one line of stitching has been done across the quilt, move to the right and stitch the next line or group of pieces to be stitched and quilt again. As row after row of quilting is done, you will be unrolling the quilt and removing the pins. When this half has been quilted crossways, roll the other half and quilt it crossways in the same way. Next, roll one side to the middle and quilt lengthwise lines or seams to be quilted. Then, roll the other side and quilt it lengthwise. Finally, any diagonal quilting can be done by rolling the quilt from one corner to the middle and quilting that area along lines parallel to the roll. Repeat this step as needed to finish the diagonal quilting.

Marking the Quilting Pattern

When quilting is not done into or near the seams, some type of marking is usually needed as a guide for the stitching. Most methods used for marking hand quilting are not satisfactory for machine quilting. Corn starch or blue chalk dust worked through perforated patterns would not survive the heavy handling done when quilting by machine. Lead pencil marks cannot be removed easily and usually show on the quilt, unless the lines are very light, which makes them difficult to follow by machine. Sometimes a sliver of soap is used for marking when sewing clothing. I would hesitate to use this method on quilts for fear that the soap would yellow the fabric in the length of time before the quilt needed laundering. If the intended heavy use of the quilt would necessitate frequent washing, this caution might not apply.

The best way to mark quilting patterns for machine quilting is with one of the new marking pens which are available from some quilting shops, catalogues and notions counters. The ink disappears quite readily when touched with a damp cloth or wet cotton. If quite a lot of this marking has to be done, hang the finished quilt on a line and spray the top with water, using a mist-type sprayer. The marks will disappear. Let the quilt hang until it dries. Some types of tailor's chalk pencils can also be used for marking, but try them on a scrap to make sure the marks can be removed. Marking may also be done with dressmaker's carbon and a marking wheel which makes a dotted line. Place the carbon with the right side to the fabric. Lay the pattern to be traced on the carbon and roll the wheel along the pattern to mark the fabric.

Whenever possible, marking should be done before the layers of the quilt are put together. It can often be done in sections instead of laying the entire top out flat. Smooth out the area to be worked on, mark the pattern and then move on to the next area. Long straight lines can often be marked along a ruler or a yardstick (meter stick). A cup, saucer or other curved edge can sometimes be used for marking curved lines. Templates of other patterns can be made or bought for marking quilting patterns or pieces for quilt blocks.

Stiff cardboard, such as poster board or from cereal boxes, can be used for making templates. If a lot of marking has to be done (especially when marking for cutting pieces), more than one template may be needed because the edges wear with use to the extent that they are sometimes not accurate enough to use. A new material has recently come into use for templates. It is the cloudy-type of "shrink-art" plastic which has one surface that is rough so that it clings to the fabric during marking.

This plastic can be found at some craft shops and can now also be found in some quilting supply stores and catalogues. It has the added advantage of being transparent, as well as having edges that do not wear with use. On either the cardboard or the plastic, mark the pattern carefully, either with a fine ballpoint or a very sharp pencil. Cut very carefully, just cutting off the lines, so that the marking around the template on the fabric will come right where the lines were marked for the template. Place the template in the desired position on the quilt piece or area to be marked and draw around it. Stitch on the line as you would sew a seam.

As a general rule, it is best to keep machine quilting patterns simple. The stitch length should be about 14 or more stitches to the inch (25 mm). Small stitches usually look better, but longer, even stitches are better than smaller, uneven ones. Larger patterns can be stitched in the usual manner, using the regular presser foot and keeping the feed dogs up to control the flow of the fabric. Free-hand quilting of smaller designs will be discussed later. When doing any quilting, remember to take care that the top fabric does not ease ahead of the needle.

Rows or parts of the quilting design should be stitched all in one direction as much as possible (see Illus. 109). This may mean that you will sometimes have to start at a given point on the pattern, stitch halfway around, cut the thread, return to the starting point and stitch the other half. The reason for this is that, no matter what you do, the fabric will ease along ever so slightly. Stitching that flows in one general direction will lie flat, while stitching that goes in reverse directions will warp the quilt at least in the area where this stitching is done. With a little planning, you should not have any problem with this. Always practice a little of what you plan to do on scraps of fabric and batting before trying it on the quilt.

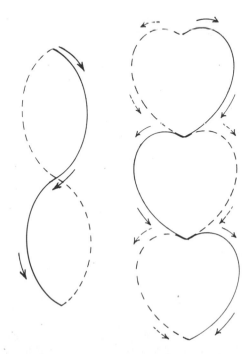

Illus. 109. Stitch rows or parts of the quilting design all in one direction as often as possible.

Diagonal Quilting

The oldest machine quilting I have seen was done by simply sewing diagonal lines across the quilt in both directions. This was done without regard to the piecing pattern of the quilt and so did nothing to add to its beauty. In fact, the pattern was almost lost because the quilting detracted from it. However, diagonal quilting can be quite attractive, in some situations, when it is used in such a way as to emphasize or to enhance the design. Diagonal quilting is the easiest way I know of quilting the layers together, which is probably the reason it was used on the old quilt I saw. It does not warp easily and the top is not as likely to ease ahead of the needle. The "Patience" quilt (color page A) was quilted in this way. Since the pieces were only 3" (7.5 cm) square, I did not even need to draw the diagonal lines, but simply sewed from corner to corner across the white squares.

In keeping with the pattern, quilt in one diagonal direction only, along each white diagonal stripe, to emphasize the design. This is an easy and attractive way to quilt this pattern and it could be adapted to other similar patterns, such as "Trip Around The World." If the piecing does not act as a guide, the pattern can be marked in one or both directions every 3" to 6" (7.5–15 cm).

If you wish to quilt diagonally, mark the quilting lines on the quilt top, if this is needed, before putting the layers together. Then put the layers together by one of the methods described earlier. When you are ready to quilt, lay the quilt out flat and pin the corner of every square through which the quilting stitches will pass. Pin every few inches (50 mm) along the line to be quilted. Roll the quilt on the diagonal from one corner to the middle so that the roll is parallel to the diagonal lines that will be stitched, rolling up about half of the quilt. Place the roll under the arm of the machine. Start quilting at one edge of the quilt and stitch to the opposite side along one line near the roll. Remove the pins just as you get to them. Do not sew over the pins unless you stop and turn the wheel by hand to make sure that the needle does not hit the pin. Cut the thread. Start at the same edge of the quilt as before and quilt the next line near the roll. You may need to unroll a little for this. Continue quilting and unrolling until all the lines in this direction on this half of the quilt have been done. Then roll the other half of the quilt and quilt it in the same way. This will

change the direction of the quilting once, but the two lines of stitching which are in opposite directions will be several inches (50 mm) apart, so no problem will result from this change.

If you plan to quilt diagonally at right angles to the first quilting lines, follow the same procedure as above.

Other Types of Quilting

Quilting designs are also done within pieces, setting blocks, sashing and borders. These should be marked for quilting before the layers of the quilt are put together. There are two ways to do this type of quilting, and the way you choose depends on the size and type of the design you use. If the blocks or areas to be quilted are to have an outline of quilting, such as quilting-in-the-ditch, do this before quilting within the areas by either method which follows.

One method is simply to follow the marked lines as you stitch, just as you would sew along a line and as you did the diagonal quilting. This method is easy to use on large or simple patterns, or on patterns requiring exact curves or parallel lines. When doing this, remember what has been said about always stitching in one general direction and about preventing the fabric from easing in front of the needle.

Machine-controlled embroidery stitches —those made with cams or with built-in pattern controls—can be used for this method of quilting. The single (not zigzag or satin type) stitches usually work better, especially the one called serpentine stitch, which makes a wavy line that curves back and forth as it advances.

The satin stitches can be used in quilting to create certain effects. A quilt might, for instance, be made of fabric with a large print instead of pieced blocks. The print might be outlined with satin stitching to resemble appliqué. The underside of the satin stitches is not attractive, however.

The other way to quilt within pieces, blocks, etc., is easier to use for smaller patterns, and for certain types of larger ones, especially if exact curves, such as circles, or precise parallel lines are not required. It is a hand-guided type of quilting which is less formal and yet very beautiful. The method is similar to that used for machine embroidery. Drop the feed dogs, remove the presser foot, and use an embroidery hoop, placing the larger of the two rings under the quilt and the smaller one on the top (see Illus. 110). This will hold the quilt to the needle plate. Without the hoop, the layers will be too loose and the machine may not make stitches. This hoop should be one made to use with the sewing machine and can be found at sewing machine shops. It will be narrower than a regular embroidery hoop and will have a screw to tighten the larger hoop onto the smaller one. You can also use a darning foot (a yarn-darning foot is not as good) *instead* of using the hoop, because this foot will press the layers of the quilt gently to the needle plate and yet permit the quilt to be moved by hand under the foot. In some cases it is better to use the hoop and in other cases the darning foot is preferable.

The embroidery hoop gives you something to hold onto in moving the quilt under the needle. The darning foot allows freedom to work over a larger area. Try both on scraps and use the one which best suits your needs. In either case, *be sure to lower the presser foot bar* even when there is no foot on the machine, because this engages the top thread tension, which is necessary for stitching. If the presser foot bar is left up, there will be loops of thread on the back of the work.

Since free-hand quilting is done with the feed dogs down, the machine will not move the quilt under the needle, so you must do this by hand. The stitch width should be set for "0." The stitch length control is not in effect with the feed dogs down.

In order to get an even stitch length, you must learn to control the relationship between the speed of the needle and the speed of your hand movement. This really is not as difficult as it may sound. A fast needle and a slow hand movement create shorter stitches. A slow needle and a fast hand movement result in longer stitches. It requires a little practice to get the effect you want, however. I prefer the appearance of about 14 or more stitches to the inch (25 mm), but you may like another length. Too long a stitch calls attention to the stitch instead of the quilted effect. If there is a relative speed control on your machine, set it for the slow range of stitching. Slow, even stitching and slow hand movement permit good control in following a marked pattern. With practice you will learn to go a little faster, but remember that speed is not the aim.

I often draw my quilting patterns free-hand, making similar, but not exact, designs of flowers, etc. These individual designs add interest and variety. On setting blocks, I sometimes do not draw any design at all, but guide the quilt by eye and ex-

Illus. 110. Using a hoop for machine quilting. Hand-guided flowers have just been quilted with free-hand quilting.

perience to make each separate quilted design a slight variation of a pattern. I might even use a variety of associated designs, such as flowers, fruits, etc.

Hand-guided quilting can also be used for quilting around a printed design. This method can be used on sheets or on strips of fabric which have been sewed together to make a top in much the same way as the quilt back is made. It makes a pretty coverlet or comforter much more quickly than if piecing were done for the top. Solid color quilts and comforters can also be made with only the quilting design as a pattern, using any of the machine quilting methods.

If you are particularly interested in this free-hand type of quilting, you will find that some of the information in machine embroidery books can be adapted to quilting. Machine-embroidered blocks also make beautiful quilts. Often, the embroidery can also be the quilting. Threads of various colors might be used for this.

The Tied Quilt

Quilts are often "tied" to hold the layers together instead of being quilted. This method is usually used on comforters because they have thicker batting, making quilting by hand difficult. It is also sometimes done on quilts because it is faster than quilting. Since the layers are not held together so well with tying as with quilting, tying should be done more closely than quilting. A quilt which will have heavy use should *always* be quilted.

Prepare the quilt for tying by finishing the edges by any of the methods you prefer. Then, lay the quilt out and pin the layers as you would for quilting. It is best to pin the places where you want the ties to go. Ties are usually made of knitting yarn. Woolen yarn must be shrunk before using or it will shrink later and cause the quilt to pucker at the ties. Synthetic yarns do not shrink and may be used instead of wool. Any size yarn up to knitting worsted size can be used, but the heavier yarn is harder to pull through the layers of the quilt. If you find it difficult to grip the needle, hold it with a rubber glove or a deflated balloon. Dazzle yarn makes a silk-looking tie.

Threads other than yarn can be used instead, such as six-strand and silk embroidery threads, crewel yarns (preshrink these), pearl cotton and crochet thread. Experiment with various yarns and threads if you are looking for unusual effects. Thread a length of yarn or thread through a needle large enough to carry the tie through the fabric without too much effort. Use the yarn or thread double by carrying the tie through twice, but do not put a double strand through the needle because this makes it much more difficult to pull through the layers of the quilt. Take a stitch through all layers of the quilt or pass the needle down and then up again if that is easier for you. Try to avoid stitching through seam allowances. You want the stitch to be almost as long on the back as on the front of the quilt. Leave the ends long enough on the top to handle easily and tie a square knot. Hold the tied ends between finger and thumb as a measure and cut off the extra length. If you hold and cut the same way each time, no other measure is needed. This tie is usually made on the top of the quilt, but it can also be made on the back.

Other types of ties can also be made. For instance, you might make a French knot on the top and tie a square knot on the bottom with the ends. This is very pretty on a quilt for a little girl. A very small knot can be made where you prefer that the tie not show very much. This is a good choice any time you do not want the ends of the ties on the top. It would also make the quilt look more reversible.

A small bow knot makes an attractive tie on a plain surface. It might be used on an unpieced top or made with the ends on the back when a French knot or other stitch is used on the top.

Various hand embroidery stitches might be used instead of a regular tie so long as all the layers are caught by a stitch in the process.

Comforters

Comforters have traditionally been tied because they are too thick for hand quilting, since more than one layer of batting is used on them. However, even very thick comforters can be quilted by machine so long as they can be rolled tight enough to go under the arm. The comforter is prepared in the same way as other quilts, by one of the methods described. The stitching is widely spaced and kept very simple in design. Polyester batting should be used, because it holds its shape better than any other type.

FINISHING PILLOWS

Quilted pillows are very popular and attractive, adding a colorful note in various rooms of the house. Many quilting patterns lend themselves nicely to use on pillows. A single block may be used, perhaps enlarged to a preferred size. A group of four or more blocks may be put together to make a pillow top. An appliqué pattern is also popular for pillows. One or more borders are often used to frame the design attractively.

You may want a ruffle or two around your pillow, quilt or comforter (color page B). Ruffles may be cut on the bias or on the straight of the fabric. They may be either hemmed or cut double the finished width plus the seam allowances and folded in half lengthwise. This method is faster and makes a very finished-looking ruffle, but it requires more fabric. Ruffles may be made of fabric that matches a piece in the pillow or that is a contrast to it. Two ruffles of different widths can often be used to good effect. Allow about double fullness for the ruffle. Join the ends in a seam. For a hemmed ruffle this should be a French seam; for a folded ruffle, it can be a plain seam. Hem or fold the ruffle and run two gathering threads, using a long stitch near one edge. The easiest way to do this is to use a double needle so that both rows of stitching can be made at one time, but only one thread (the one from the bobbin) needs to be pulled for gathering (see Illus. 111). With pins, mark off regular spaces along the edge of the pillow. Then mark off spaces on the ruffle, before gathering, that are twice as long as the spaces on the pillow. Pin the ruffle right sides together to the pillow, matching the marking pins. The bobbin thread can be caught with the head of a pin at any desired point and pulled to gather in the extra fullness in the ruffle to fit the pillow. If there are to be two ruffles, they should be gathered in separately, with the narrower one next to the pillow top and the wider ruffle on the narrower one. Baste the two in place with machine stitching.

A sawtooth edge is sometimes used on pillows or quilts (color page D). This is quite easy to make and is very attractive with pieced patterns and appliqué designs. Start by cutting squares of fabric. Experiment a little to see what size is best for your needs. Fold the squares on the bias and press. Fold the resulting triangle in half with the cut edges together. This cut edge is placed along the seam allowance of the quilt so that the pieces overlap halfway by placing the single fold of one triangle within the two folds of the one next to it (see Illus. 111).

Pillows, quilts or comforters may also have a corded edge. Cording in various sizes may be found at fabric shops. It must be covered with bias-cut fabric (see Illus. 112 for how to cut this). Cut the bias strips 1½″ (37 mm) wide, or as needed to cover the cord, and join the ends to make one long strip. Fold this a little off center so that the edges will be graded and lay the cording in the fold (see Illus. 112). Use a long machine basting stitch and a cording foot to sew the cording in place. Place this line of stitching right over the stitching line for the edge of the quilt top with the cording toward the middle of the quilt. Machine-baste it in place and then proceed to assemble the quilt as desired.

When the pillow top is finished, including any edging to be used, lay it on a piece of batting with a piece of lining fabric on the underside. This lining may be any scrap which is large enough for the purpose, even used fabric, such as the back of a shirt or a piece of a skirt. Quilters traditionally make use of salvageable materials whenever possible. This lining is not subject to much wear, so new fabric is not needed to insure long service. Quilt the top, if desired, in any way that pleases you. If no quilting is done, the layers of batting and lining will still be needed to help create a smooth surface when the pillow is stuffed. Machine-baste the layers together within the ¼″ (6 mm) seam.

Cut a back for the pillow the same size as the top. Lay it on a piece of batting and lining as you did the pillow top and quilt it if you want. Machine-baste the layers together. Place the back with its layers of batting and lining right sides together with the top and sew all layers together just within the basting lines. Leave an opening on one side to turn the pillow and then stuff polyester fluff stuffing or bits of batting between the lining fabrics. I have sometimes used two layers of batting under the top and the back of the pillow for an even smoother finish. This is a bit more bulky to handle, so leave a larger opening for the turning of the pillow after the top and the back are sewed together. You may make your pillow as soft or as firm as you like, but remember that the use of the pillow will, in time, settle the stuffing somewhat, so make allowances for this when you are adding the stuffing. The finished pillow will be completely washable.

If you want your pillow to have a removable cover, make and quilt the top as before. Make the layered back with a zipper or with an overlapped opening (see Illus. 113). Lay this right sides together with the top and sew all around the sides. Turn the pillow right side out through the overlap or the opened zipper. Make an inside pillow of muslin the same size as the top. Stuff it with polyester fluff and insert it into the finished pillow cover.

For a boxed pillow, make the top and back as before. Make layered sides the same way. A layer of stiff non-woven interfacing may be used as the side lining to give more shaping there. The zippered or lapped back can also be used for this pillow. The seams of the inside pillow should be top-stitched in a crease to create a pinched or corded effect which will help support the boxed sides and keep them squared.

Pillows filled with foam pillow forms always have an understuffed look and are not as professional-looking as the ones that are stuffed. The bolster-type pillow is a possible exception to this. The cover for the bolster form must be quite snug in order to look well. To accomplish this, make the cover just a fraction smaller than the form. This cover may be made removable by inserting a zipper into the seam of the tube part.

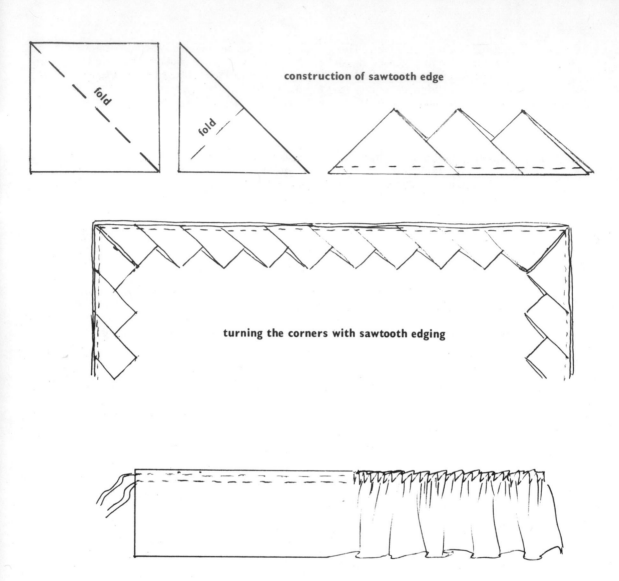

construction of sawtooth edge

turning the corners with sawtooth edging

construction of ruffle (may be hemmed or folded double): stitch gathering thread with two rows of stitching or with a double needle, which is faster and easier to gather

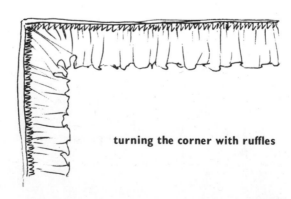

turning the corner with ruffles

Illus. III. Folding and sewing sawtooth edge, and ruffle.

slash seam allowance to stitching at corner
It is better to round corner a little and slash two or three times—this
makes a better "corner"

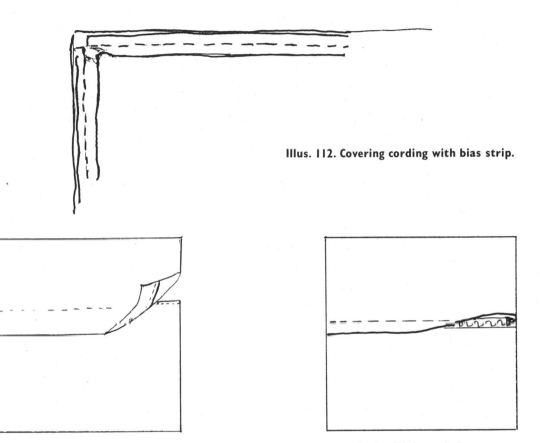

Illus. 112. Covering cording with bias strip.

lapped back for pillow

back with lapped zipper

stitch back to top in the usual way

wrong side of boxed pillow cover
with lapped back

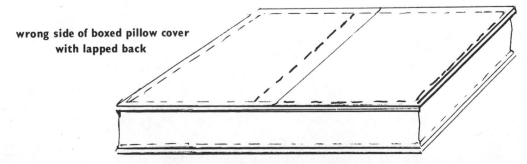

Illus. 113. Joining sections of a pillow.

SECTION 6

Apartment Quilting and Quilting-As-You-Go

Some people feel that they do not have enough room to work on a large quilt, but they would like to make one anyway. Others do not enjoy working with large quilts, finding them awkward for one reason or another. Still others prefer a project which can be taken along to meetings or when visiting. All of these people, as well as many others, will find something in this section to suit their needs.

In making the quilts in this section, you will be using some of the methods you have used before and you will also be learning some new methods. Keep in mind not only the procedures you have learned, but also the other points which have been discussed, such as the interplay of color and value and space.

QUILTING IN SECTIONS

This type of work is sometimes called apartment quilting because no large area is needed for spreading out the layers of the quilt so that they can be pinned or basted together. The quilt discussed here is made up in sections to be joined when most of the work is completed.

Begin by planning your quilt in the usual way with a color diagram and decide the size of the sections to be made. These will divide naturally, such as between rows of blocks. Mark the fabric and cut the pieces as for other types of quilts. Make the top of the quilt in two or three sections as planned. Lay one top section on its batting and back of the same size. All of the quilting can be done on the section just as though it were a complete unit. Finish each section to this point before putting them together. Now lay two sections top sides together and pin them along the edge to be joined. Add a strip of 1" (25 mm) wide bias or straight-cut fabric, with its right side to the back of one section. Sew the layers together with a ¼" (6 mm) seam (see Illus. 114). Trim or pull out as much batting as you can from the seam allowances. Turn the seam allowances away from the narrow strip and baste them to the back of the quilt, since you want them to lie as flat as possible. This basting should not show on the top because it will not be taken out. Turn under the edges of the fabric strip and baste to cover the seam allowances, then slipstitch the turned edge to the quilt back. This narrow strip looks best if it is of the same fabric as the back. Add other sections in the same way. Finish the outside edge of the quilt with binding.

Single quilt *blocks* may also be quilted and then joined together to make a complete top. Set the finished blocks in strips as though they were little sections. There should be as many of these blocks in a strip as there are in the length of the quilt. Use the inch- (25 mm-) wide fabric to finish the seams between the blocks as you would for the sections. These strips may either match the back of the blocks or may be made of any fabric that looks well with it. In this case it has the appearance of sashing and the quilt looks more reversible. You may also choose to make the backs of the blocks of various prints and/or solids to create an attractive pattern with them. The strips of blocks are then joined in the same way as described for joining sections.

If sashing is to be used between the blocks on the top of the quilt, the process is even easier. Place a piece of the sashing that is to go between the finished and quilted blocks right sides together along one top edge of a block (see Illus. 115).

stitch together

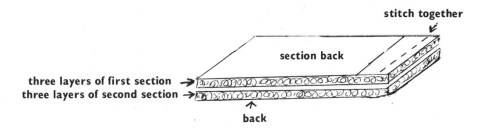

three layers of first section →

three layers of second section →

section back

back

fold this edge back—do not catch in stitching

lay the free back edge over the stitched seam, turn the edge under and slipstitch in place

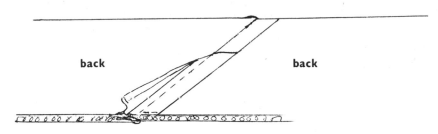

back

back

Illus. 114. Joining sections of a quilt.

three layers of block

back

← back sashing

stitch layers as shown

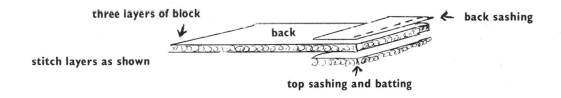

top sashing and batting

join another block to the top sashing

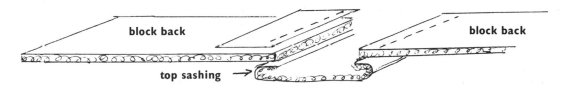

block back

block back

top sashing →

lay back sashing over seam and slipstitch

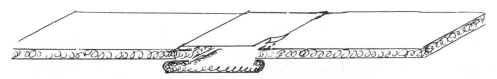

Illus. 115. Joining blocks with sashing.

Place a strip of batting of the same size on the sashing. Add a piece of back sashing to the same edge on the back of the block. Pin all the layers together and sew a ¼″ (6 mm) seam. Fold open the top sashing and the batting and lay another block right sides together on it. Sew a ¼″ (6 mm) seam to join all layers. Turn under the free edge of the back sashing which was sewed into the previous seam and slipstitch it to the seam line just sewed. Add enough sashing and blocks, alternately, to complete a lengthwise strip for the quilt. To one of these long strips add a lengthwise top sashing and a batting strip to match. On the back side, add a strip of back sashing and sew a ¼″ (6 mm) seam. Make enough strips with sashing for the width of the quilt.

Do not add any sashing to the last strip of blocks unless you intend the sashing to form a border around the quilt top as well as to separate the blocks.

Borders can be added in the same way as adding sashing. They can be mitered if you like. Finish the edges with binding.

QUILTING-AS-YOU-GO

With this type of construction, the quilting is done as the pieces are sewed together to form the blocks or units, which are then joined together and the edges finished to complete the quilt. Several types of patterns fall under this heading, though they are quite different in construction.

String Quilts

String quilts grew out of the necessity to make use of every possible scrap of fabric. Long narrow bits of material were often not wide enough for cutting into conventional pieces, but did contain good, usable fabric when they were sewed together side by side. The earliest examples of this type were likely to be quite simple and casual. The pieces are not matched in size or shape, but are sewed together more or less in whatever shape they were when left over from other sewing projects. Traditionally, to save fabrics, as little trimming as possible was done. The strings were often sewed into long strips, beginning at one end and adding string after string until the strip was long enough for the quilt size desired.

These strips are easy to quilt as the seams are sewed. Lay a piece of batting on the fabric that is to be used for the back. Each should be about ½″ (12 mm) larger all around than the finished strip is to be. Begin at one end and pin a string of fabric right side up along the edge. Add another string right sides together and sew a ¼″ (6 mm) seam, stitching through all layers. This way, the quilting is done "as-you-go." Fold open the string and continue to add enough strings to finish the strip (see Illus. 116). Strips can be joined by the method described for joining sections.

Sometimes blocks of strings were made and sewed together. Later, the blocks were set together in such a way as to create very interesting patterns (see Illus. 117).

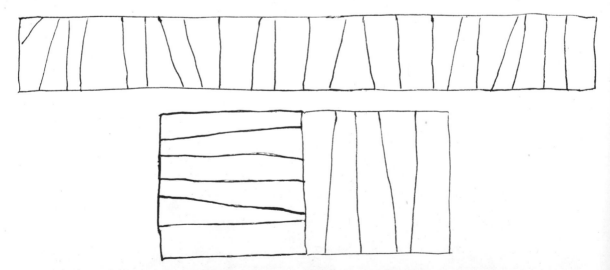

Illus. 116. Simple string patterns and blocks. Make long strips of strings and join them like a "Stripey" quilt, but with strips of fabric on the back to cover the seams, as for apartment quilting sections. Join string blocks with string going in opposite directions.

My own string pattern, named "Broken Square," was created especially for this book (see Illus. 118). It is a block of two half-square triangles which are pieced of alternating wide and narrow strings. (Half-rectangles could be used for a different effect.) This block can be set together in groups of four to make at least three different designs. Two of the blocks, set with two setting blocks in opposite corners, make another variation. As with most patterns, by using different color combinations—the arrangement of dull and bright hues, and coordinated prints and solids—you can create many different effects with this design.

Illus. 117. "Spider Web" pillow made of a string pattern. Eight triangles form the block. The web is created in the middle of the block. Other webs are formed as the blocks are joined together.

1.

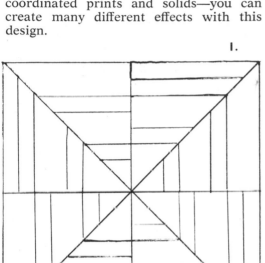

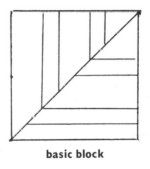

basic block

2.

3.

Illus. 118. "Broken Square." Three variations of joining the basic block are given to create three different effects. Set these blocks with lattice the width of the wider stripe in the block.

Another of my designs, "Autumn Leaf," also falls into this group (see Illus. 119). The rectangles fit together in such a way as to require a small square in the middle of the block. Follow the easy instructions in the illustration for adding this center square.

If the pattern is pieced of spring greens instead of fall colors, I call it "Spring Leaf." Two narrow rectangles, covered with random-width strings, are sewed together to form the wider rectangle used in the block.

this is the easy way to set in the middle square

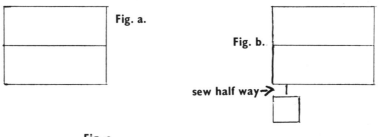

Fig. a.

Fig. b.

sew half way→

Fig. c.

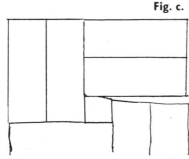

add next pair of pieces across ends of first pair and the square

continue around in this manner, finishing the seam of the square to the first pair of pieces as the ends of the last pair are sewed

Illus. 119. "Autumn Leaf"—a string pattern piece to make in fall colors.

Log Cabin

Log Cabin is the most popular of the string quilts. It can be pieced in the usual way (without batting) or constructed by the quilt-as-you-go method, which is described here. Cut squares of back fabric and batting as a foundation for sewing the block. They should be 1" (25 mm) larger all around than the measurements of the block before it is sewed to the other blocks. Cut one square of backing fabric and one square of batting for each block to be made. Cut an equal number of small squares to be used in the center of the blocks. These are usually about 1" to 3" (25 mm–7.5 cm) square, but may be any size needed for the effect you want. They were traditionally made of red fabric to simulate the flames in the fireplace of the cabin, but other colors are often used now.

The color of the center square must be the same in all the blocks, even though the "logs" may be a variety of scrap fabrics. This center square gives a unity to the quilt, tying all the blocks together. The strips for the logs may be from ½" to 2" (12 mm–5 cm) or more wide, plus seam allowances. One huge block of the wide strips could form an entire quilt. You can cut several layers of strips at a time if you pin carefully. Mark and cut them crossways

of the fabric. By working with your diagram you will be able to decide the width of pieces you need for the block you want.

Another decision you need to make is the arrangement of the fabrics. Imagine the block divided diagonally into two triangles. The two triangles usually have a contrast of some sort, such as light and dark. The idea originally was that one was the sunny side and the other the shady side of the cabin. For either or both sides, you can use all prints, all solids, a mixture of prints and solids, prints on one side and solids on the other, or any combination your imagination may come up with. The effect can be either traditional or modern, even psychedelic! It can be very masculine or completely feminine or neither. I have seen striking examples made of striped silk ribbon. The use of a rectangle in the center around which a rectangular block is built is an unusual change. These and all the other possible variations contribute strongly to the continuing popularity of this versatile pattern. Quilters are as intrigued by exploring possibilities as any other artist or craftsman.

In addition to these variations, there are numerous ways to set the blocks together to form completely different designs on the quilt top. See Illustrations 120 for a few ideas, or make up some of your own.

Illus. 120. Several settings for "Log Cabin."

Construction of the basic block is quite simple, yet a bit tricky (see Illus. 121). The trick is to center the middle square, making sure that it is parallel to the sides of the back fabric, and then to sew each "log" with an accurate seam allowance. First, place the batting on the quilt back, which is right side down. Since you cannot draw a line on the batting, to determine the exact center, fold the back in half lengthwise and then widthwise and put a pin through the central point where the lines cross, sticking the pin straight up through the batting. Locate the center of the small square and add it to the pin (Illus. 121-a). Then, make sure that the sides are parallel to the sides of the block back and pin the small square in place. Follow the diagrams in Illustration 121 as you read these instructions.

Choose a strip of the first fabric to be sewed and lay it right sides together on the small square. Sew a ¼" (6 mm) seam, using about 14 stitches to the inch (25 mm). Cut off the extra length of the strip even with the square. It is not necessary to cut the thread. It can be cut on the back later and the ends worked under, or it may be left on the inside.

Open the piece flat and pin it down at both ends (Illus. 121-b). Sew another strip of the same fabric across the end of the piece just sewed and the side of the square. Cut off the extra length and lay it aside. Open out the second piece and pin it at both ends (Illus. 121-b). Now, sew the first two pieces on the other triangular half of the block by the same method used for the second piece just sewed. Use the first fabric for the second half of the block (Illus. 121-c). Next, sew two logs on the first half of the block, using the second fabric as you have planned (Illus. 121-d). Continue to sew pairs of strips alternately on each half of the block (Illus. 121-e) until all are sewed. On the *last four strips sewed*, start sewing ½" (12 mm) from the ends of the pieces and back stitch. On the final strip, leave both ends unstitched for ½" (12 mm). This is done to leave the back fabric free for joining the blocks.

Pin the ends of these pieces into place with the unstitched part of the seam allowance turned under. When you sew across them later they will not pull out. Illustrations 122–124 show diagrams and a template to help in your construction of "Log Cabin."

An aid to sewing Log Cabin blocks

If you have difficulty getting your "Log Cabin" blocks to come out square and true to size, here is an easy method I have developed to correct the problem. It takes a little more time, but your blocks will turn out right and fit together properly. On a large sheet of white paper, draw a diagram of your block exactly the size it is to be. Add the seam allowances beyond the stitching lines as indicated in Illustration 123. When you are sure it is just right, go over the lines for the seam allowance edges only, using a pointed felt pen that makes very black lines. A ballpoint pen is too fine for this. If the backing fabric for the blocks is a light color (muslin is traditional), the lines of the block diagram will show through the fabric. Trace the lines on the *wrong* side of the fabric, using the special fabric marking pen mentioned earlier. Use a ruler when tracing the lines to be sure that they are straight and in the right place. If you do not have the special pen, perhaps tailor's chalk or a pencil line will work. It should not show through to the right side of the fabric, but must be dark enough to show through the batting.

If the fabric for the back of the blocks is too dark for the pen marks to show up on it, another method can be used. Trace the lines on the sheer nonwoven material used for tracing patterns (look for this among the interfacing fabrics). Trace one of these squares for each block to be made and lay it on the wrong side of the block back or on the batting. Pin the center square in place and proceed to stitch the strips to the block in the same order as before. Each cut edge should rest on a line when the strip is opened and pinned down. If it does not, the seam was either stitched too wide or too narrow. A slight variation can be accommodated by placing the next strip to be joined here *with its edge along the line* and sewing it in place. If there is more than a little variation from the line, the piece should be taken off and resewed correctly. By keeping to the lines as a guide, the block can be made true to size.

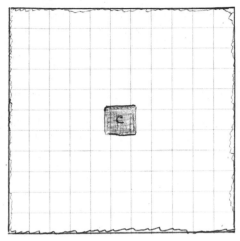

Fig. a. beginning the block: batting on back piece, central piece in place

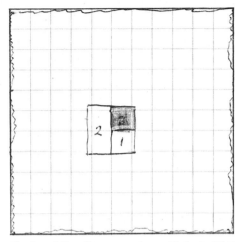

Fig. b. adding first two pieces (light half of block)

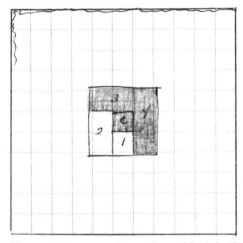

Fig. c. adding second two pieces (dark half of block)

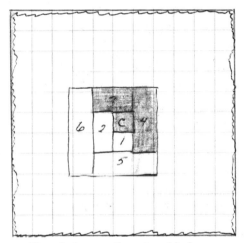

Figs. d. & e. continue to add pieces

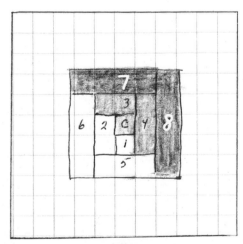

Fig. e.

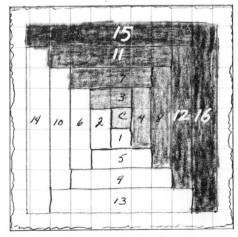

Fig. f. the finished block

Illus. 121. Construction of "Log Cabin."

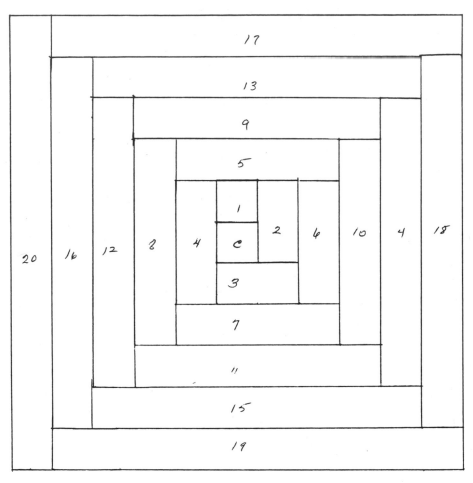

Illus. 122. Diagram of "Log Cabin" block. Add pieces in order according to the numbers, following either the half-square or the border arrangement of the lights and darks.

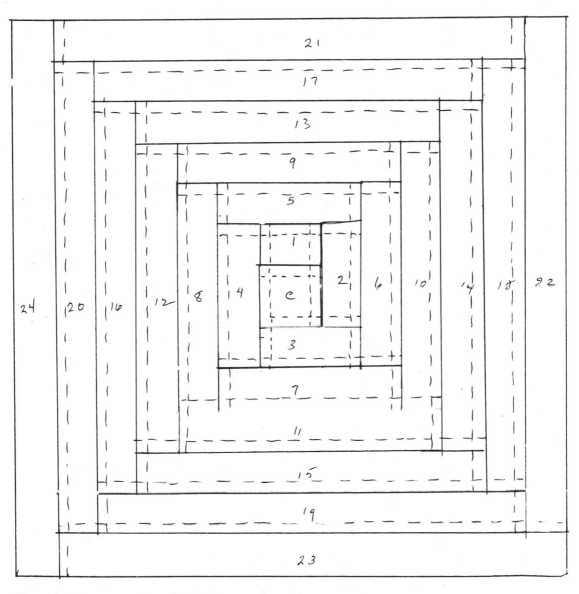

Illus. 123. Diagram for "Log Cabin" tracing template.
Finished pieces will be 1″ (25 mm) wide. The solid lines indicate the cut edge of the pieces when in place. The dash lines indicate the stitching line for each piece. They are used here for clarity, but are not needed when making your template. Mark very black lines in this manner on white paper or poster board. Trace the lines onto the block backs.

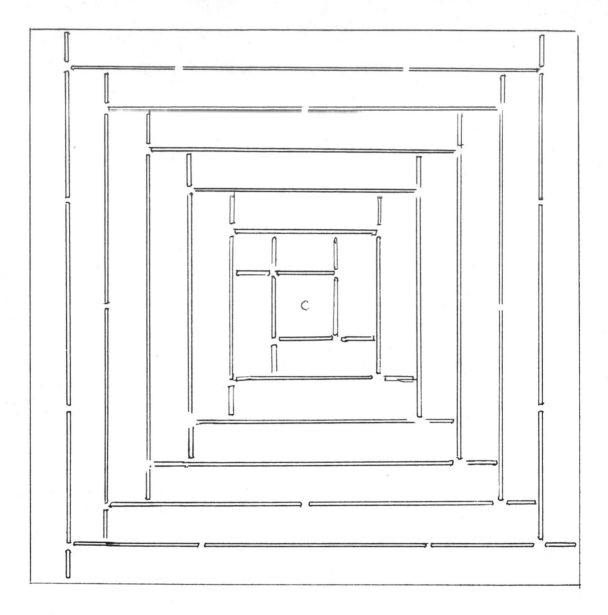

Illus. 124. Diagram for "Log Cabin" plastic template. Mark the diagram on plastic according to the size and number of pieces. Cut the slits ⅛" (4 mm), or less, wide. The edge nearer the middle should be the guide for the lines marked. Slits indicating the ends of the pieces may be omitted if you prefer. Place a metal-edged ruler along the line to be cut. Use a mat knife, a razor blade, or some other very sharp blade for cutting the slits. Cut both sides, then the ends of the slits. Long slits are in sections to add strength. The outside edges are the lines for the last pieces added.

Instructions for use — Lay the plastic template on the back, or lining, fabric and mark the lines through the slits, guiding the marker next to the edge nearest the middle. Lay the batting on the lining fabric. The lines should be dark enough to show through it. Place the central piece in the square marked for it. Its edges should touch the lines of the square. Pin it firmly in place.

Consult instructions on page 126.

There are two variations of the "Log Cabin" block. (All variations are often simply referred to as "Log Cabin.") The first variation is similar in appearance and construction to the original, and is called "Courthouse Steps." The difference be-

tween this and the usual "Log Cabin" is the order in which the strips are added around the center. "Logs" are added in adjoining pairs, while "steps" are added on opposite sides of the center square (see Illus. 125–128).

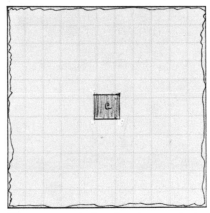

Fig. a. central piece in place on batting and back

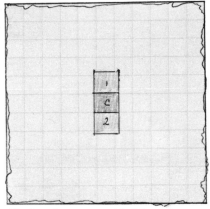

Fig. b. pieces are added in pairs on opposite sides of the central piece

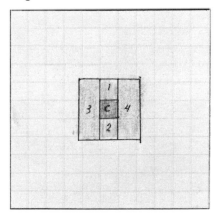

Fig. c.

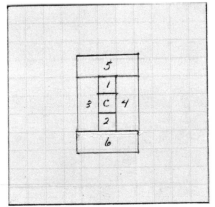

Fig. d.

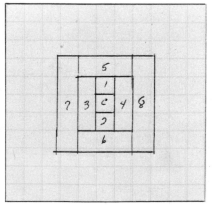

Fig. e.

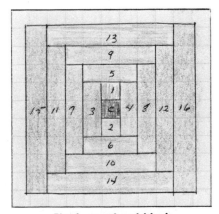

Fig. f. completed block

Illus. 125. Construction of "Courthouse Steps."

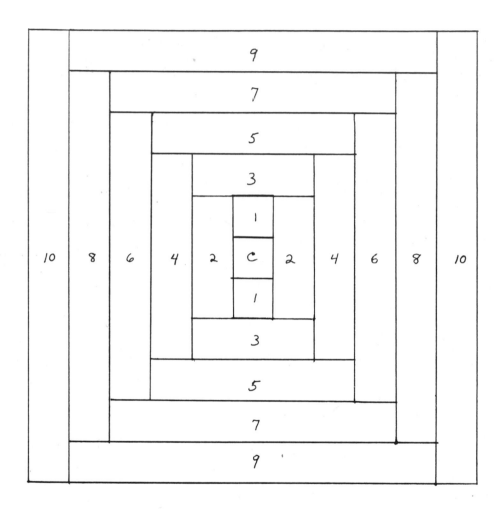

Illus. 126. Diagram of "Courthouse Steps."

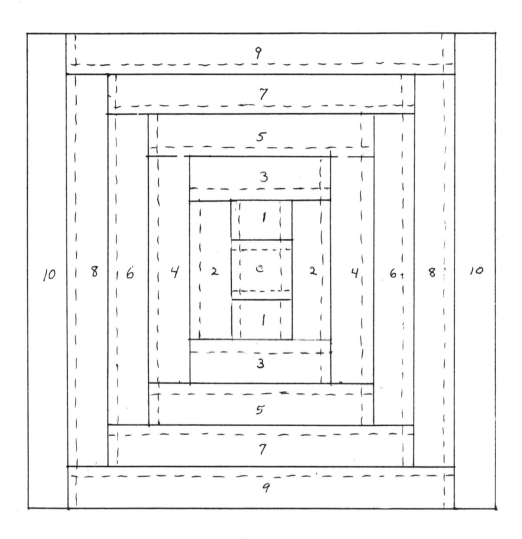

Illus. 127. Diagrams for "Courthouse Steps" tracing template. Finished pieces will be 1″ (25 mm) wide. Follow instructions in Illus. 123.

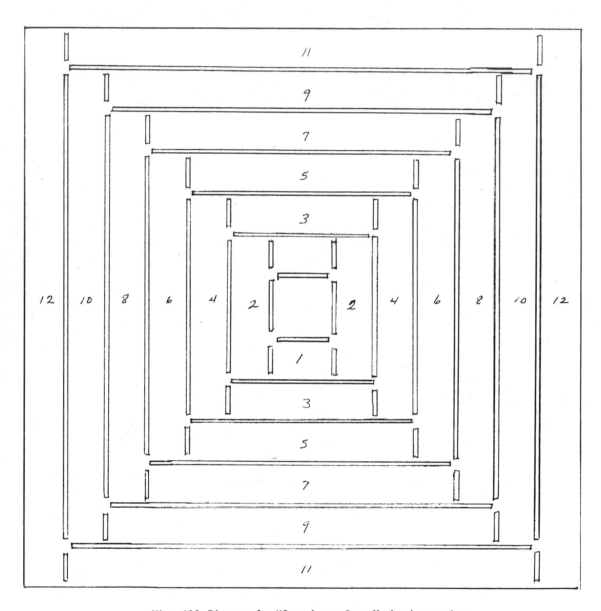

Illus. 128. Diagram for "Courthouse Steps" plastic template.
Follow instructions in Illus. 124.

The other variation of "Log Cabin" is called "Pineapple." It is quite different in appearance from the basic "Log Cabin," but the construction of the block is related (see Illus. 129). Pineapples are a favorite decoration in other crafts, also, and are found carved on bedposts and other furniture, and crocheted into lace table cloths. It is a symbol of hospitality, which is one reason for its frequent use in the home.

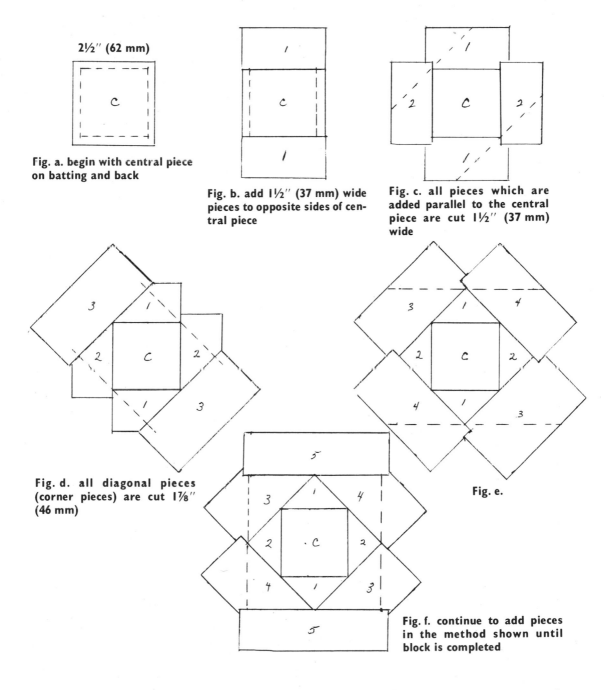

Fig. a. begin with central piece on batting and back

Fig. b. add 1½" (37 mm) wide pieces to opposite sides of central piece

Fig. c. all pieces which are added parallel to the central piece are cut 1½" (37 mm) wide

Fig. d. all diagonal pieces (corner pieces) are cut 1⅞" (46 mm)

Fig. e.

Fig. f. continue to add pieces in the method shown until block is completed

note: strips 1½" (37 mm) and 1⅞" (46 mm) long each can be cut for the pieces—cut off the length needed as they are sewed

Illus. 129. Construction of "Pineapple." Dash lines are stitching lines for next pieces.

When I first began thinking of "Log Cabin" as a half-square pattern (since it usually has a light triangular half and a dark one), it occurred to me that this block might be set together in a way similar to other half-square patterns—again, something I had not seen done. As I began to experiment with this idea, I became so caught up in it that I worked out several settings, either in arrangements of the block by itself in the same patterns used for half-squares, or in combination with setting blocks to create exciting new effects. I have included some of these here (see Illus. 130–131). The idea is far from exhausted by these and I am still having fun exploring other possibilities. I hope that these samples will stimulate your own ideas, not only for "Log Cabin," but for new settings and combinations of other patterns.

Fig. a.

Fig. b.

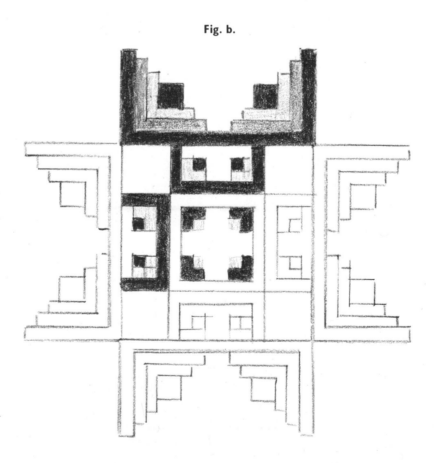

Illus. 130, 131. "Log Cabin" variations. (Fig. a.) "Log Cabin on the Square"—a group of four Log Cabin blocks with setting blocks of equal size. (Fig. b.) "Rising Log Cabin Star"—this can be set solid or with lattice to create quite different effects. Quarter-size blocks of two different color orders form the center of the star.

Puff Patterns

If you like to carry needlework with you, this is the type of quilt for you. The quilt can be made of small or large pieces. Before the pieces are put together, they will be finished individually, including backing and batting, and any quilting to be used will be done. The pieces will be of squares, triangles, rectangles or hexagons; or you may use a combination of shapes, such as octagons and squares or squares and triangles. They can be set together in any pattern which these shapes or combination of shapes would make if they were pieced in the usual way.

To make the pieces, first count on your diagram the number of each color that will be needed for the design you have chosen. Mark the pieces on the fabric. If the pieces are to be square, rectangular or triangular, they can be marked in a method similar to that which was described earlier in this book, by laying the fabric on your cutting board and marking the pieces with the use of a yardstick (meterstick). In this case,

however, the pieces will be marked on the stitching lines instead of on the cutting lines. To do this, measure and mark the exact measurement of the finished pieces and leave ½″ (12 mm) between each marked piece for the two seam allowances (see Illus. 132). It is not necessary to mark the cutting line between the pieces. Always mark the pieces on the *wrong* side of the fabric to be used for the back of the pieces. *Do not cut the pieces apart.* Stack the layers with the batting on the bottom, the fabric for the top of the pieces wrong side to the batting, and the fabric for the back of the pieces right side to the top fabric.

Hexagon and octagon shapes must be marked with a template. *Do not* include seam allowances in any templates for puff patterns. Mark the pieces on the wrong side of the fabric to be used for the backs of the pieces and assemble them as instructed above. This way, the seams will be next to the back of the pieces when they are finished.

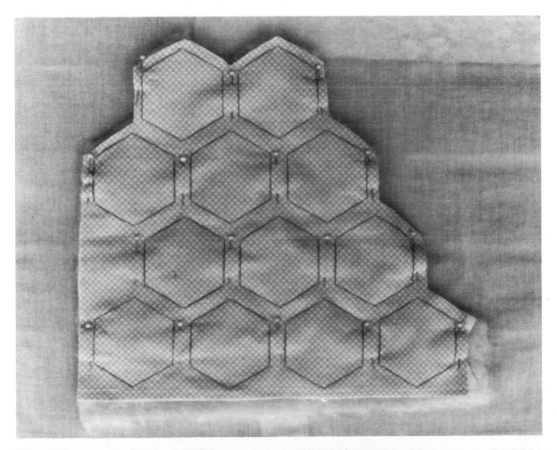

Illus. 132. Fabric marked for hexagon puffs, showing ½″ (12 mm) spaces left for seam allowances. Puffs are always marked on the stitching line instead of the cutting line, even for machine stitching.

Pin within the seam allowances, using enough pins to hold the layers firmly together. If a large number of pieces have been marked, cut the marked fabric (*after* it has been stacked and pinned for sewing) into sections of a size that is not awkward for you to handle (about 18″ to 24″ [45–60 cm] both ways). Cut between rows of pieces where the cutting line should be. The reason for working on small sections is that you will be turning the work frequently as you sew the pieces.

The special method I use makes it much easier to sew all these little pieces. You have been instructed not to cut the pieces apart. It is much easier and faster to sew around each one first, rather than to handle all the little pieces in the separate steps of marking, cutting, stacking in layers and pinning.

Begin the stitching at the approach to one corner of a piece and stitch all around that piece *on* the marked line. At each corner, set the needle into the corner, raise the presser foot and turn the work to the position needed to continue stitching. End the stitching a little beyond the last corner, leaving a space between the beginning and the end of the stitching large enough for turning the piece inside out. Be sure that there are at least a few stitches before the first corner and after the last corner to make a neater finish and to make the final slipstitching easier when you close the open space. Move to another piece and repeat this stitching process. Continue sewing pieces until you have stitched all of them like the first one.

Now we come to the part of the work that you can take along on trips and such. Trim off any extra fabric and batting around the edges, leaving a ¼″ (6 mm) seam allowance on all sides of the pieces. Cut halfway between the stitching on the pieces to separate them. At the same time, trim away any materials beyond the ¼″ (6 mm) seam allowances. It is not necessary to remove any batting from the seam allowances, since this extra soft bulk will make the puffs nice and puffier. Turn the pieces right side out through the opening left for this purpose. Close the opening with slip-stitching.

The pieces may be left unquilted if you like, but any quilting used should be done before the pieces are put together. If you like a lot of hand work to take along, you may hand quilt the pieces near the edges or with a small pattern in the middle of the piece. Otherwise, a small, simple pattern, such as a circle, may be machine quilted in the center of each piece or you may machine quilt ¼″ (6 mm) from the edges.

Lay out the colored pieces according to your pattern and slipstitch adjoining pieces together. You must slipstitch *both* the front edges and the back edges. If one is not stitched, it looks unfinished (see Illus. 133). Here is another piece of work to take along. Do not try to whipstitch all four layers (the two backs plus the two tops) at the same time as you hold the pieces together, because one side will be puffy at the seam but the other will not. Smaller stitches are required if it is done this way, so no time is actually saved. Sew the two

Illus. 133. Construction of a block of hexagon puffs: 2 unquilted; 2 with narrow quilting back; 3 with wide quilted border. Three are joined together. The two quilted ones are slipstitched together on both sides. The other one is slipstitched only on the back, leaving a space between the pieces on the front. This shows why both must be slipstitched.

tops or the two backs as they are held right sides together, stitching as near to the seam as you can.

By using a different group of fabrics on the backs of the puffs, you can have a reversible quilt in the same pattern but with a different color scheme. If you are very clever at planning and following your diagram, you can even create an entirely different design of the same shapes on the back of the quilt from that which is on the front (perhaps two versions of "Ohio Star" or "Grandmother's Flower Garden"). You will have to plan very carefully to have the right pairs of fabrics made into each puff. If you want to try this, make two color diagrams of the front design and two of the back design. Number all the pieces of one design (both copies alike). Lay one pair of diagrams aside to use as guides in checking the patterns later. The second pair of diagrams must be large enough (perhaps ½" [12 mm] or larger shapes) so that the individual shapes can be cut apart and handled easily. Cut away any paper outside the diagrams and paste the two diagrams together carefully, back to back, so that the patterns are in line. Mark every individual shape in the pattern for the top with an "X" so that you will not confuse the front and the back sides of the shapes after they are cut apart.

Cut the shapes apart and separate them by color. For instance, if the top of the quilt is to be made up in pink, green and yellow, and the back is to be red, white and blue, first separate the pink, the green and the yellow shapes into piles. An egg carton or other divided container is useful for this. Use a separate carton for each color. Then, work with the pink pieces, putting those with blue on the back in one section, those with white on the back in another section and those with red on the back in a different section. Do the same with the green shapes and with the yellow shapes. When you are finished, you will be able to count the number of finished pieces of each color combination and shape that will be needed.

Work with each combination separately in this manner: count the number of pink shapes with white backs that are needed. Mark the fabric for the back as described above and proceed to make these pieces. Then mark the pink pieces with blue backs, and so on until all the different combinations have been finished and are ready to set together. Keep the groups of finished pieces in separate plastic bags for convenience. Bags with a lock-type closing are ideal.

Paste your other diagrams together, back

to back, or fasten the edges together with tape so that one is positioned exactly on the other. Stick a pin in the first piece in the upper left corner. Suppose that it is pink. Look at the diagram on the other side to see the color of the piece with the pin (it should be in the upper right corner). Suppose that it is white. Select a finished pink piece with a white back and lay it nearby.

Now, stick the pin into the next shape to the right on the first row. Suppose that it is green on the front and blue on the back. Select a piece with those colors and sew it to the first piece. Leave the pin in place in the diagram while you sew. The pin and the pinholes will help you to keep your place as you proceed. Continue in this way until you have sewed all the pieces in the first row across the top of the quilt. Then, begin with the first piece on the left end in the second row and add the pieces in that row, one by one, to those in the first row and to the previous one in the second row. Continue to add row after row in this manner until all the pieces have been joined to form the quilt. This completes the quilt.

Here is a variation of the method just described. Piece or appliqué *full-size blocks* of any shape and pattern that pleases you, and then make them up by the puff method, finishing each block completely. Since these blocks will be larger than the simple pieces, you can work with them as separate units. Mark the fabric for the back, lay it on the batting, pin the two together and cut them as one. Add the completed top of the block right sides together with the back and stitch around the outside, leaving an opening for turning. Turn the block and slipstitch the opening closed. You will likely want to do more quilting on a full block than you would on small pieces. Do this in any type of quilting that you like before you put the blocks together. Sashing strips, setting blocks and borders can also be made up by this method and used with the blocks in the usual arrangement.

The Biscuit Quilt

The biscuit quilt, sometimes also called a puff quilt, is quite a different-looking quilt from any other, and equally different in construction (see Illus. 134). It is a one-patch type of pattern and is related to the puff quilt described above, in that the name designates the construction rather than indicates a pattern. Many different allover designs may be created with these pieces, simply by the way the different colored biscuits are set together. They can be

Fig. a. lining piece

Fig. b. top piece

Fig. c. fullness eased in

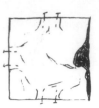

Fig. d. fullness pleated in

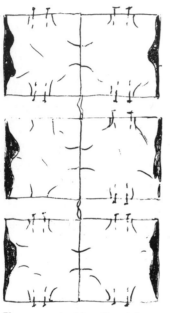

Fig. e. empty biscuits string-sewed

Fig. g. a stuffed biscuit

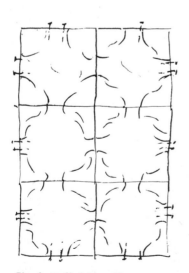

Fig. f. stuffed biscuits

Fig. h. biscuit pillow top (a pillow would be filled between the biscuits and the back, but no batting is used in a quilt besides the stuffed biscuits)

Illus. 134. Construction of biscuit quilt.

joined to resemble any pattern that is made up of squares (rectangular biscuits could also be made, but I have never seen this). The design should be kept quite simple for the best effect.

The pieces can be made of any size that is practical, but are usually about 3″ to 4″ (7.5–10 cm) square for the lining piece. The top of the biscuit is made about 1½″ (37 mm) or more larger in both directions than the lining. Larger biscuits may need even more extra fabric in the top piece to get the raised look you want. Cut these pieces by the same method that you used for the one-patch patterns, such as "Patience" in Section 2.

Fit the top piece to the lining piece, *wrong* sides together. One way to do this is to case in the extra fabric in the top piece by basting the two together on three sides. An easier way is to pin two little pleats, spaced a little distance apart and turned toward the corners, along three sides of the piece. One side is left open for stuffing, which is to be done later. String-sew the pieces, right sides together, in pairs of rows with ¼″ (6 mm) seam, using your diagram to show you which colors to join together. Next, sew the pairs of pieces together with ¼″ (6 mm) crossways seams. Now, you have strips of two rows of pieces which are open on opposite sides of the strips. Use equal size pieces of polyester batting or fluff to stuff each biscuit. Pin the little pleats or ease in the extra fullness along the open sides. Join the strips of stuffed pieces with ¼″ (6 mm) seams. This will leave the two outside edges still not stitched. These edges can simply be bound. A back can be added to the quilt to be bound on the edges, or it can be pillowcased and turned. The back should be tacked between the biscuits to hold it in place.

Cathedral Window

"Cathedral Window" has such a strong appeal to people today that separate classes are taught for this pattern only. I have included this pattern in this section because it is made up of small units which are joined to make the top. Large areas of space are not required for its construction, so you can take it along with you easily.

"Cathedral Window" is traditionally made of unbleached muslin which is folded and stitched over small squares of print fabric. Other color combinations are now being used also. No batting is used in the construction and, by the strictest definition, no real quilting is done. For these

reasons, it is not a true "quilt." However, this in no way dampens most quilters' enthusiasm for the pattern.

About half of the work can be done easily by machine, which saves you a lot of time. After the fabric has been washed, straighten it as much as you can when ironing because it is better to have the large squares cut on the grain of the fabric both ways. The squares should measure 9″ (22 cm) if cut. If you prefer to tear 100% cotton fabric, the seam allowances should be ½″ (12 mm), so tear 9½″ (23.7 cm) squares. The finished squares will be about 4″ (10 cm) after folding. Two small squares of print, not less than 2½″ (6 cm) across, will be needed for each large square that is cut. Follow the diagrams in Illustration 135 as you read these instructions.

Fold the large square in half on the straight of the fabric and sew a ¼″ (6 mm) seam across each end (Illus. 135-a, -b). Now open the resulting "envelope" (Illus. 135-c) and bring the ends of these two seams together and pin them right sides together (Illus. 135-d). Two new folds will result from bringing the raw edges together. Stitch from each fold to about ¾″ (18 mm) from the pinned seam, leaving an opening (Illus. 135-e). Turn the piece right side out through the opening (Illus. 135-f). This is usually slipstitched closed, but you can machine stitch it. Set the stitch length for about 14 stitches to the inch (25 mm). Set the stitch width for about one-fourth the width of the zigzag. Lay the piece with the turned-under edges of the opening one on the other. Stitch so that the needle goes alternately into the very edges of the fabric and then off the edge (Illus. 135-g). This is a little like overcasting the edges together, but when the piece is opened, the seam will lie flat (Illus. 135-h). These stitches will be covered later.

You now have a square with bias folded edges. Fold the corners in so that they meet in the center over the intersection of the machine-stitched seams, and make a crease in the fabric at each fold line (Illus. 135-i). Lay two squares like this back to back and sew a seam along one crease only, to join the two squares (color page D). Around one of these squares, join three more squares. Fill in the corners with other squares and add more rows of squares. Before the piece becomes too large, begin joining the loose corners. Bring the four loose corners of one square to meet in the middle of the square and tack them together. Repeat this on all the inside squares. Leave the loose corners on the outside squares free so that

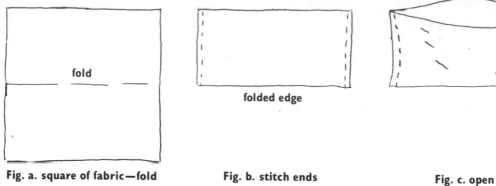

Fig. a. square of fabric—fold

folded edge

Fig. b. stitch ends

Fig. c. open

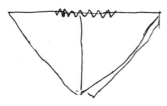

Fig. d. bring seams together

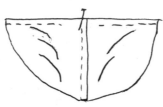

Fig. e. stitch from folds at end to leave opening on each side of seam

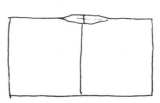

Fig. f. turn right side out through opening

Fig. g. overcast opening closed with narrow zigzag stitching (catch only the edges of the opening)

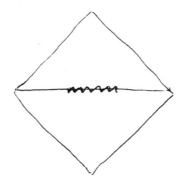

Fig. h. seam will lie flat

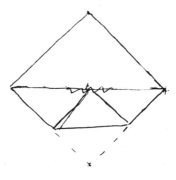

Fig. i. fold corners to the middle and press

Illus. 135. Construction of "Cathedral Window."

other squares can be machine stitched to them later.

Now, work with those squares whose points or corners have been tacked together in the middle. Lay a square of print fabric over one of the seams which joins two squares. Turn the bias edges of the two corners of the folded square over the raw edges of the print square to cover them. Slipstitch the turned edge to the print square (color page D). The stitches should not catch so deep that you cannot slip your finger under two opposite corners of the print square. In this same way, add another print square over each seam which joins two larger squares. Add more large squares as needed and finish them with the print squares until the piece is as large as you want it.

Secret Garden

A variation of this pattern, which I have not seen anywhere else, is one I call "Secret Garden." Make the large squares the same way as described above, using a small green-and-white-print fabric. Sew the squares together across the corners as directed. Before joining the points of the square in the center, add a bright solid-colored square. This square piece should be cut large enough so that it measures the same as the distance between the seams that join the larger squares. Lay this bright square in that area and backstitch around the edges. Tack the points of the folded square together over it. Turn back the bias edges of the corners in the same way as before (no small square will be included this time) and slipstitch them down to the loose corner. When this is done on each bias edge, it will reveal a hidden four-petaled flower underneath (see Illus. 136). The flowers may be made of one color or of many colors, arranged either into a pattern or randomly placed in a casual manner like wild flowers scattered across a green field.

Illus. 136. Construction of "Secret Garden."

SECTION 7
Seminole Piecing and Hawaiian Quilting

SEMINOLE PIECING

The Seminole Indians, who live in the swampy Everglades of southeastern Florida, are a small branch of the Creeks. Having separated themselves from all other Indian groups, they have developed a completely distinctive art of patchwork. Their intricate designs have been developed since about 1920 and are directly related to the introduction of the sewing machine in 1880. Without this tool it is very doubtful that this fascinating type of piecing would ever have developed, for it would be impractical to do by hand.

Seminole women work with strips of solid-colored fabrics. I have seen prints used in the same ways by other people, and the results are attractive but in a different way—the authentic feeling of the piece is lost.

The fabrics usually used for quilts lend themselves perfectly to Seminole piecing. Though these designs were originally used on clothing, they have, in recent years, been adapted for use on other items, including quilts. The interest in these patterns is growing rapidly for obvious reasons: the designs are very interesting, and the color combinations are usually strong and lively and are handled with a feeling and a skill for playing one hue against another for greatest effect.

Seminole piecing looks very intricate and tedious to construct. This is deceptive, however, for the clever methods that are used make it much easier than you might imagine. The ¼" (6 mm) pieces are not that size when the seams are sewed. Instead, they are much longer and quite easy to handle. Two or more long, narrow strips are sewed together like stripes. These are cut crossways and the resulting pieces are sewed together to create the various designs. Some of the designs are quite simple,

while others are more involved, but the basic methods are the same for all. Once you understand the steps in the construction of the designs, you may find yourself creating some of your own.

Some of the patterns which follow are accompanied by diagrams that show how to cut and piece them. These are taken from actual examples of the work, though I have seen some variations in the proportions and some adaptations and modifications of the patterns. Any of the measurements could be changed, if you so desire, to create innumerable variations for each

Illus. 137. A Seminole-design pillow. (See also Illus. 140 and color page B.)

144

one. The scale can be enlarged or, in some cases, decreased, to suit the project you have in mind.

The patterns given can be used as lattice or borders for quilts. They would be effective used alternately with plain bands around a pieced, plain, or appliquéd medallion. Start with these easy patterns and advance, as your interest leads you, to more involved ones. I am sure you will become more intrigued as you do so.

In planning your color combinations, you can work your designs out on graph paper. Plan the size and color of each strip and how the strips will be sewed together, cut and then pieced to make the final design. Be sure to plan for the seam allowances required also.

For your first project, it might be wise to enlarge the scale of the pieces to make them easier to work with while you are learning the methods. For other projects, use a scale that suits the item, or one that will give the effect you want.

String-sew the long strips of fabric and press the seams. If two different combinations of strips are to be used, press the seams so that they will lie in opposite directions when the segments are sewed. Mark the segments with a template, then string-sew the segments in pairs. Cut the pairs apart and string-sew pairs together. For some patterns, this will complete the design. For others, continue to string-sew groups of segments until the band is completed.

Where small pieced squares are set into unpieced setting strips, add setting strips or setting pieces to opposite sides of the squares. Then join these like segments, matching the corners of the squares.

Pieced bands are bordered with plain fabrics so that they look like stripes of pattern in a solid color fabric. The illustration for the pillow shows you how to do this.

Fabrics which are a blend of 65 per cent polyester and 35 per cent cotton ravel badly on the raw edges—much worse than 100 per cent cotton usually does. The fabric is also quite soft, as a rule, after it has been washed. I like to starch it (spray starch works well) before cutting it and also spray starch when pressing seams as I sew. This gives more body to the fabric and helps keep raveling to a minimum.

All strips should be cut crossways from the fabric, which is a little stretchy in that direction. This helps when matching seams on tiny pieces, for if there is a slight difference in the width of the piece, the narrower one will "give" a little to adjust to the wider one.

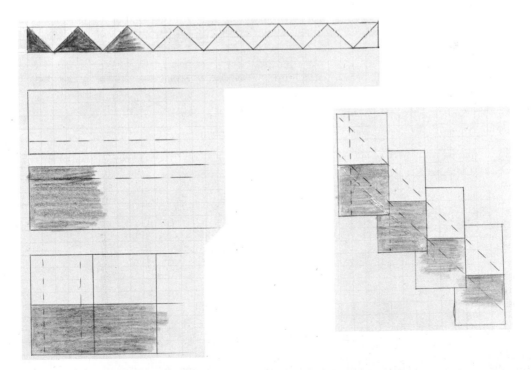

Illus. 138. A Seminole pattern with construction diagrams.

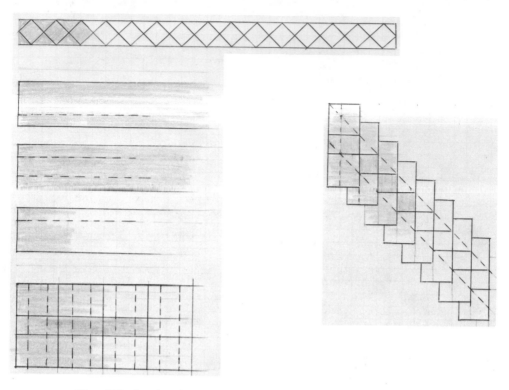

Illus. 139. Another Seminole pattern with construction diagrams.

Illus. 140. Section of pattern for Seminole pillow shown in Illus. 137. The design may be enlarged for use as a "Stripey" quilt, since Seminole patterns are especially suited for these quilts.

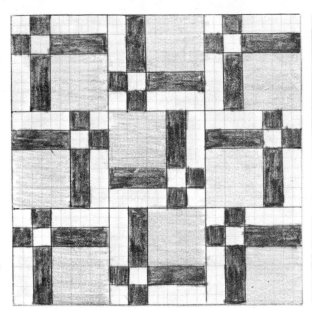

Fig. a. a group of nine Seminole blocks turned four ways and set solid—notice the windmill created where the corners come together.

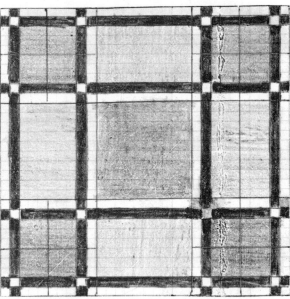

Fig. c. group of four of the same block turned differently and set with a pieced stripe block the same size and a plain block in the center—all are the same size blocks.

Fig. b. groups of four of the same block set solid in a different design.

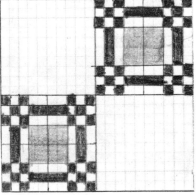

Fig. d. four-block group of a different design set with plain blocks.

Illus. 141. Seminole designs adapted to quiltmaking. Each design can be repeated as needed for full quilt size. Border is optional. Most Seminole block designs can be adapted to these arrangements. The blocks can be made large or small to achieve the desired effect. (Variations adapted by author.)

HAWAIIAN QUILTING

The ingenious women of Hawaii have developed a style of quilting all their own. Its mood is as lovely and carefree as the land in which they live. The patterns are taken from the flowers and other natural forms which are so profusely evident on the islands. They have both a strength and a delicacy which cannot fail to appeal to all who see this distinctive type of quilting, for they reflect the air of freedom and openness of the people. The designs are quite intricate, while the construction is comparatively simple, though certainly not easy when executed by hand. The women of Hawaii frown upon the use of the sewing machine for this work. However, the visual effect of the lovely color combinations and the fanciful designs is virtually the same when done by machine as when done by the traditional methods. The time required is considerably less, of course, but care and skill are still important for fine workmanship.

Hawaiian quilting is a type of appliqué. Sometimes the design is appliquéd to the quilt top. At other times the "background" may be appliquéd to the design, instead—this is called reverse appliqué. Many design variations have been extensively explored by these talented women. The design may have only one large central pattern, with or without a border. It may be bound. The edges of the quilts I have seen are always straight. The border, when used, may be quite simple or it may have an elaborate pattern which is closely related to the central motif. A large- or medium-sized central pattern may be surrounded by a related pattern which does not reach the edge of the quilt. A medium-sized central design may be adapted for use in the four corners of the quilt also.

Hawaiian quilters may use two values of one color or two entirely different colors. Usually only two colors are included, though a third may be introduced as an accent. The lighter color, whether it is used for the design or for the background, is usually placed on the bottom because the darker color tends to show through the lighter one. (In cases where this would not occur, either color could be used on top.) If the design is on the lighter color, and so on the bottom, it is set into the darker color which is appliquéd to it. (This is reverse appliqué because the "background" is appliquéd to the pattern.)

Although Hawaiian quilters cling to the tradition of an all-handmade quilt, the machine is being used by other quilters. This type of design is being adapted to block-size for easier handling and used for quilts, pillows and other items. I recently saw a very beautiful machine-appliquéd quilt which was hand quilted and had taken a Best of Show prize.

Hawaiian quilters make no two patterns alike, and it is forbidden to appropriate someone else's design. Even if permission is given to use one, a small change, at least, is made so that the pattern is a little different from the original. Do not hesitate, therefore, to make your own designs. Perhaps you would like to turn to the flowers or foliage of your own locale for inspiration, as the Hawaiians have done. Keep the patterns very simple, whatever you choose.

Whether you make your own designs or use ones you have seen, the method for cutting the pattern is the same. Use a piece of paper that is the size the design is to be. Fold it in half twice to a fourth of the original size. Fold once more to make a triangular shape. Draw the design on the triangular-folded paper and cut it out—or cut it as you go (see Illus. 142). When you are satisfied with your pattern, cut two pieces of fabric the same size as the finished piece will be. Include seam allowances on all sides. Unfold the pattern and pin it to the lighter fabric. Draw the entire design on this fabric, even if you intend the design to be made from the other color.

Pin the two layers of fabric together along the lines of the design. Then, stitch all around the design with tiny stitches. Now, you may trim away *either* fabric, leaving the desired color appliquéd to the other color. Thus, if you want a light-colored design, trim away the dark fabric within the design and leave the light fabric showing. Satin stitch on the dark fabric with thread to match either color. If you want a light background, trim away the dark fabric outside of the design. This way, no dark fabric can show through the lighter one. Here, also, satin stitch on the dark fabric. The tiny stitches will help prevent raveling along the cut edge, even though you trim very close to the stitching. A narrow satin stitch looks best. A contrasting color might be very attractive, but it would not have the same visual effect as the Hawaiian designs.

Sometimes a difficulty arises because the zigzag satin stitching tends to draw the fabric together under the stitching. This is one reason for using a narrow satin stitch. Iron-on interfacing or typing paper under the fabric may prevent this. If this doesn't

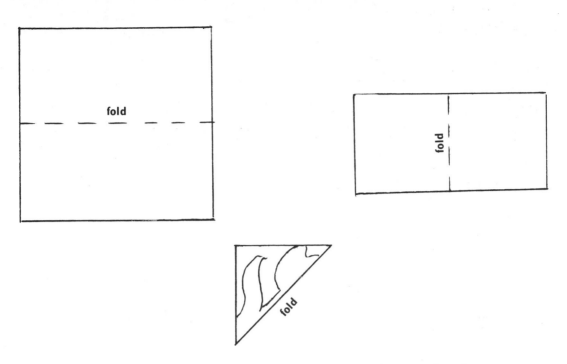

Illus. 142. To cut a Hawaiian design, mark design on folded paper and cut it out.

work, try using a hoop while satin stitching. You may prefer to try this before the iron-on interfacing, which tends to stiffen the fabric.

Quilt blocks may be quilted as a unit and the blocks joined afterward (see Section 6). This would be the easiest method. A small quilt might be assembled by the pillowcase method or bound and then quilted by machine. It would be difficult to quilt a very large piece by machine because of the way the quilting is done. Hawaiian quilting follows the lines of the design, both within the pattern and on the background, so that the quilting echoes the pattern, like the waves of the ocean around an island (which is what it is intended to resemble). The quilting is begun near the appliqué stitching and continued in an *unbroken line* (it is considered bad luck to break the quilting line), easing over from one row to the next until the entire area is quilted or until it meets the "ripples" from the border or another part of the design. The rows of stitching are done a finger's width apart, but this sometimes varies.

I have included some of my own designs for your inspiration (see Illus. 144). You are welcome to use them if you want to. If you like the idea of making at least a small change when doing so, change the length or size of some shape; indent a curve more or make it more shallow. Perhaps a small part may be omitted or something added to comply with custom.

Illus. 143. One block for a Hawaiian sampler quilt.

TULIP

IRIS

ROSE BOUQUET

ROSE GARDEN

Illus. 144. Some Hawaiian designs.

IRIS GARDEN

SECTION 8

Figuring Yardage

There are several ways of deciding how much fabric to buy for a quilt. The simplest of these is to guess. This sounds rather haphazard, but if you find fabric you cannot pass up for possible future use, it is better to guess than to have no rule of thumb at all to guide you.

TWO WAYS TO "GUESTIMATE"

If I am in doubt as to how much fabric to buy and have no particular pattern in mind, but just like the color or print, I usually buy 4 yards (meters). This is long enough for even a king-size quilt border with some left over for pieces of the pattern as well. Three and a half yards (meters) are enough for other size borders with some left over for pieces. When the time comes to use the fabric, if I do not need 3 or 4 yards (meters), I consider the extra fabric as a bonus to be used on another project.

If I am buying fabric for a pattern I have in mind, but do not have time to figure the yardage, I estimate. I know from experience, or can very quickly estimate, the amount of fabric required for the back of the quilt in the size I want to make. I then study the pattern and decide what percentage of the entire top, or even of a single block, is made from a certain fabric in the pattern. In the case of "Rail Fence," for instance, it might be ⅓ or ¼ of the area, not including the border. In the case of "Nine-Patch," it might be ¼ or ⅕ of the area, not including border and lattice.

If I buy enough fabric to equal that portion of the yardage required for the back, I am fairly safe. For example, if the back required 9 yards (meters) (three lengths—for a double bed) I would know that part of that fabric would be left over after the back was made. Then, if the pieces covered

⅓ of the area of the top, 3 yards (meters) of fabric would be enough, even though many seam allowances which do not show must also be provided for. This is an educated guess, of course, because I know that fabric is usually left over after making the back of a quilt, so that the fabric bought for it is more than is actually used. Thus, ⅓ of the area of the top might not be more than ¼ of the fabric bought for the back. The difference will cover the extra material needed for the seam allowances of the pieces. I take into consideration possible shrinkage and any extra material needed to straighten the end of the fabric. These things gradually become "second nature" to the quilter. If I feel that my guess is a little close, I usually buy a little extra fabric just to be on the safe side. Granted, these are rough estimates, but they serve pretty well and any leftover fabric can always go into a small project, such as a pillow or lap quilt.

There are times when it is important to know within a few inches (50 mm) the amount of fabric needed. These are the times to sit down with pen and paper and take the time to figure just what is required. It is not difficult if you understand the process and follow the steps required to arrive at the correct figures. It does take quite a bit of time, however, for the more involved pattern. Sometimes it is necessary to figure the exact amount for only one fabric which is in limited supply at the shop or in your own collection. When a large purchase is involved, you may want to figure all the yardage very closely.

In order for you to have a picture of the various parts of the quilt which are involved in figuring the measurements and the yardage, draw a rough diagram of the quilt you plan to make. Indicate the pieced blocks and any setting blocks, sashing or borders that will be included. Using this diagram as a guide, you can proceed to figure all the information you will need for planning the actual size of the quilt and all the parts. Sometimes, such things as whether or not to use lattice or how wide to make the lattice or the border must be adjusted to fit the number of blocks required for the pattern. For some patterns, such as "Windmill," an even number of blocks across and down is needed to balance the pattern. In other cases there must be an odd number, as for "Nine-Patch" with setting blocks. Sometimes the block itself must be made larger or smaller to fit the size limit of the quilt, especially the width. When you have come to a decision about all these things, make a finished color diagram of the quilt and you are ready to figure the yardage required.

FINDING THE ACTUAL MEASUREMENTS OF THE QUILT

First, we will consider what is involved in a simple quilt having only pieced blocks. Later we will look at the more complicated setting arrangements and variations.

Suppose that you would like your "Rail Fence" quilt to be approximately 94" x 108" (235 x 270 cm), and you plan for the blocks to be 9" (22.5 cm) square, *finished* size. *Do not* include seam allowances in figuring the measurements of parts of the quilt top. Seam allowances *will* be included when figuring yardage, of course. The width of the quilt is less adaptable than the length because the length of the quilt on the bed can be adjusted where the quilt tucks under the pillow, but the width must be accurate in relation to the distance from the floor. If the size or the number of blocks cannot be made to fit within the needed width, some alternatives in regard to lattice or border may be considered. Otherwise, a change from full-spread size to coverlet size or vice versa may be necessary. There are certain patterns which simply will not fit into a given area and a different pattern must be chosen in these cases.

To estimate the quilt size, begin with the measurement of the mattress and add the distance to the floor (the drop) on three sides, as well as the amount to be tucked under the pillow on the fourth side. A double-bed mattress is 54" x 75" (135 x 187.5 cm). If a drop of 20" (50 cm) is desired (measure yours, since there is a lot of variation in the height of the mattress from the floor), that would make the quilt 94" x 108" (235 x 270 cm) with 13" (32.5 cm) to

tuck under the pillow. We will start with that measurement and divide the block size into the width to find how many blocks are needed across the quilt.

$$
\begin{array}{r}
\text{number of blocks} \\
10 = \text{across the quilt} \\
\text{(block size) } 9\,\overline{)\,94''}\text{ (quilt width)} \\
90 \\
\hline
4'' = \text{left over}
\end{array}
$$

$$
\left(\begin{array}{r}
10 \\
22.5\text{ cm}\,\overline{)\,235\text{ cm}}
\end{array}\right)
$$

The 4" (10 cm) can be divided into two 2" (5 cm) borders. If you must have an odd number of blocks, or if this makes no difference but you would like a wider border, use nine blocks across and add the 9" (22.5 cm) from the tenth block to the borders, which will give you two borders 6½" (16 cm) wide.

Now that these measurements are established, proceed to figure the measurements of the length of the quilt, which we would like, in this case, to be about 108" (270 cm).

$$
\begin{array}{r}
\text{number of blocks} \\
\text{down the length of} \\
12 = \text{the quilt} \\
\text{(block size) } 9\,\overline{)\,108''}\text{ quilt length} \\
9 \\
\hline
18 \\
18 \\
\hline
0
\end{array}
$$

$$
\left(\begin{array}{r}
12 \\
22.5\text{ cm}\,\overline{)\,270\text{ cm}}
\end{array}\right)
$$

We find that the quilt will be 12 blocks long by 10 blocks wide, totalling 120 blocks in the quilt. Four inches (10 cm) must be added to the length for the two borders, which will make the length of the quilt 112" (280 cm). Again, you have the choice of using one less block for the reasons mentioned above, but it must be eliminated in both directions or the border will be affected.

Let us say that we now know that the quilt will be 94" x 112" (235 x 280 cm) with 2" (5 cm) borders and that the pattern is "Rail Fence" with four stripes. The fabrics we have selected are all 45" (112.5 cm) wide, not including selvages.

FIGURING THE YARDAGE FOR THE QUILT BACK

The first thing we want to figure is the amount of fabric needed for the quilt back.

If the back is to be no wider than the fabric, one length of fabric would be enough. If the back is wider than the fabric, two or three lengths of fabric would be needed. (For sewing the back, see Section 5.) In the case we are working on in this section, our quilt is wider than two widths of the fabric, so three lengths must be purchased (3 x 112″ = 336″ or 9 yards and 12″) [3 x 280 cm = 840 cm or 8 m and 40 cm]. Add about 4″ (10 cm) for straightening the fabric and 9″ to 10″ (22.5–25 cm) for 3 per cent shrinkage, and we have the figure of 9 yards 26″ (8 m 77 cm), so we will buy 9¾ yards (approximately 9 meters) of fabric for the back.

FIGURING THE YARDAGE FOR THE PIECES OF THE BLOCKS

Now we will figure the amount of fabric needed for the top. Since the pattern is "Rail Fence" with four stripes, this means that we will need one pattern piece cut from each of four different fabrics for each block. Our quilt is to have 120 blocks, so 120 pieces of each of four fabrics will be needed. These pieces will measure 2¾″ (2.75″) x 9½″ (9.5″) [6.8 x 23.7 cm] *cut size*—that is, including seam allowances. The width of the fabric is 45″ (112.5 cm), so we will divide 45″ (112.5 cm) by 2.75″ (6.8 cm) to find the number of pieces which can be cut across the width of the fabric.

$$
\begin{array}{r}
16. = \text{number of pieces} \\
2.75″)\overline{45.00″} \\
27\ 5 \\
\overline{17\ 50} \\
15\ 50 \\
\overline{2.00} = \text{left (not enough for}
\end{array}
$$
another piece)

$$
\left(\begin{array}{r} 16. \\ 6.8\,\text{cm})\overline{112.5\,\text{cm}} \end{array} \right)
$$

We find that a strip of 16 pieces can be cut across the width of the fabric. We now need to know how many of these strips of 16 pieces are needed to cut all the pieces required. We will divide the 16 pieces into the total number of pieces needed to find the answer.

$$
\begin{array}{r}
7 = \text{full widths} \\
16)\overline{120} \\
112 \\
\overline{8} = \text{pieces still to be cut}
\end{array}
$$

We find that 7 full crossways strips of 16 pieces will be needed and that 8 more

pieces must be cut on another strip, so a total of 8 strips will be needed.

The length of the piece is 9.5″ (23.7 cm). Since we need 8 strips of this measurement, we multiply 9.5″ (23.7 cm) x 8 to find the yardage

$$
\begin{array}{r}
9.5″ \\
8 \\
\overline{76.0″} = 2 \text{ yds.} + 4″
\end{array}
$$

$$
\left(\begin{array}{r}
23.7\,\text{cm} \\
\text{x } 8 \\
\overline{189.6\,\text{cm}} = 1\,\text{m} + 89.6\,\text{cm (approx. 2 m)}
\end{array} \right)
$$

Most fabrics will shrink as much as 3 per cent, so you must add a little more than 1″ (25 mm) for each yard (meter) of fabric to allow for this. If the fabric has been cut from the bolt at an angle, more inches (millimeters) are needed to allow for straightening the ends. We will add 7″ (17.5 cm) for these reasons, making 2 yards plus 11″ (2 meters plus 7 cm). This is the amount we will need of each of four different fabrics to make the blocks for the quilt.

When figuring the yardage for your own quilt, just *substitute your own measurements* for those used above for the quilt size, block size, size of pieces (rectangular or square) and width of fabric, and you will be able to figure the amount of fabric needed for square or rectangular pieces in any pattern.

If triangular pieces are used, draw the triangle pattern just as it is done in Section 3, Illustration 37 (on page 54), including the seam allowances. Measure the square or rectangle formed by two of these triangles and use these measurements for figuring the yardage.

Remember that there are two triangles to the square or rectangle, so you would plan for only half as many of the squares or rectangles as the number of triangles that is needed. For instance, if 138 triangles are needed, figure the fabric needed to cut 69 squares or rectangles which will then be divided into triangles.

Other pieces can often be adapted to the shape of a square or a rectangle for the purpose of estimating yardage by drawing the pieces on a square or rectangular shape and estimating the yardage for that shape (see Illus. 145).

For some pattern pieces, it is easier to mark a strip on paper that is half the width of the fabric and measure the number of pieces which will fit into that strip, then figure the number of strips needed to cut the number of pieces required. Shelf-lining

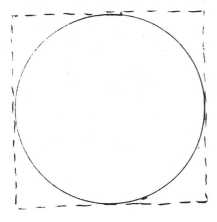
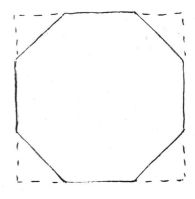

some pieces will fit into a square—
estimate the yardage for that square

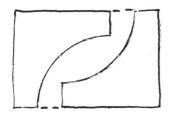
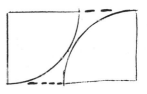

some pieces fit into a rectangle—measure
yardage for the number of rectangles
needed

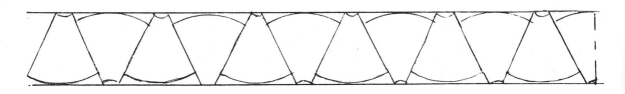

some pieces can best be measured in strips—count the number of pieces that will fit in a strip across
the fabric and figure the yardage for the number of strips required to cut the number of pieces
needed

Illus. 145. Estimating yardage for odd-shaped pieces.

paper or sheets of newsprint or computer print-out paper may be used for this. To figure pieces marked on a strip of paper, first make a template of the piece, including the seam allowances. On a large piece of paper, draw lines to indicate the width of the fabric, either folded or unfolded. Draw another line joining the first two lines as though you are straightening the end of the fabric. Then, using the template, mark the paper with the piece shapes, fitting them together to the best advantage as you would mark them on the fabric. Mark a strip of these shapes across the paper and count how many of them can be drawn in that width of fabric. Draw a line across the bottom of the strip of pieces. Measure the distance between the "straightening" line and this last line to find the lengthwise measurement of the strip. From these two figures, you can determine the yardage. For example: if 15 pieces can be cut across the width of the strip or fabric, and 70 pieces are needed, divide 15 into 70 and you will find that 4 full crossways strips are needed, plus 10 pieces must be cut from a part of another strip. So, 5 strips are needed in all. If the lengthwise measurement of the strip is 5″ (12.5 cm), multiply that by 5 strips, which equals 25″ (62.5 cm) of fabric needed for cutting the number of pieces required. Be sure to add a little extra for shrinkage and for straightening the end of the fabric.

Figuring yardage for hexagons presents a slightly different situation because hexagons fit together at an angle when marked in one position and overlap when marked in the other direction. Study the diagram in Illustration 146 to guide you. Circles may also be figured in this way more accurately than by adapting them to squares. Notice that after you figure the number of strips needed, half the measurement of the hexagon (or circle) must be added to the sum of the strips because half the figure overlaps the strip each time onto the following strip. On the final strip, there is no "following strip" so this half of the figure must be added extra.

FIGURING THE YARDAGE FOR OTHER PARTS OF THE QUILT

The Border

Quilts have other parts besides the pieced blocks. The border is the most common addition. Very often there is enough fabric left over from the side pieces cut from the quilt back to make the border, if you want it to be of that fabric. These pieces will already be the length needed for the side borders, so their use for this purpose can be very economical. You need only measure the width of two pieces to see if there is enough to cut the width (plus seam allowances) of the four border strips. When these have been cut, there is often additional fabric left, from which pieces of the blocks can be cut if you want to do so.

If the border is to be of a different fabric from the back, you will need the same amount of fabric as the length of the quilt plus 4″ (10 cm) for ease in handling the mitered corners if you are using these.

Setting Blocks

Plain blocks are often used alternately with pieced blocks. These are setting blocks. They are the same size and shape as the pieced ones. They are usually cut from muslin or solid colors, but prints are sometimes used. The plain fabric offers an opportunity to display a quilting design. The yardage for these plain blocks is figured in the same way as for any other square. Your diagram will tell you the size and number needed. If the setting block is of any other shape than square, figure the yardage in the same way as you would for that shape.

The Lattice or Sashing

Lattice pieces are long rectangles, so the yardage for them is figured by the method for that shape. There are sometimes little corner squares used at what might be called the "crossroads" of the lattice strips. These are, of course, figured like the squares. Consult your diagram, as usual, for the size and number of pieces required. Lattice, and borders also, are sometimes pieced instead of plain. In this case, yardage must be figured for the pieces instead of for the solid strips.

Borders on Blocks

Sometimes each block has its own border in addition to or in place of sashing. The pieces for this are, again, rectangles and squares and the yardage for them is figured by the method used for those shapes. Your diagram is your guide to the size and number you will need.

FIGURING THE MEASUREMENTS OF QUILTS WITH LATTICE AND BLOCK BORDERS

The quilt which has lattices and borders on blocks is more complicated to plan

Fig. a. if hexagons are marked with the flat side at the top:

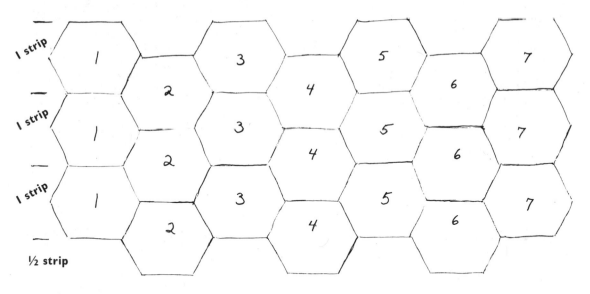

Fig. b. when hexagons are marked with the point at the top, figure repeats of strips of the length indicated and add the length of the point area extra.

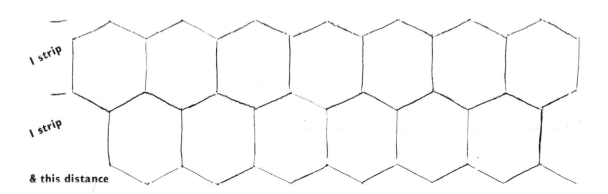

Illus. 146. Figuring yardage for hexagons. There are seven hexagons to the strip. The width to figure is equal to the length of the hexagon. Figure repeats of that width of fabric, then add ½ of the width to allow for the hexagons that extend below the strip.

when it comes to figuring the number of blocks required for a quilt of a given size. In the case of blocks with borders, the border becomes a part of the block. Add the finished width of both borders to the measurements of the block and figure the number needed as you would for other pieced blocks. When there are lattices, add the finished width of only *one* lattice to each block when figuring the number of blocks required. When you have done this, subtract the width of *one* lattice from the total measurement of the blocks needed because there will be one less lattice than there are blocks. However, when the lattice is to surround the pieced top like a border, as well as to separate the blocks (color page A), there will be an *extra* lattice instead of one less. In this case, *add* the width of one lattice to each block as before, and then *add* one extra lattice width after the final number of blocks-plus-one-lattice has been figured. The logic of all this will be clear when you draw your diagram.

AFTERWORD

Endings always fill me with mixed feelings. When I have finished a good book, returned from a visit with loved ones, or completed a series of classes I have taught, it is always the same. It is not really surprising that I find myself feeling those same emotions as I approach this ending also.

Years of growing and experience, followed by many months of intricate plannings and writing have produced this book. It has been a challenge, a trial, and a joy all at the same time. I have tried to think of each one of you as an individual with your own interest, capacity and need as related to quilting, just as I do with each person in any of my classes. I have tried to anticipate your questions and to give you the best answers I know at this moment in as concise and full a manner as I can within the space allotted.

This does not mean that I shall not continue to learn and share just as you will. For growing, learning, and sharing are basic qualities of life. It does not mean, therefore, that there will never be anything more to say on this subject. It simply means that I have had the pleasure of sharing with you many things that I have learned and which I hope will contribute to your learning and to your pleasure as you pursue your interest in quilting.

Endings have also left openings for new beginnings, the next visit, the next class, a new experience.

HETTIE RISINGER

SOURCES OF SUPPLIES

To order quilting supplies:

Hearthside Mail Order
Box 24, Dept. QN
Milton, Vermont 05468

Mail-In Quilt Supplies
Box 630
Woodcliff , New Jersey 67675

Quilts and Other Comforts
Box 394
Wheatridge, Colorado 80033
   (attention shop)
(303) 423-8442

The Walrus Quilt Shop
4614 East State Street
Rockford, Illinois 61108
   (815) 399-9462

To order quilt pattern compendiums:

Quilting Publications
566–30th Ave.
San Mateo, California 94403
   (415) 573-9243

INDEX